D1289536

391.209 L666v   F V

LEVITT
VICTORIANS UNBUTTONED : REGIS-
TERED DESIGNS FOR CLOTHING,
THEIR MAKERS ...   34.95

 St. Louis Community College

Library

5801 Wilson Avenue
St. Louis, Missouri 63110

VICTORIANS UNBUTTONED

Registered Designs for Clothing, their Makers and Wearers, 1839–1900

VICTORIANS UNBUTTONED

Registered Designs for Clothing, their Makers and Wearers, 1839–1900

Sarah Levitt

London
GEORGE ALLEN & UNWIN
Boston   Sydney

George Allen & Unwin (Publishers) Ltd,
40 Museum Street, London WC1A 1LU, UK

George Allen & Unwin (Publishers) Ltd,
Park Lane, Hemel Hempstead, Herts HP2 4TE, UK

Allen & Unwin Inc.,
9 Winchester Terrace, Winchester, Mass 01890, USA

George Allen & Unwin Australia Pty Ltd,
8 Napier Street, North Sydney, NSW 2060, Australia

First published in 1986

British Library Cataloguing in Publication Data

Levitt, Sarah
    Victorians Unbuttoned
1. Costume – Great Britain – History – 19th century
I. Title
391'.2'0942   GT738
ISBN 0-04-391013 0

Set in 10 on 12 point Erhardt by Fotographics (Bedford) Ltd
and printed in Great Britain by William Clowes Limited, Beccles and London

Contents

Acknowledgements

I would like to thank the staff of the Public Record Office, Ruskin Avenue, Kew, for all their help, especially for their cheerful fetching and carrying of hundreds of large, heavy, dusty books. I would also like to thank my family and friends for their encouragement and useful advice. I am particularly grateful to Peta Lewis, June Swann and Gaby Porter for their comments on the sections dealing with hosiery, footwear and hats respectively, and to David Welding and Alan Jenkins for access to unpublished manuscripts. I am indebted to Mr J. Knapman and Mrs I. Spouse for showing me material relating to H. T. Greenlaw & Co. Ltd. Finally, thanks are due to Judith Dempster of C. & J. Clark Ltd, Gordon Drew of Welch Margetson and Co. Ltd and Maria Potempski of Corah PLC for their help, and kind permission to use photographs.

All illustrations asterisked in the list of illustrations are closely copied by the author from the original drawings of registered designs. Unless otherwise indicated, all photographs are reproduced by permission of the Public Record Office, at which place they and the originals of the author's drawings may be consulted. All crown copyright records from the Public Record Office are used by permission of the Controller of HM Stationery Office.

For reference, a list of the registered designs referred to and full sources for quotations are given at the end of the text. I am grateful to the following for permission to use extracts from published works: the Society of Authors as literary representative of the estate of Compton MacKenzie for Compton Mackenzie: *My Life and Times*, the estate of H. G. Wells for *Bealby, Kipps*, and *Love and Mr Lewisham*, and the editor's literary estate and the Hogarth Press for *Life as We Have Known It* by Co-operative Working Women, ed. Margaret Llewellyn Davies.

To my parents

Illustrations

(NB Full details of registration numbers are given at the back of the book.)

6   Complete Dress to Be Sold as One
    Andrews & Williams (Commission
    Agents)
    3 Old Fish Street, City   1861
7   Costume
    Henry Robinson
    12 Watling Street, City   1869
8   Skirts for Ballgowns
    John Hunt
    349 Edgware Road, London   1871
9   'The Princess Costume'
    Henry Robinson
    12 Watling Street, City   1875
10 Costumes
    Rosa Salter
    2 Crombie Row, Commercial Road,
    London   1873
11 Mantle
    Scott & Son
    8 Cannon Street, City   1876
12 Costume
    George Henry Lee & Co.
    Liverpool   1883
13 Mantles
    Spencer, Wicks & Co.
    4, 5, 6 Watling Street, City   1890
14 Evening Dress*
    Felix d'Alsace & Co.
    24 Rue St Marc, Paris   1898

9   Millinery

1   Plaited Straw Bonnet
    Possibly G. Long
    Loudwater, nr High Wycombe   1849
2   Paper Hat
    Simeon Miles
    89 Bunhill Row, City   1870
3   Tulle Cap
    Fisher & Watson
    20 Milk Street, City   1849
4   Bonnet
    George Smith & Co.
    Union Hall, Union Street, Borough,
    London   1853
5   Bonnet*
    Charles Clark
    10 Austin Street, Hackney   1858
6   Amazon Hat*
    Robert Heath
    18 St George's Place, Hyde Park Corner,
    London   1859

7   Hat
    Robert Heath
    25 St George's Place, London   1860
8   Hats
    Munt Brown & Co.
    85 Wood Street, City   1860
9   Cloth Hat
    Sadok Schneiders & Son
    Buck's Row, Whitechapel,
    London   1888
10 Hats
    Jay's Mourning Warehouse
    247 Regent Street, London   1873
11 Straw Beret
    White & Auborn
    57 Upper Prince's Street, Luton,
    Bedfordshire   1896

10   Men's Coats and Boys' Suits

1   H. J. & D. Nicoll's Establishment,
    Regent Street
    from *A Visit to Regent Street*   1860
2   Paletôt
    H. J. & D. Nicoll
    114, 116 and 120 Regent Street and 22
    Cornhill, London   1848
3   'Oude Wrapper: Cape or Coat'*
    Benjamin Benjamin
    74 Regent Street, London   1856
4   'Dustcoat to Be Called "The Traveller's
    Friend" '*
    (featuring ticket and map pockets)
    Lewis and Co.
    Ranelagh Street, Liverpool   1867
5   'Coat with Rever in One Piece'*
    H. J. & D. Nicoll
    Regent Street and Cornhill,
    London   1849
6   Convertible Overcoat*
    Samuel Shirley
    28a Market Street, Manchester   1884
7   Overcoat
    Stone & Forster
    5 York Street, Saint James's Square,
    London   1874
8   Overcoat
    John H. Wilson & Co.
    24 Love Street, Liverpool   1876
9   Boy's Costume*
    Donald Nicoll & Co.
    St Paul's Church Yard, London   1870

xiv

10 'The Duplex Waistcoat'
Elias Moses & Son
Minories and Aldgate, City   1849
11 Surviving Example of Barran's Boy's
Suit   late 19th century
(Leeds Industrial Museum, Armley
Mills, Leeds)
12 Boy's Jacket with Cloth Bands*
John Barran & Sons
Chorley Lane, Leeds   1884
13 Boy's Suit
Joseph Hepworth & Son
Wellington Street, Leeds   1884
14 Boy's Suit
Macbeth & Co. King Street,
Manchester   1879
Joseph Hepworth & Son
Wellington Street, Leeds   1884
15 Girl's Coat
John Barran & Sons
Chorley Lane, Leeds   1884
16 Boy's Sailor Suit
Stewart & MacDonald
Park Lane, Leeds   1891

11   Men's Hats

1 'The Bonafide Ventilating Hat'*
John Fuller & Co.
95–6 Long Southwark, London   1849
2 Metal Hat Ventilator*
James Marlor & Sons
Taylor Lane, Denton, Cheshire   1885
3 Adjusting Ventilator*
Daniel Lever
Denton, Cheshire   1888
4 Top Hat
Christy's
Canal Street, Stockport,
Cheshire   1853
5 'An Elastic Dress and Opera Hat'*
James Bickerton Junior
36 Stamford Street, Blackfriars,
City   1844
6 Ventilating, Expanding and Contracting
Hat Lining*
Charles F. A. Rider
61 Red Cross Street, Borough,
London   1847
7 Hat Tips
Wareham and Hollingsworth
Hyde, Cheshire   1878

8 Hat Leather
William Bracher & Co.
Stockport, Cheshire   1895
9 Cap
David Nyman
St James's Barton, Bristol   1851
10 'The Perfection Roll Curl for Soft Hats'
Sadok Schneiders & Son
7 St Mary Street, Whitechapel,
London   1870
11 Bowler Hat with Leather Brim
James Hague, Hooley Hill, nr
Manchester   1886
12 Hardening and Planking
Battersby's Hat Factory
Offerton, Cheshire   1911
*Reproduced by permission of Stockport
Museums and Art Gallery Service*
13 Flat Cap
Andrew & Watson
403 Gallowgate, Glasgow   1899

12   Hosiery

1 The Hosier at Work
Ure's Useful Arts and Manufactures,
SPCK   1850
2 Child's Striped Stocking
Billson & Haines
Leicester   1855
3 Seamless Shirt*
John Biggs & Sons
Leicester   1843
4 Gussetless Shirt*
John Biggs & Sons
Leicester   1854
5 Knitted Polka Jacket
Richard Harris & Sons
Leicester   1850
6 Fashion Plate
The World of Fashion (February 1853)
7 Crocheted Undersleeves (with net
trimming registration in between)
Sarah Nathan
20 London Road, Southwark   1851
8 St Margaret's Works, Leicester
Reproduced by permission of Corah PLC
9 Registered Trademark
of Cooper, Corah & Sons (Corah's)
St Margaret's Works, Leicester
10 Jersey Bodice*
Alfonso Boccardo

8　'The Watteau Lawn Tennis Shoe'
　　Samuel Winter
　　22 Sussex Place, South Kensington,
　　London　1878

9　*Punch* Cartoon　1878

10　Man's Tennis Shoe
　　Joseph Dawson & Sons
　　Overstone Road, Northampton　1891

11　Bicycle Motif on Belt
　　D. B. Harris & Son
　　73–5 Newhall, Birmingham　1897

12　The Fred Wood Champion Suit
　　N. Corah Sons & Cooper
　　St Margaret's Works, Leicester　1883

13　Tricycling Dress
　　William James Harvey
　　14 Victoria Gardens, Nottinghill,
　　London　1884

14　Tricycling Skirts
　　Fébes Wahli
　　144 Westbourne Grove, Kensington,
　　London　1894

15　Handkerchief Printed with the English
　　Football Team
　　Samuel Higginbotham, Sons & Gray
　　Glasgow　1886

16　Knee Protector*
　　Nurse Angelina Coles
　　20 Simpson Street, Battersea,
　　London　1891

17　Football Boot*
　　Owen Tilley
　　Sullington Road, Shepshed, nr
　　Loughborough, Leicestershire　1896

18　Football Boot*
　　Benjamin Ladds
　　Wellingborough Road, Rushden,
　　Northants　1892

19　'The Cert'
　　Football Boot (without sole)
　　Broom & Foster
　　Manchester　1894
　　Reproduced by permission of Leicestershire
　　Museums and Art Galleries Service

20　'The Registered Cricket Guard'*
　　William Redgrave
　　Grafton Street, London　1852

21　Jacket for Rowing and Cricketing*
　　Ben Nicoll
　　42 Regent Circus, London　1849

22　Cricket Dress*
　　Robert Shaw (Gentleman)
　　22 Baker Street, Lloyd Square,
　　Pentonville, London　1890

23　Cricket Jumper
　　William Thomas Pitchers
　　Regent House, Church Street,
　　Surrey　1893

24　Sporting Motifs: (a) Watch and chain
　　like bicycle chain, Saunders and
　　Shepherd, Bartlett's Buildings, Holborn
　　Circus, London, 1896; (b) Button like
　　horseshoe, Speyer Schwert & Co., 35
　　Monkwell Street, London, 1894;
　　(c) Brooch like golf clubs, James
　　Fenton, 74 Great Hampton Street,
　　Birmingham, 1892; (d) Buckle like
　　cricket bat, ball and wickets, Alexander
　　Black Fergusson and Robert John Key,
　　42 Stamford Street, London, 1894;
　　(e) Buckle like tennis racquet and balls,
　　Alf Stanley, Wednesbury Road, Walsall,
　　Staffordshire, 1892

Introduction

AT THE beginning of Victoria's reign, most people's clothing, rich and poor alike, was either home made or produced by small independent craftspeople such as tailors, dressmakers and hosiers. By the close of her reign, much of the clothing worn by ordinary people was made by large scale manufacturers and sold through retail networks. This book is an attempt to trace some aspects of the development of the mass clothing trades and their products. It uses as its starting point a hitherto unexploited source of information, the records of registered designs 1839–1900 kept at the Public Record Office, Ruskin Avenue, Kew, in West London.

This institution is like a great filing cabinet of British history. Every so often it makes the news when time restrictions on confidential documents lapse, revealing to the world the long forgotten affairs of, say, the Foreign Office or the Ministry of Defence. However, most visitors to Kew from both sides of the Atlantic are less likely to be pursuing dead politicians than to be seeking their family histories, buried among the official forms, lists and logs which chart our lives.

The PRO knows its users as 'readers', thus emphasising its character as a place of written information. Yet few readers know that the Public Record Office also houses within some of its volumes one of the most important collections of nineteenth-century textiles in the country, together with hundreds of made-up garments, and thousands of illustrations of clothing. They provide first-hand information about Victorian clothes and their manufacturers, showing not just the fashionable ideal, but real clothes intended to be worn by ordinary people. Garments recorded here rarely survive elsewhere, being either too cheap or commonplace to have been treasured, or so serviceable that they were worn until they fell to pieces. Made by large scale manufacturers for the mass market, they are thus of particular interest since little is known about the appearance of early ready-made clothing. Nineteenth-century garments surviving today can rarely be associated with a maker, but at Kew every manufacturer is named and all the designs are dated. The remarkable survival of these objects is because all were registered designs, lodged with the government Designs Office under the provision of Copyright of Designs Acts from 1839 onwards. In the following chapters I hope to give some insight into this wealth of material.

PART I

1
Registered Designs 1839–1900

THE IDEA of registering a design to protect it from being pirated by other manufacturers developed gradually in response to the changing needs of British commerce and industry. The right of an inventor to manufacture a completely new product without competition has long been recognised. This right was, and still is, protected by the issuing of a patent. The first patent was granted by Edward III to the inventor of a technique for colouring glass in 1449. Only comparatively recently, however, has similar protection been given to the originator of a new design for an existing object.

Before the Industrial Revolution, most goods were individually made in small local workshops. Each area had its own craftworkers, making and selling their wares. Traditional patterns were used, changing only slightly, and varying from one part of the country to another. Choice was limited to what could be bought from a pedlar's pack, a local maker, or on the occasional foray to a nearby town. This situation was changing in the eighteenth century as goods began to be made in large quantities and distributed nationally and internationally.

As production became more sophisticated, so too did marketing techniques; manufacturers courted the ever growing population of town dwellers, with enough money in their pockets to enjoy not just the necessities of life but also a few of its luxuries.

The textile trade was in the vanguard of the Industrial Revolution. As a result of the inventions of Arkwright, Hargreaves and Crompton cotton production soared from the 1760s. As each innovation speeded up a process, others were made to enable the rest of the machinery to keep up with the increased output. A ban on the sale of printed cottons which had been imposed in 1721 at the instigation of the silk trade was lifted in 1774. This gave a tremendous boost to the cotton industry. Manufacturers raced to copy one another's designs almost before the dyes had dried and the situation was soon intolerable.

In order to safeguard printers against the attentions of unscrupulous rivals, in 1787 an Act was passed by Parliament which gave two months' protection to printed cotton designs as an experiment. This was not an unprecedented step: the authors of books had been granted copyright in 1709, and engravers in 1734. Copyrighting printed

1 A mosaic of Victorian clothing preserved in a volume of design 'representations' 1859

cottons was so successful that the Act was renewed annually from 1789. It was made permanent in 1794, and the period was extended to three months. Protection was conferred automatically on publication, as it had been during previous copyright legislation, and so there are no record books to consult.

-New markets opened and the pace of British industry quickened following the French Revolution and the Napoleonic Wars. However, as the French trade recovered and trade barriers between England and France were lifted in 1824, Britain began to move into a recession. France was renowned for exquisite luxury goods, while British industrialists were apt to prefer quantity to quality. They sought to make use of their great technical expertise to supply large markets with cheap goods. In the short term this may have been an acceptable policy, but overall trade must eventually suffer if inferior goods only are produced.

This, at any rate, was the opinion held by the government. In 1835 Melbourne set up a committee 'to inquire into the best means of extending a knowledge of the arts and principles of design among the peoples of this country'. The committee sat for two sessions of Parliament, hearing evidence from witnesses concerned with almost every aspect of art, industry and commerce. They were unanimous in their criticism of the British attitude to design, and in their praise of the French, whose wonderful products were filling British shops. The final report 'adverted with regret to the inference received, that, from the highest branches of poetical design, down to the lowest connexion between design and manufacturers, the arts have received little

2 Rare surviving
   example:
   manufacturer's
   copy of a
   registered mitten.
   Russell Bowlett
   and Russell,
   Welford Place,
   Leicester 1877.
   Now in Leicester
   Museum and Art
   Gallery

encouragement in this country'. The proposals made included the setting up of schools of design, and an increase in the number of museums and exhibitions to be opened for the benefit of the lower orders. One of the most important recommendations was that a copyright system for all ornamental designs should be established, like that in operation in France. This was essential, since, without it, manufacturers had no incentive to invest in their own designs, rather than stealing other people's.

This report was to have great significance. Those early schools of design were the forerunners of today's art schools. It set off a chain of events culminating in the Great Exhibition of 1851 and the establishment of the museums at South Kensington. But its most immediate impact was felt in 1839 when the Design Copyright Act was passed. All earlier legislation conferred protection automatically on publication. By the 1839 Act, copyright could be secured only after the article itself, an illustration or model of it had been deposited with a registrar employed by the Board of Trade. On payment of fee, it was given a registration number, glued into the 'representations' book and the depositor's name, address and occupation recorded in a separate register. Ornamental designs were protected for twelve months, or three years in the case of metalwork. A manufacturers' index was kept for quick reference.

In 1842 thirteen classes of object were established, with periods of protection varying from nine months to three years, depending on the class. These were as follows:

1. metal;
2. wood;
3. glass;
4. earthenware;
5. paperhangings;
6. carpets;
7. printed shawls;
8. woven shawls;
9. printed warps and yarns;
10. printed fabrics with small patterns;
11. printed fabrics with large patterns;
12. damasks and other woven fabrics;
13. lace, and anything 'not included elsewhere'.

3

3 The mimosa or flower cornet; 'it will appear evident that by forming the trumpet so as to present the appearance of a flower it will be less unsightly than the trumpet ordinarily used by deaf persons', William Blackmore Pine, The Strand, London, 1849

The penalty for infringement of copyright was £5. From that year also a diamond-shaped emblem had to be displayed on each object made according to the design registered. This mark gave, in code, the object's class, date of registration and parcel number. A copy of the design with an attached certificate of registration was kept by the proprietor. Very occasionally these copies survive: Clark's Shoe Museum at Street, Somerset has several drawings of registered shoe designs, and some samples of fitted fingerless mittens registered by the firm Russell, Bowlett & Russell in 1877 are preserved in Leicester Museum and Art Gallery.

One flaw in the Act was that it made no provision for functional, as opposed to decorative designs. While the 1839 and 1842 legislation protected the livelihood of, say, a milliner; a plumber, who may have spent years perfecting the ideal shape for a tap, could have no redress if it were copied the day after he launched it. To rectify this anomaly, a further Act was passed, in 1843, which gave three years' protection to any kind of useful design. Protection was obtained in the same way as for the ornamental designs, but the designs were registered by drawings, and later photographs, rather than examples. The useful designs class also differed in that each registration was accompanied by a description beginning, 'The purpose of utility to which the design has reference'. This makes them particularly informative.

In 1875, the Patent Office took over the administration of registered designs from the Board of Trade. In 1883 the Patents, Designs and Trademarks Act was passed, amalgamating and rationalising a mass of legislation which had built up since 1839. After being in operation for over forty years, the registered design scheme needed modernising. For instance in the field of textiles, shawls had been fashionable in 1842 and two classes were allotted to them. 'Hardly anybody' wore shawls by 1880, and so these classes were obsolete. A scheme which had enabled objects to be provisionally registered for six months, so that they could be exhibited but not sold, was dropped, as was the distinction between ornamental and useful designs. The manufacturers' index was discontinued. Designs were no longer grouped according to their class: instead they were glued in the books numerically. The diamond mark was replaced by the registration number.

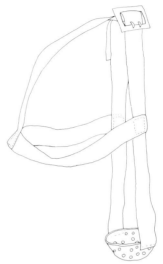

4 Belt for keeping the mouth closed while sleeping, devised by John Tucker 'of independent means', Birch House, Old Lenton, Nottingham, 1885

From 1883 the system became more efficient. While the price of registering a textile design remained constant at 1s, other types of designs were reduced from up to £5 to 10s. The £5 stamp duty payable on all designs since 1870 was abolished. Protection was now granted for five years, but copyright was lost if the design was not marketed within six months of registration. The fine for infringement of copyright was raised to £50. A tremendous increase in registrations followed. The new numbering which began in 1884 had reached 368,154 by January 1901. This caused the registrar of designs to economise on space. The meandering written descriptions and large meticulous illustrations which had characterised the scheme disappeared as designs were crammed into the volumes. Sometimes they were even folded up.

The 1883 Act rectified a particularly unfortunate omission from the original legislation, in that it created a new class for 'articles of wearing apparel'. Seven out of the thirteen existing classes had referred to flat textiles, but in 1842 Parliament had not seen fit to create a separate category for clothing. The clothing trade in the 1840s had been rapidly growing and was highly competitive. Those involved tended to be progressive enterprising people, and they were quick to take advantage of the new scheme for registering designs. All kinds of garments, accessories and trimmings were registered in great numbers from 1839. They were generally allotted to class twelve for woven fabrics, thirteen for lace and miscellaneous goods, or they were

5

registered as useful designs.

Together, they make up a fascinating collection, in which can be found examples of almost every item of Victorian dress, from trouser fastenings, hair pieces and pink elastic garters, to luxurious wraps and overcoats. The designs were registered in a variety of ways: rough sketches on scraps of paper were submitted alongside neat watercolours with copperplate explanations, or smart engravings. From the mid-1850s onwards, stiff whiskery gentlemen and bemused children, awkward in their new clothes, peer at us from photographs. Perhaps most interesting of all are the actual garments such as straw bonnets and slender kid gloves. Each one is like a pressed flower in an old book, which, although flattened and desiccated, preserves the memory of a forgotten time.

All types of people registered designs. A small minority were obviously the brain-children of eccentric amateurs. They can be identified by their descriptions in the registers, since they tend to be styled 'gentleman' or 'military officer' rather than 'manufacturer' or 'warehousemen'. Untrammelled by the need for commercial viability, they registered some of the most amusing and intriguing designs. A bootlace emblazoned with the Stars and Stripes, a nose-warmer, foot-shaped hollow rubber hot-water bottles for wearing while convalescent, or an apparatus for keeping the mouth closed while sleeping are just a few examples.

Most designs were registered by commercial enterprises. These were obviously intended to be marketable. It is reasonable to assume that most were produced. However, before 1883, the fact that a design was registered does not necessarily mean that it was ever manufactured. While most were typical of their period, a few were very much in advance of their time and may not have been widely used.

Some of the biggest manufacturers, wholesalers and retailers in Britain submitted designs, and some even came from abroad: particularly from Germany, France and the USA. Their names appear in the register alongside those of what were obviously one-man bands. High-class tailors registered their exclusive cutting systems side by side with garments made in the country's most notorious sweatshops. Passing fashions were registered, as well as utilitarian dress meant to last a lifetime. While some designs were clearly intended for the bespoke market, most garments registered would have been mass produced by firms catering for the growing ready-made market. From the several hundred volumes of representations which include garments can be recreated a detailed picture of the British clothing industries in the last century, when the great centres of commerce, places such as Glasgow, Manchester, Leeds, Leicester, Bristol, the City and East End of London clothed not just Britain but much of the world.

The registered designs recall mighty warehouses which darkened the City's streets from Aldermanbury and Addle Street, to Gutter Lane and Old Jewry. This *was* the City to many people, but the Blitz and redevelopment put an end to it. Today all has gone except the names of the old thoroughfares.

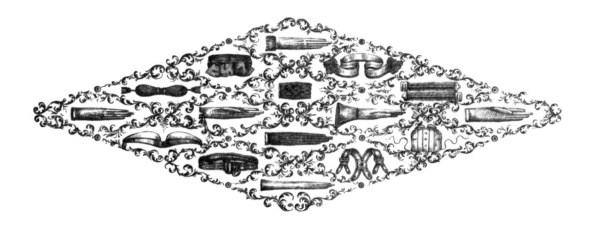

5   Box lining paper with outfitter's stock. Wellington Williams, Gutter Lane, City, 1852.

2
Customers and Tradesmen

T THE beginning of the Victorian era, very few ready-made clothes could be bought, by rich or poor. When a woman from the better-off sections of society wanted a new outfit she was likely to have it made by a dressmaker, or by her servants. Poorer women made their own clothes or bought them second hand. Some garments, such as shawls and stockings, could be bought ready-made at drapers' shops, emporiums and warehouses, but these were exceptions. Even if more ready-made garments had been available, no respectable lady would have dreamed of buying them. To display social status was one of the main aims of dress, and this end could be achieved most effectively by means of expensive, individually-made garments. It was not socially acceptable for members of either sex to buy their clothes 'off the peg'. A gentleman would have his tailor, his shirtmaker and bootmaker.

Then, as now, the best clothes were very expensive. While aiming for roughly the same sartorial impact, those members of society living at less elevated levels patronised correspondingly humbler establishments. One of the problems for the would-be fashionable was the rigidly hierarchical nature of society. Fashions were created by and for the people at the top. Clothes were intended to demonstrate the wearer's wealth and station, or those of whoever paid for them, such as husband, lover, parent, or employer. The gentleman, with his shiny top hat, perfectly fitting coat, brand new gloves and pristine collar and cuffs immaculately laundered, who may have dressed with the aid of a valet; or the lady in her hampering draperies bedecked with lace, silk frills and artificial flowers and cocooned in furs, both set fashions which were inappropriate for the lifestyles and pockets of the mass of people who sought to emulate them.

The vast differences in incomes, even among the middle and upper classes, can be gleaned from the evidence of contemporary memoirs and literature. While reading the following examples, it should be remembered that as late as 1900, the average man's wage was about £1 a week.

The major fashions of the last century were created for women whose 'pin money' might amount to over a thousand pounds a year. Such people thought little of paying £300 for a court presentation dress from 'Madame Elise'. (Jane Welsh Carlyle, *Letters and Memories*). It has been estimated that the early Victorian middle class family needed an annual income of at least £300: yet Lady Dorothy Nevill's mother was not unusual in having a dress allowance of precisely that amount in the 1840s, while she, as a young girl, had £45 a year pin money. (Lady Dorothy Nevill, *Under Five Reigns*).

1 One of the great City Warehouses in its heyday. Welch Margetson & Co.'s Moor Lane headquarters from their 1903 catalogue

Inflation was no stranger to the Victorians. Commenting on rising prices, the author of *How to Dress Well* wrote in 1868:

> Now the most ordinary dinner gown suitable for wear only at a family dinner party, cannot be made for less than fourteen or fifteen pounds . . . We remember to have heard it said five hundred a year pin money was a very small allowance for a young married woman.

Mr Pooter, G. and W. Grossmith's narrator of *The Diary of a Nobody*, which appeared in *Punch* in the late 1880s, probably earned much less than five hundred pounds as a senior clerk in the City. Yet he considered himself well off with his house in Holloway and a maid. H. G. Wells's hero, Kipps, a respectable draper's assistant in the 1890s, earned his keep and £20 a year. There were women who, while considering themselves part of the respectable middle classes, were happy to buy the many books published with titles such as *How to Dress Well on a Shilling a Day* (by 'Sylvia') or *How to Dress Neatly and Prettily on £10 a Year*.

In 1878, in Leicester, a skilled male shoemaker earned 27s for a 54-hour week, while most women in that trade earned 14s a week as sewing machinists.* Even as late

* Leicester Chamber of Commerce Report quoted in Leicester Footwear Manufacturers' Federation 100th Annual Report and Centenary Supplement 1871–1971.

as 1906, Board of Trade figures were to show that 'half the women in industrial Britain earned under 10s for a week's work of seldom less than 54 hours'. (Robert Roberts, *The Classic Slum*).

For the poorest, to be adequately clothed was simply a matter of covering themselves. For those with a little money to spare for self-decoration, clothing was still a major problem, particularly when their work called for a 'respectable' appearance which often meant maintaining a standard of dress higher than they could easily sustain on their income.

Looking back on her 1860s childhood in Bethnal Green, a woman remembered being inadequately fed and clothed while her father, in an office job, had to spend considerable sums on dress.

> My father, a well educated man, was employed in a government situation, working from 10 a.m. to 4 p.m. My father's position compelled him to keep up an appearance which an ordinary workman, earning the same wages, would not have had to do. He always went to business in nice black clothes and a silk hat. His appearance was quite out of keeping with the neighbourhood we lived in, and when he and my eldest brother came home in the evening I do not think people quite knew what to make of them. (Cooperative Working Women, 'Memories of Seventy Years' from *Life as We Have Known It*.)

Clerks and shop assistants were among the chief patrons of such devices as shirt fronts, paper, rubber and celluloid collars and cuffs. When the only possible fashions were dictated from above, it was also hard on working girls responding to their natural desires to appear attractive when they were castigated for 'aping their betters' and ridiculed because of their tattered finery.

> The maid of all work does not hesitate to copy, to the utmost extent of her power, the dress of the greatest lady in the land ... Did our readers see a London house maid cleaning the doorsteps of a London house? It is a most unedifying sight. As the poor girl kneels and stoops forward to whiten and clean the steps, her crinoline goes up as her head goes down, and her person is exposed to the gaze of policemen and errand boys who are not slow to chaff her upon the size and shape of her legs ...
>
> Persons in humble class of life will often ape their betters, dressing after them, and absolutely going without necessary food in order to get some piece of finery. Fine gowns of inconvenient length, expanded over large crinolines; silk mantles, richly trimmed, often conceal the coarsest, scantiest, and most ragged underclothing. We have seen the most diminutive bonnets, not bigger than saucers, ornamented with beads and flowers and lace, and backed up by ready-made 'chignons' on the heads of girls who are only one degree removed from the poor house. (*How to Dress Well.*)

The poor were often forced to buy second-hand clothing, and throughout the nineteenth century, this was a flourishing trade, carried on to a large extent by Jewish and Irish people.

Worn clothes were, of course, always procurable in the purlieus of Whitechapel and St

Giles. A nobleman's or wealthy commoner's cast off garments went to his domestics and from his domestics to the old clothes men, and from the old clothes men to the mechanics, and from the mechanics to the sweepers at the street crossings. In fact, the poor of all classes were glad to wear at second hand the costumes of the rich, for clothes made to order were most disproportionately costly. The would-be fine gentleman, with a consumptive purse, was compelled to deck himself in faded finery that ran the chance of being recognised in the streets by its former owner . . . and the humblest members of the community, in their second-hand Sunday garments, often exhibited the most grotesque and hideous caricatures of high life. If the coat did not fit the purchaser, it was altered and re-altered until it somewhat nearly approximated to his figure; but by no letting out or curtailments was the fact concealed, that the garment was never originally intended for the wearer.

This extract is from a work published by the outfitters E. Moses & Son of the Minories and Aldgate in the City, entitled *The Growth of an Important Branch of British Industry* (1860). It praised the recent increase in shops, particularly their own, selling new men's clothing at prices to suit most pockets. Some crude male clothing had long been available ready made, however. Called 'slopwork' because it originally consisted of loose sailors' garments of that name, by the nineteenth century it included all kinds of simple working clothes, and complete outfits intended for emigrants to the colonies. The slopwork trade grew up around ports, notably in East and South-east London, Portsmouth, Bristol and Liverpool, not only because it catered for the requirements of travellers, but also because newly arrived immigrants tended to congregate around the docklands. These people, often poor and unskilled, created a ready supply of cheap labour: seafaring towns were centres for the clothing trades throughout the century.

Moses & Son were among the first firms to go 'up market', rising from the style of 'slopseller' to 'clothier and outfitter'. From the early 1840s they made clothes intended for a wider clientele. They kept their working men's department, but also made fashionable coats, trousers, waistcoats and overgarments and, like all the best tailors, ladies' riding habits. In addition to these, all kinds of undergarments and accessories could be bought. Moses's rise to fame is charted in their pamphlets issued throughout the 1840s and 1850s. They even started a bespoke department with a servants' waiting room, and a glamorous showroom which was, we were told in *The Exhibition of 1851 for All Nations*, 'in itself the most perfect bijou ever thrown open to the public gaze'. With this, and a scheme for 'self-measured' bespoke suits, the distinction between tailor made and ready made was deliberately blurred. Moses & Son were unusual for their time in that their prices were fixed and ticketed on the garments. Their trade was based on quick sales and low profits and they offered a money-back guarantee. In the 1850s they had three London shops, and branches in Bradford, Sheffield and Melbourne, Australia. Other similar operations were emerging in the 1840s. H. J. and D. Nicoll of Regent Street set their sights even higher. They sought, and gained, royal patronage.

These shops seemed to offer good value for money. Their clothes were cheap and easy to buy. But it was soon found that one reason for this was their practice of contracting out work to sweatshops.

The clothiers Henry J. and Donald Nicoll were both rich and influential. In 1850 following Henry Mayhew's revelation of their dubious practices in his letters to the *Morning Chronicle* on the life and labour of the London poor, the brothers engineered his dismissal from the paper. This cost them the price of eighteen inches of front page advertisement daily for several weeks.

Although these outfitters had wholesale departments they were primarily retailers. It was only later when the advent of the sewing machine encouraged the factory system that wholesale manufacturers such as John Barran of Leeds emerged to supply

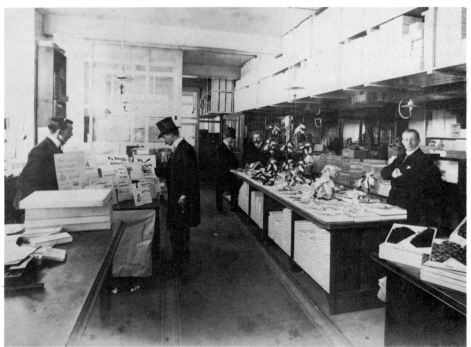

2 Examining the goods at the necktie manufacturers H. T. Greenlaw & Co.'s Golden Lane Warehouse. From an album c. 1905 (private collection)

small shops on a large scale. In other clothing trades such as hosiery and shoemaking, as well as general textiles, the wholesale system was firmly established by the start of the century. Large country manufacturers found it advantageous to set up warehouses in London where the drapers who sold most kinds of ready-made garments as well as textiles could visit them easily to buy their stock in trade. Once a warehouse had been started, it was easy to diversify, supplying the drapery trade with more and more types of goods. By the mid-century the hosiers I. & R. Morley, in common with many other firms, sold not only a wide range of knitted garments in addition to stockings, but also such things as neckties, collars, parasols and leather gloves. They registered many of their products and from these a picture of their stock can be built up. Other warehouses originally started in different areas, but all became less specialised as the years went by. Cooks of St Pauls began in cotton piece goods and Thomas Vyse & Sons as milliners, but both had moved into clothing by the 1860s.

Welch Margetson & Co. always specialised in men's wear. The firm began in 1832 when Joseph Welch and John Stewart Margetson purchased for £500 the stock and bracemaking business of Margetson's sister. They rapidly moved into other fields; before 1850 they were printing silk bandannas, and manufacturing shirts and collars at their works in Northern Ireland. The range of products continued to increase and many were registered throughout the century. Their 1903 catalogue is one inch thick, and apart from every imaginable type of shirt and collar, includes raincoats, bathing drawers, cricket and smoking jackets, umbrellas, trouser presses, chest protectors, stocking suspenders, travelling rugs, walking sticks, in fact, everything needed for the manly wardrobe. Much of it would have been bought from other specialist manufacturers.

The warehousemen largely congregated around the Wood Street area, where they were well placed for several of the new railway terminals. These brought in buyers, would-be employees and consignments of goods with every train, and sent them out again. They were also close to the City finance houses, and the huge sorting office set up to meet their needs near St Paul's. Through here passed packages carefully wrapped for every conceivable climate and eventuality: gloves for India and China had to be packed in separate tin boxes to keep them dry in the monsoon, goods for South America had to be in bundles small enough for mules to carry and those for the Belgian Congo were made into coffin-shaped parcels for carrying on heads. (Robert Finch, *The Flying Wheel*).

If there was one factor above all others which encouraged the development of this area, it was the export trade, which grew to keep pace with the insatiable demands of new markets throughout the British Empire, and even in the most far flung corners of the earth. In the 1850s a contemporary told the following story about the products of Richard Harris & Sons, the famous Leicester knitwear manufacturers:

> The various fabrics ... are suitable for clothing in every part of the globe. They are equally adapted to the climate of the equator and that of the poles. A demand is consequently found to exist for them in every continent and in every island which British commerce finds its way. Nations, savage as well as civilised, are glad to possess them for their warmth, beauty and utility. A young man, formerly residing in King Street, near the warehouse of Mr Harris, but now in South America, was travelling a short time ago in the trackless wilds of that continent for scientific purposes, when he arrived at a miserable hut on which he saw fastened, as a sort of architectural ornament, a strip of material which appeared to him to be of English manufacture – what was his astonishment on examination to find that it was a band, for the tying up of goods, on which was the name of R. Harris & Sons, King Street, Leicester. The sight of this sign of civilisation amongst

widespread barbarism coming as it did from his own doors, naturally awakened in his mind overwhelming associations of home, friends and by-gone hours of happiness. (Reverend T. Lomas, *A Memoir of the Late Richard Harris MP.*)

3
Methods and Machinery

HE GROWTH of the warehouses was seen as one of the marvels of the modern age, and their emergence was due to the effects of others. The Reverend Lomas wrote in his memoir of Richard Harris, published in 1855:

> The railway and the telegraph have brought a complete revolution in commercial affairs. The manufacturer no longer carries, as was very commonly the case fifty years ago, his goods on a pack horse for sale in the various villages and market towns far and near, but employs the modern methods of locomotion and communication, places his agents in the metropolis and other large towns and cities, and is visited at his own stately warehouse by merchants from every part of the globe.

Mass clothing manufacture would have been impossible without the introduction of new technologies and production techniques. By far the most important of these was the sewing machine. This invention had been attempted several times before the American Elias Howe created a lock-stitch machine in 1846. Penniless and unable to find a sponsor, he took it to England where he sold his patent rights to William Thomas, a Cheapside staymaker. Thomas jealously guarded his patent until it expired in 1860. Meanwhile, back in America, Isaac Merritt Singer had improved the lock-stitch machine and taken out an American patent. It was rapidly adopted there but its widespread introduction was held back in England by Thomas's patent. When in 1856 Singer opened his first British agency, he chose Glasgow, not only because it was a clothing centre but also because, being in Scotland, he avoided paying a fee to Thomas. The sewing machine was used to some extent in Britain in the 1850s, notably in shirt factories in Ireland and by the Leeds clothier John Barran. A few designs were registered for machine stitched collars in the late 1850s, but the sudden upsurge in the use of machines from 1861 is reflected in the flurry of designs registered for machine stitched items around that time.

Large scale clothing production depended on the introduction of steam engines. Their tall chimneys had transformed the appearance of many textile towns by the 1850s. At Barran's and at the Irish factories, rows of sewing machines were harnessed to central, steam driven shafts from the start, so that they could be worked more efficiently than by foot power. At the same time, in hosiery towns such as Leicester and Nottingham, the old hand-knitting frames were giving way to steam driven machinery.

The sewing machine completed in minutes work which had previously taken hours to accomplish by hand. It was soon found that it was hard to supply the machinist with enough pieces. John Barran's invention of the band-knife enabled the cloth to be cut out as quickly as it was sewn. This continuous looped blade sliced through many thicknesses of cloth like a block of cheese. Above all other inventions, this enhanced the commercial potential of the sewing machine. Barran got the idea in 1858 from a band-saw for wood which he saw at a furniture exhibition, and commissioned its makers, Greenwood & Batley, to produce a modified version.

However, despite many new developments in the clothing trades of Britain and the United States, even after 1900, a substantial proportion of processes continued to be carried out by hand for many years. Clothing production was always labour intensive, and one of the main features of the industry was the way in which manufacturers sought to bring down the cost of manpower. Bringing the workforce under one roof was the most efficient way of utilising modern machinery, and although employers had to comply with the Factory Acts, it had the advantage that, with improved working conditions, output increased. Many firms built new model factories towards the end of the century, which were proudly described in contemporary commercial handbooks. However, capital outlay was high and there was less flexibility than with the old system whereby the work was given out to contractors who paid people to make it up. Contracting-out, or sweating, as it came to be called, co-existed alongside factories. It inevitably led to abuse. In 1887 the first of many government reports on the subject pointed out:

> The system may be defined as one under which subcontractors undertake to do work in their own houses or small workshops, and employ others to do it, making a profit for themselves by the difference between the contract prices and the wages they pay their assistants.

Most people involved in the sweated trades were paid a fraction of the real value of their work and suffered extreme hardships as a result. A succession of public outcries were raised against the system, from the early 1840s when *Punch* published 'Moses Brothers Versus the Widow Biddell'. This recounted a court case in which a woman was charged by the Tower Hill clothiers with theft because she had pawned some shirts in order to feed her family while she made the rest of the order.

Immigrants, arriving in Britain without friends, money, or often skills, were glad of any employment whatsoever and were prepared to work hard for little remuneration. These people suffered most from the sweating system. Britain experienced successive waves of Jewish immigration, reaching a peak in the 1880s, as people fled from persecution in Russia and Eastern Europe. Most passed through on their way to the United States, but some stayed. Starting from humble beginnings, they eventually became a significant economic force in the clothing trades. These, especially tailoring, were traditional Jewish occupations in Europe, neither proscribed on religious grounds nor prohibited by the conventions of Christian society. Many new techniques, such as the sewing machine and the division of manufacture into small semi-skilled processes, were resisted by traditional craftsmen, anxious to protect their time honoured practices. Immigrants accepted the new methods willingly, which was an additional reason for employing them. This problem also led many firms to set up in areas with little tradition of clothing production, such as Northern Ireland.

Working conditions in all the clothing trades were generally very poor throughout the century. Government concern was shown by the many enquiries set up on different aspects of the industries, such as those investigating the condition of the framework knitters (1845), children's employment (1843 and 1863–7) and the sweating system (1888–90). All heard pathetic tales of hardship. The conditions in some industries were improved following the Factory Acts of 1825, 1833, 1847, 1878 and 1891. However, many clothing workers, particularly women employed in small workshops and at home were not protected by them.

A great deal of public concern was felt for the plight of female workers who suffered some of the worst conditions in the trades. In 1843 the Association for the Aid and Benefit of Dressmakers and Milliners was set up, and it was active for a number of years. Other schemes encouraged the wholesale emigration of surplus woman workers. In the end, however, the gradual improvements seen in the lives of clothing workers were due largely to their own efforts. Many Trades unions were successfully organised, for instance the National Association of Tailors set up in 1846, and the United Framework Knitters' Society of 1866. The history of Trades Unionism in the clothing trades is a subject in itself, which has been well documented elsewhere.

4
Selling the Goods

THE CLOTHING trade was a fiercely competitive business. Traders enthusiastically touted new lines as fast as they could be churned out in the cut-throat race to gain custom. The latest novelties were widely and unscrupulously advertised; in newspapers, across vans and omnibuses, on the backs of sandwichboard men giving out handbills, plastered across gable ends and written in letters six feet high over shop windows.

The constant efforts of manufacturers to devise new patterns for the most mundane garments can be traced through the registered design sample books: exciting new seams for shirts, or stripes for mittens and socks. Fashions come and go as the pages are turned — each one an invitation to buy more. Salesmen exploited passing crazes, and carefully registered their inventions to protect them from the certain forgery which would inevitably follow success. For example, several 'anti-garrotte' cravats were registered, to reassure the nervous on dark nights; street lighting was by no means general in the early years of Victoria's reign, and brutal atacks were common.

The discovery of electricity brought about a widespread belief in the healing properties of 'Galvanism'; that is, the chemical production of electricity from metals. In March 1844, Noel Jefferey Dixon of Billacomb Hymstock, Devonshire, registered a hat with a 'metallic Galvanic circle placed within the crown' presumably to increase the brain power, and a few days later, John Derring of 85 The Strand registered his adjusting galvanic band, which could be made to fit around the required part of the body by means of a stud and groove.

Sometimes novelties were aimed at a less sophisticated clientele, as, for example, the gentleman's necktie shaped like a plump female leg registered by George Edmund Geach of 4 Champion Terrace, Camberwell, in 1886, or the lovely corsets embroidered with either brides or cupids registered by Farcy & Oppenheim of Paris the following year.

A large proportion of the designs reflect the Victorian need to 'keep up appearances'. Most of these feature novel ways of avoiding the expense and discomfort that this could entail. For example, an abundance of hair was much admired throughout the period. The huge buns of the 1860s and 70s in particular could often only be achieved artificially. While the rich bought undetectable real hairpieces, cheap imitations deceived no one. Some were registered by actual examples, and these survivors are possibly unique. Mulloney & Johnson of Priory Row, Coventry, registered examples from 1867 onwards which are especially interesting since they are composed of rows of sausage curls made from coarse brown cotton thread with a glazed finish, fastened to a hair net.

The combination shirt waistcoat, registered by John Smith of Lawrence Lane,

Cheapside, in 1849, would have combined coolness with economy. It was important that the two parts of such garments were washable. The rigid dress code which led English men to wear stifling collars, ties and jackets, even in the far flung tropical outposts of the British Empire, gave rise to many similar devices for deception. The collar made from a single band of fabric with a necktie piece stitched in front, registered by Richard Mullins Moody, an Aldermanbury tie manufacturer, in 1885, may have been intended for use in hot climates.

A garment's originality could owe as much to its name as to its appearance. The Victorians loved pseudo-scientific terms and must have enjoyed wearing the 'Anuphaton' cloak, the 'Dicanum' trousers, the 'Acme' lapel collar or the 'Sternophylon' chest protector. Some names conferred manifold attributes; as in 'Madame Blangy's Parisian Hindoo Cloth Petticoat'. This name craze did not go unnoticed. In 1861 Andrew Wynter wrote in *Our Social Bees*: 'There seems a rage just at the present moment for re-christening all articles of wearing apparel'. He went on to describe the amazement of a Somerset farmer, when faced, in 'one of the splendid outfitting establishments in the City', with the 'Carratzza Shirt', the 'Hydrotobolic Hat with a Patent Ventilator', and the 'Calcarapedes' or self-adjusting galosh.

Famous people were a useful source of names for goods. Among the registered designs we have the 'Beaconsfield Bow Tie', the 'Livingstone Bracebuckle', the 'Elcho' necktie, the 'Lady Peel Jacket'. Alternatively, their portraits could be used as decoration: Cobden and Mr Punch were both the subjects of umbrella handles in the mid-1840s, along with Shakespeare, all manufactured by Roberts & Metham of Sheffield. Political allegiances could be secretly maintained by one's braces: in 1885 George Statham of Coventry registered webbing for braces which incorporated woven portraits of Disraeli, and in 1887, George John Flamank, an inland revenue official with inclinations towards the USA, registered braces embellished with the Stars and Stripes. Heel plates were moulded to depict famous men, so that one could leave a hero at every tread. A General Gordon heel plate was registered in 1884. One of the largest categories in the registered designs was printed cotton handkerchiefs, through which nearly all the major social and political events of the late nineteenth century can be charted.

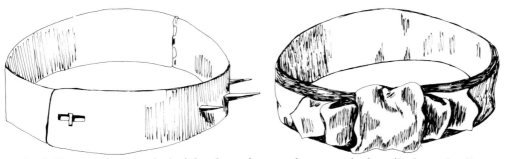

1   **Self-protection on a dark night: the anti-garrotting cravat had a spiked metal collar hidden behind its bow. Walter Thornhill, cutler and dressing case maker, 144 New Bond Street, 1862**

19

Then as now, the Royal Family enjoyed a great deal of public interest. Manufacturers found it an especially fruitful source of names, particularly since it expanded at such a pace that new names could easily be found every year. To begin with, names like the 'Victoria and Albert Elastic Gaiter' were chosen or the 'Registered Royal Ladies' Drawers'. Later came the 'Albert Edward Scarf' and the 'Dane' shirt cuff, in honour of Princess Alexandra. Another royal wedding was celebrated by the 'Kaiser Cape'. Victoria's Golden Jubilee in 1887 was commemorated by many garments decorated with royal emblems: Graham & Hummel of 3 Trump Street, Cheapside, manufactured panels for corsets embroidered with crowns and thistles and gentlemen's slippers could be purchased with similar motifs.

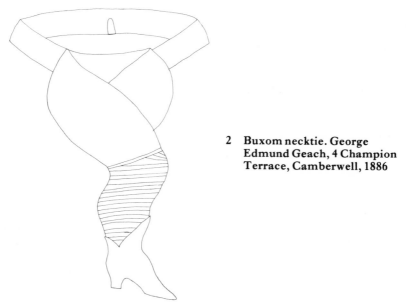

2   Buxom necktie. George
    Edmund Geach, 4 Champion
    Terrace, Camberwell, 1886

The succession of international exhibitions held from 1851 onwards were a great stimulus to trade, not least because they provided an excuse for manufacturing yet more novelties. Perhaps the nicest idea to be concocted for visitors to the Great Exhibition of 1851 was a glove with a map of London showing the Crystal Palace on its palm, enabling the wearer to find her way around the metropolis with discretion.

Each succeeding exhibition inspired a number of registered designs. Wareham & Hollingworth of Hyde, Cheshire, registered a hat lining with a view of the Paris International Exhibition of 1879.

It would be hard to say for certain that many designs were registered in preparation for entry into the various exhibitions: while an increase in registrations is detectable in the months leading up to the 1851 exhibition, this is not so with later ones. The catalogue of the 1851 exhibition gives about a dozen references to registered garments among the firms' entries, but others may have been exhibited also. They

3 'All that glitters is not gold'. Glazed cotton hair-piece mounted on an elasticated net. Mulloney & Johnson, Coventry, 1867

included W. Cutler's 'Duplexa' combined morning and evening coat, Eliza Devy's 'Registered Riding Stays', Price & Harvey's registered carriage bonnet and W. Reid's 'Sans Pli' shirt. Entering the international exhibitions was a useful means of publicising products, and if they won medals, these were proudly printed on labels, advertisements and letter headings. Such medals appeared to give an official sanction almost as convincing as the presence of a royal coat of arms.

If recognition could not be gained through competition or patronage, then it could be bought. Many firms found that by either registering or patenting their product, they obtained not only protection from piracy, but also a useful sales feature. Taking out a patent was very expensive and time consuming. The idea had to be completely new, and the length of protection was unnecessarily long in some cases. Registered designs were much cheaper and easier to obtain, and gave a more appropriate period of protection. They, therefore, became an extremely useful means of achieving an effect similar to that of a patent. A registration not only protected a saleable commodity, but also made it more saleable through the act of registration. The ordinary mass-produced object immediately acquired a cachet of individuality. The word 'registered' appended to a product made it sound special, almost as special as if it had been hand made exclusively for the buyer. Proprietors of registered designs derived added value from them through the confusion which existed, and which they

4 Combination garments helped to 'keep up appearances'. Shirt and waistcoat by John Smith, Cheapside, City, 1849

helped to foster, in the public mind between a registered design and a patent. In Kelly's Directory of 1850, H. J. and D. Nicoll styled themselves 'Patentees of the Registered Paletôt', and W. C. Jay, proprietor of Jay's Mourning Warehouse of Regent Street, advertised the 'Patent Eupheima Bodice', in the *Illustrated London News* in 1866, which was, in fact, a registered design rather than a patent. Both firms, and many others who registered designs, also took out patents for other inventions. Garments were often advertised as 'registered' long after their registration period had elapsed.

Although cases were brought to court for infringement of registrations, and at some places in the sample books designs have been deleted, on the whole, until 1883, registering a design was a lax affair. Many of the designs were virtually indistinguishable from one another. As one firm hit on a good idea, it was quickly followed by its competitors. This happened in the autumn of 1869: a small tie maker, Roger Gresty of 77 Packington Street, Islington, registered an ingenious device which incorporated a necktie, and an extension of it made to look exactly like a waistcoat front. Within days several giant Wood Street firms had registered almost identical garments. In a sense, registering a design made the copyist's task easier, since the garment or an

5 Collar and tie, Richard Mullins
Moody, Aldermanbury, City,
1885

illustration of it was kept for inspection at the office of the registrar of designs.

It is possible that the manufacturers themselves did not think much of the protection conferred by registering a design. While some firms made registrations throughout the period, such as Welch Margetson & Co., they cannot have formed more than a tiny fraction of their output. The vast majority only ever registered a few: the shoe manufacturers C. & J. Clark registered around half a dozen designs. Some of the biggest firms never bothered with the scheme at all. Some types of garments occur more frequently than others: overcoats heavily outnumber jackets, far more corsets were registered than crinolines and bustles, and hardly any drawers or stockings were registered for either sex. The reasons for this are difficult to pin down – why should one product be considered more worthy of protection than another? It may be that

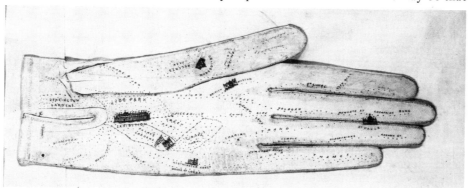

6 An indispensable souvenir of the 1851 Great Exhibition: map glove registered by
George Shore of New Oxford Street

they were registered when the proprietors felt particularly threatened by competition, or just because an individual happened to be enthusiastic about the idea. The random nature of the designs would suggest that the privilege of advertising their products as being 'registered' was often as important a consideration for the manufacturers as the protection so conferred.

23

7 Like many large corset
manufacturers, R. & W. H.
Symington of Market
Harborough registered many
designs

This view is supported by the fact that when the Trade Marks Act was passed in 1875, the scheme was an immediate success. The registered trademark rapidly became a guarantee of authenticity suggesting exclusiveness. It was a useful advertising tool, even easier to obtain and cheaper in the long run than a registered design, since one trademark could be used to 'authenticate' a firm's entire output for an indefinite period. Many of the trademarks registered in the early years, such as Corah of Leicester's 'St Margaret', are still in use today.

8 Welch Margetson &
Co.'s trademark, which
is still in use today.
From their 1903
catalogue

9 'Mr Punch' pressed horn
umbrella handle, celebrating a
daring new magazine. Roberts
& Mettam, Sheffield, 1845

The advertising function of the registered design was to some extent taken over by
the trademark. After the 1883 Act, the character of the designs began to change. Good
business propositions gradually took over from ingenious gimmicks, and there was no
longer a place for the far fetched ideas of amateurs. To some extent this is
compensated for by the enormous increase in designs registered in the last decades of
the century, once the term 'registered' became more meaningful. But overall these late
designs are more sensible and humdrum, and less attractive than the earlier ones.
Less information is given about the manufacturers, and all explanations are omitted.

PART II
5
Women's Underwear

Corsetry

STAYS WERE traditionally made by a professional staymaker. This was because of the difficulty of dealing with several layers of fabric and inter-lining, with cord or whalebone stiffening held down by countless rows of tiny, regular stitches, and the fact that the fashionable figure depended for its shape on precise contours. Nearly all women wore stays; they were essential for decency, and to go without them was to risk being considered a 'loose woman'. One also risked looking peculiar, since the popular idea of the female shape was based on the shape created by whalebone and lacing rather than by nature.

While many women preferred to have them made to measure, by the early nineteenth century, there was a substantial market for ready-made stays. In *The Lady's Shopping Manual and Mercery Album* of 1834, E. E. Perkins stated that stays were available in each colour and white, of jean, jean sateen, drill and satin. Girls' and maids' had waists from seventeen to twenty-one inches, women's twenty-one to thirty inches and outsize thirty to forty inches.

The aim of the stay was to create a smooth hard outline. It reduced the waist measurement by forcing it into a circular section, rather than a kidney shaped one, and accentuated the hips and breasts. Many women exaggerated the effect by tightly pulling up the laces at the back. Tight lacing was self-limiting as long as the eyelet holes were stitched; beyond a certain point the cloth ripped. But in the late 1820s metal eyelets began to be used, and waists could then be wrenched smaller still. It was reasoned that if the need to unlace stays every night was removed, then they would be quicker to put on. Experiments were made with front fastening stays, and various attempts were registered, such as Sarah Pearce's 'Sevigné Stay' of 1851 with its clumsy arrangement of straps. In 1853, Caleb Hill, a stay manufacturer of Cheddar, Somerset, registered a version of what was soon to become the standard fastening: a split metal busk, one side bearing studs, locked into 'keyholes' in the other. Many firms followed suit. Christopher Page wrote that this was a French invention. (About this time the word corset began to replace stays, the 1874 edition of Perkins stated that stays 'laced behind' and corsets 'fastened in front'.)

Front fastening stays could be laced even tighter – a quick gasp and they were on. Throughout the 1840s and 50s a great deal of concern was expressed about tight lacing. Edward J. Tilt wrote in his *Elements of Health and Principles of Female Hygiene*

1 'The Sevigné Stay', named after
a famous 17th century beauty,
by Sarah Pearce, New Bond
Street, Bath, 1851

of 1852, that because of the practice, 'can we, then, wonder that the sex suffers from shortness of breath, palpitation, indigestion, hysteria and a host of maladies, which, though not immediately fatal to life, are incompatible with sound health'. Staymakers were aware of this problem, and throughout the period, many exercised their minds to devise healthy garments — with varying degrees of success. Some examples of registered reformed corsets look as vicious as the unreformed.

One of the best known dress reform pioneers was Madame Roxy Anne Caplin, author of *Health and Beauty, or Corsets and Clothing, Constructed in Accordance with the Physiological Laws of the Human Body* 1856, and *Woman and Her Work: The Needle, Its History and Utility* of 1860. She was married to Jean François Isidore Caplin, proprietor of the Royal Hygienic Gymnasium at 9 York Place, and was proprietress of a staymaking business and ladies' anatomical gallery at 58 Berners Street. The latter was 'quite distinct from the rest of the establishment, and a visit to one does not necessarily involve a sight of the other'. (*Woman and Her Work*). The Caplins were inveterate inventors. They patented a front fastening stay as early as 1838, which had

2 'Caplin's dress and corset
model', Jean François Isidore
Caplin and probably his wife
Roxy, 58 Berners Street,
Oxford Street, London, 1841

27

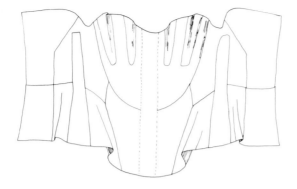

3   The Caplins'
'Hygean or
Corporiform
Corset', 1849

pulleys and wheels behind and springs and grooves in front, and registered a dummy
for displaying stays in 1841. Caplin's main claim to fame was her hygienic corset
which 'gave freedom to every organ and support where it is needed' by means of
elastic panels. The juries of the Great Exhibition awarded it a medal. In *Health and
Beauty* she complained that 'it is either pirated or attempted by almost every
staymaker in London and Paris', and her newly invented skirt band would share the
same fate.

> Within six months after this is published it will be displayed and advertised in all
> directions, cut and twisted into every shape to make it look unlike ours; and we should
> not be surprised if some genius or other should turn it upside down, just to display her
> originality. Well, so be it, the only thing that we desire is, that those who use it will use it
> properly, and have the good taste and honesty to award the credit of the invention to the
> parties to whom it is due.

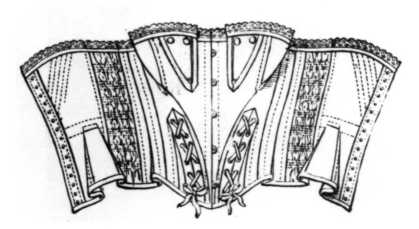

4   Maternity corset, W. Hull King & Son, off Oxford Street, London, 1896

5 Device for the 'expansion of the chest, strengthening of the shoulders and prevention of stooping of the wearer'. Charles Cross, Hallatrow, Bristol, 1871

Caplin obviously felt strongly about copyright, and presumably to avoid piracy, she registered an improvement to her corset under her husband's name, in 1849, called the 'Hygean or Corporiform Corset'. The novelty consisted of a specially shaped panel which helped in the fitting – Caplin's corsets were custom made. The Caplins had many admirers: James Torrington Spencer Lidstone included sections on them in *The Londoniad: A Grand National Poem on the Arts* published by Universal Patronage in 1856. Madame Caplin's eulogy went as follows:

Madame Caplin

How shall the poet, in a single lay,
the glory of her age and time portray?
Suffice if for the wondering world to mark
She took from all beside the medal in Hyde Park;
The only prize that was for corsets given
to any manufacturer under heaven.
Lo! the dazzling splendours of her fame advance
O'er 'All England' and the whole of France
She, the beloved, who now fills Brunswick's throne
Deals with Madame Caplin – her alone;

- - - -

Why need I paint the heroine of my lays,
Or tell the land where passed her virgin days;
'Twas Canada!' – above all colonies renowned –
that heard my heroine's praises first resound,

- - - -

You'll an incarnation of the graces meet
at No. 58 in Berners Street.
Science and pure benevolence combined,
A deity in human form enshrined;
Gracious demeanour, and courtly mien,
Learning and worth are thine, great Native queen.

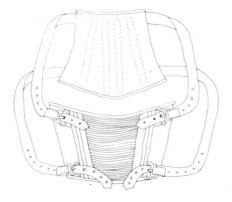

6 Cavé's Abdominal Supporter,
registered prototype. Anna
Maria Cavé, 1880

One variation of Caplin's hygienic corset was a 'gestation stay': even dress reformers considered that it was necessary to be corseted during pregnancy. Dr Tilt considered the busk should be removed, and that:

> In pregnancy the form of the stays should be moulded to the changes of the figure, and they should be sufficiently excavated at the breasts not to depress the nipple. Many young married women, from those most condemnatory feelings of false delicacy . . . try, by tight lacing and the application of a stronger busk, to conceal pregnancy as long as possible, and by so going, they not only increase their own sufferings but may do harm to the child.

Gestation stays were the only maternity garments to be widely advertised. Often marketing them as being constructed on scientific principles, many manufacturers liked to protect their special features by registration. They remained remarkably similar throughout the century. Most had adjustable hip gores, and could be used to help restore the maidenly form after the happy event. They also had openings to allow

7 Advertisement for Cavé's
Abdominal Supporter. Leicester
Museum and Art Gallery. Anna
Maria Cavé, 25 Union Grove,
Clapham, 1880. Note that the
three (6, 7, 8) are all slightly
different.

30

8 Surviving example of
Cavé's corset, Leicester
Museum and Art Gallery

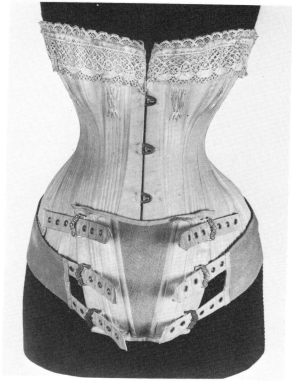

breastfeeding; unlike their Georgian grandmothers, even rich and fashionable Victorian mothers believed it was their duty to feed their own babies, rather than put them out to wet nurses.

Other pseudo-medical contraptions for controlling the body were registered, such as the back straighteners inflicted on countless children, and abdominal belts, providing secondary reinforcement for the especially corpulent. This one is a surviving example of a type of which versions were patented and registered by Madame Cavé in 1880. The original advertisement included a recommendation from *The Lancet.*

From the 1860s, firms such as R. & W. H. Symington of Market Harborough began to build factories in which rows of sewing machines operated from a central steam driven shaft turned out highly finished articles; up to forty whalebones could be stitched into casings to form complex patterns. In the 1870s developments in machine embroidery techniques allowed criss-cross stitching to be added to strengthen and embellish the casings. Steam moulding was used from the 1880s; the garment was brushed with wet starch and put on a heated block which 'set' it in a permanent shape. By this method more sophisticated undulations were possible than ever before. It is hardly surprising that corset making was a very competitive field. Firms made corsets

9 Clever photograph used to register Walter Helby of Portsea's elegant plagiarism, 1886

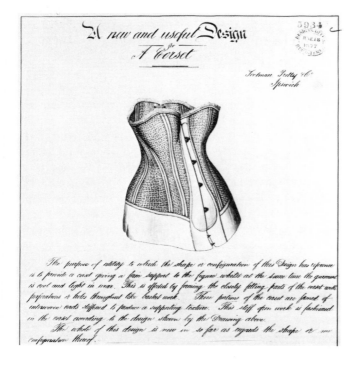

10 Hot weather corset registered in 1877 by Footman, Pretty & Co., an old established Ipswich firm now part of the Debenhams group

for every occasion from weddings to emigration – for every requirement of figure or taste. The classified pages of journals such as *The Queen* and *The Graphic* were full of advertisements of a particular firm's speciality. More often than not, these would state that the corset was registered or patented, or would give the registered trade-mark. Corset manufacturers were among the most frequent users of the registered design scheme, with good cause. Symington's kept copies of their rivals' advertise-ments and products as well as their own which are now in the care of Leicester Museum. Among the collection is a Symington corset which fastened by means of buckles in front. It had adjustable shoulder straps, but otherwise was identical in virtually every respect to the garment registered by Walter Helby, a notable Portsea corset manufacturer, in 1886. Just who was copying whom will never be known.

Other Underwear

Despite the widespread feeling which survived well into the present century, that only exquisitely hand-sewn underwear was acceptable for the true lady, the market for the ready-made variety increased steadily. Even in the 1840s, many large shops calling themselves 'ladies' outfitters' sold nothing but baby linen and female underclothing, designed primarily for brides and emigrants. However, this is not an area in which designs were often registered. Drawers, chemises and petticoats did not change radically and were not objects of high fashion. Being loose and simply shaped, they could be easily made in the home. The major exceptions to this were examples of superbly woven cotton and flannel made to imitate the complex tucks of con-temporary petticoats, registered by firms in Manchester and Glasgow.

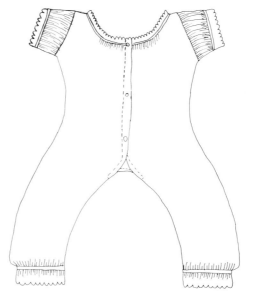

11 Lady's combination garment,
George Langridge & Co.,
Temple Street, Bristol, 1877

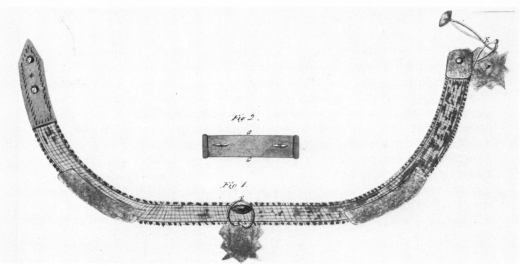

12   An early example of a 'ladies' belt', in red and blue silk with chamois leather pads at the hips and under the toggle towel fastenings, to prevent chafing. Adjusted by elastic piece in front. Theresa Lawrence, Ludgate Hill, City, 1849

13   Chemise registered by Galbraith, Stewart & Co., 43 Mitchell Street, Glasgow, 1868

Registered underwear tended to be produced by large firms who dealt in, and registered, other types of clothing, such as corsets. George Langridge & Co. of Bristol registered corset fastenings as well as, in 1877, a 'lady's combination garment'. The fashionable figure was at that time particularly svelte, with the dress tight fitting well down the hips. Combinations, which did away with many layers of underclothing, were popular. As a new line, it was probably considered particularly worthwhile to register them. Charles Bayer of London Wall was another corset manufacturer who registered a chemise in 1888. He is notable as an early maker of sanitary wear, for in that year, he also registered a 'lady's belt'. These had been registered occasionally, since 1849, but it was only from the close of the century that they became widely available and openly advertised.

Bayer & Langridge also manufactured and registered bustles and crinolines. Like corsetry, these were vigorously marketed through advertisements in the national press. A great number were registered, to protect their charms, but far more were

14 Chemise registered by Mrs Hornblow, St Anne's Square, Manchester, 1867. At that time, several chemise designs offered a tight fitting alternative to the traditional loose garment. It is significant that within a few years the chemise passed out of use.

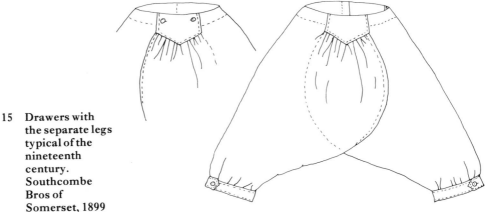

15 Drawers with the separate legs typical of the nineteenth century. Southcombe Bros of Somerset, 1899

patented. The metal cage crinoline was patented in 1856 and marketed by the American W. S. Thomson in the United States, England and France. There is evidence in the registered designs, however, that petticoats with hoops were worn well before that date, whilst Alison Adburgham in *Shops and Shopping* notes Mayhew's testimony to their use in 1851, and the Frenchman Francis Wey describing them as an English novelty in 1856. W. S. Thomson's patent was one stage in the fashion cycle of the skirt. The trend towards wider skirts began in the 1830s, and as they grew, more and more petticoats were worn to support them. The original 'crinoline' was a horse-hair fabric petticoat; its name was derived from the French words for hair and thread. The fancy warehousemen Salomons & Sons of 42 Old Change registered this type of crinoline in 1854 by means of a miniature sample with two double flounces, rippled by a goffering iron.

The idea of an underskirt with hoops was a natural development, which must have occurred to many people. 'Madame Blangy's Parisian Hindoo Cloth Petticoat' of 1849, registered by John Heather of 3 Bedford Court, Covent Garden, was described as having 'springs' slotted into tucks at the hem. These were probably sprung steel. It was, however, not until 1856 that Henry Bessemer perfected his method of making sprung steel on a large scale, which enabled steel crinolines to be widely worn. This light, pliable structure effortlessly performed the function previously carried out by layers of heavy petticoats. Even Mrs Amelia Bloomer gave up wearing her radical bifurcated costume when introduced to the crinoline. It was a most persistent fashion. It evolved into the crinolette, then various stages of bustle; women were to carry cages around with them for the next thirty years. The crinoline looked solid, but actually bounced about with every step or gust of wind. Lady Dorothy Nevill was not alone when she wrote of an experience with:

that monstrosity 'The Crinoline' which once came near costing me my life . . . It was in the drawing room one evening after dinner at Dangstein before the gentlemen had joined us, and at the time my dress caught fire, I was showing a lady an engraving of Mr

36

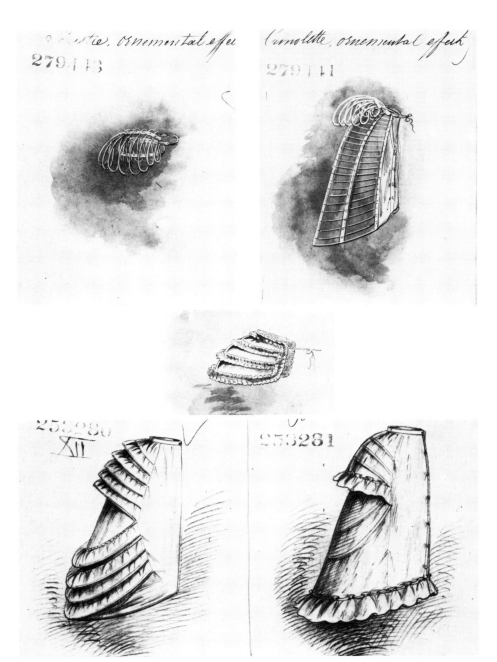

16 Flexible steel crinolettes and bustles gave a fashionable 'tournure'. Léonce Bernard
Schmolle, 55 Aldermanbury, City, 1872–4

FASHIONS FOR NOVEMBER.

"L r! Mr. Tomkins, I wish you wouldn't meddle with what doesn't concern you. If you must know what it is—It's an Air Tube Dress Extender."
(*Ed.* "What next!")

17   *Punch* 1849

Cobden, which he had just given me, and which hung near the fireplace. Somehow or other my voluminous skirt caught fire, and in an instant I was ablaze, but I kept my presence of mind, and rolling myself in the hearthrug, by some means or other eventually beat out and subdued the flames . . . none of the ladies present could of course do much to assist me, for their enormous crinolines rendered them almost completely impotent to deal with the fire, and had they come very close to me, all of them would have been ablaze too. (*The Reminiscences of Lady Dorothy Nevill.*)

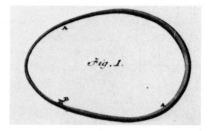

18   George Lander's inflatable rubber petticoat, 1848

38

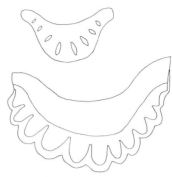

19 'Ladies' Bussels –
material air-proof',
Thomas Foot
Piper, 94
Cheapside, City,
1843

The designs prove the existence of another type of crinoline. In ridiculing the fashion, *Punch* referred as frequently to inflatable rubber hoops as to metal ones. A parody of a poem by Thomas Moore (1779–1852) pleaded:

> *Believe me if all those voluminous charms*
> *which thy fondness for fashion betray*
> *And keep e'en thy honest relations at arm's*
> *   distance some paces away,*
> *Were those air-tubes now blown up, exploded outright*
> *and those hoops trundled off thee as well,*
> *with less ample skirts thou wouldst look less a fright*
> *and move belle-like when less like a bell.* (Vol. 32, 1857, p. 60.)

The phenomenon was first illustrated in *Punch* as early as 1849, and a comparison between the garment in this cartoon and the 'Dress Extending Zephyr Belt' registered by George Lander of Cheltenham in 1848 would suggest that they were perhaps one and the same thing.

Even so, the concept was not new. Ever since 1822, when Charles Macintosh first sandwiched together two cloths with rubber softened by naptha, and so perfected the first truly impermeable fabric, 'Mackintosh' had been used for 'airwork', such as inflatable mattresses, cushions and life-belts. Among the earliest registered designs were some which exploited this air-proof quality for a novel purpose: on 12 September 1843, two rough sketches were used to register 'Ladies' Bussels' (sic), 'Material Air-Proof'. They show no mouthpiece, and so must have been inflated during manufacture. They were made by Thomas Foot Piper, a 'stay and corset manufacturer' who in 1845 had two branches in London and one in Portsmouth.

'Airwork' manufacturers answered another heartfelt need of certain women. Throughout the period, inflatable rubber bust improvers could be bought, enabling the flat chested to conform to the voluptuous ideal. The prevalence of strategically placed wadding in the linings of surviving dresses shows that a good many did not hesitate to gild the lily. Inflatable bust improvers could be worn loose, of the type registered by Rebecca and Emma Alcock of Doctor's Commons in 1849, or they could form an integral part of the corset, as in the 1881 'Corset with Expansible Busts' registered by F. Parsons, of 30 Gracechurch Street, London, and Sunnybank, Chipping Norton, whereby:

> The inconveniences attendant upon the use of loose pads are avoided. Pockets hold India rubber or other air-proof bags which are made of a form to represent as nearly as possible when distended the shape of the human breasts and they are provided with a short tube filled with a suitable mouthpiece whereby the busts may be expanded as required when the corset is on the body.

20 **More sophisticated 'airwork' by Foot Piper's neighbours, Simister & Holland, 66 Cheapside, City, 1847**

6
Elastic

NOTHER EARLY application of rubber to clothing was in the form of elastic. At about the same time that Charles Macintosh was experimenting with naptha–rubber solutions in Glasgow, an Islington coachbuilder with a scientific turn of mind, Thomas Hancock, was also devising ways of making the material usable. In 1820 he patented 'an improvement in the application of a certain material to various articles of dress and other articles, that the same may be rendered more elastic'. Hancock applied his invention to gloves, first stitching, then later sticking with Macintosh's solution, a piece of rubber to their wrists. He claimed that 'an immense quantity' of these gloves were sold in the 1820s. (*A Personal Narrative of the Origin and Progress of the Caoutchouc and India Rubber Manufacture in England*).

Shortly, however, Hancock's little rubber strips were superseded by a covered braid, the prototype of modern elastic. Hancock remembered how in the early 1830s:

> A German whose name I am not acquainted with conceived the idea of introducing a thread of rubber into a woven web of fabric, so as to form a warp, and by keeping it confined in an extended state during the operation of weaving, and then releasing it, the fabric would be gathered up and elasticated.

This man enlisted the help of the English managers of Hancock's Paris India Rubber Showroom, who perfected the thread, which was produced in some quantity in France. The receptive Hancock quickly copied the idea in England. Rubber was imported from South America in small bottle-shaped pieces. To obtain strands, these were painstakingly sliced into five inch by one-sixteenth of an inch strips. Gangs of girls then spliced the ends together thus forming a continuous thread. It was soaked in hot water, stretched and cooled in that position, before being woven into a tape which was ironed to regain its elasticity. Hancock was soon tired of this fiddly process, and eventually collaborated with a Manchester ribbon manufacturer.

Hancock was not on his own. Caleb Bedells, a Leicester hosiery and haberdashery manufacturer, produced elastic web in the same way. Then in 1839 Bedells patented a method of incorporating elastic into knitted goods. Such was his success that elastic web manufacture was taken up by many Leicester entrepreneurs, and became an important sideline for that town already the home of the woollen hosiery industry.

Elastic thread was still expensive and time consuming to produce when registration began in 1839, but it was exciting a great deal of interest, and in the early years many designs incorporating elastic can be found. A favourite use was as a back fastening for waistcoats, to give the fashionable 'nipped in' look to the male torso. These disappear

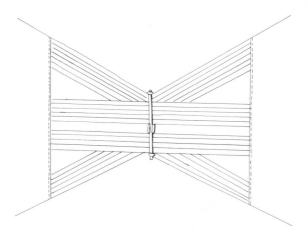

1 'Improved spring
for waistcoats,
trousers, et-
cetera', John
Smerton, 9
Edmond Place,
London, 1841

after 1841, perhaps because it was found that elastic lost its stretching qualities under constant strain. Early India rubber goods were unsatisfactory in other ways. They tended to become distressingly soft in the heat, and brittle in the cold; and began to decompose on exposure to sunlight or sweat. If rubber was to be universally accepted, these interesting characteristics would have to be eliminated.

The problems were even more acute in the United States with its extreme weather conditions. Many disastrous attempts to market rubber products had been made when in 1835, a chance visit by Charles Goodyear, an impecunious inventor and failed businessman, to the Roxbury India Rubber Company's New York showrooms led to his spending the next nine years seeking a way to stabilise rubber. After more than one false start, he found that, when mixed with sulphur and exposed to very high temperatures, it became less sensitive to ordinary temperature changes. He patented his process in America on 30 June 1844. But even at the brink of success his luck was marred: two weeks earlier, Thomas Hancock had patented an identical method in England. Ever since then, fierce controversy has raged over the identity of the real inventor. Goodyear may have given Hancock a clue when in 1842 he sent a sample of

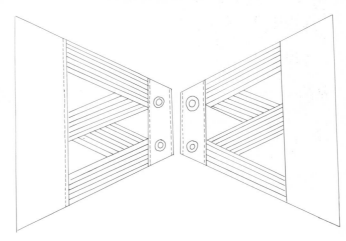

2 And another;
George Barnett,
Jewin Street, City,
1841

his work to England in an attempt to find sponsorship. Whoever invented the process, it was Hancock who coined the term 'vulcanisation', after Vulcan, Roman god of the forge.

Vulcanisation revolutionised the use of India rubber. The 1851 Great Exhibition devoted a sizeable section to it, and the Jury commented:

> From the moment in which vulcanisation of India rubber first became known, all the inconveniences which ordinary caoutchouc presented having disappeared, its employment received an extension which is continually increasing and each year sees new applications of this product spring into use.

3   A tantalising glimpse of a bright pink garter. John Checkley, a haberdashery manufacturer, Blackfriars Road, City, 1853

From 1844 there had been a flurry of activity among manufacturers and protection had been sought for all kinds of designs incorporating elastic, including gloves, boots, stays and the waistbands of men's long drawers. Elastic was less frequently the subject of a registration after the mid-1850s. This can be seen as an indication of the way it was passing out of the vanguard of technology and into the humdrum of everyday existence.

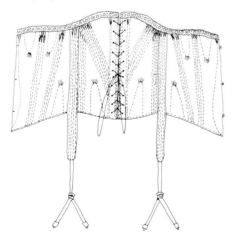

4   The garter's successor: corset with suspenders 1883. William Rushton, Landport, Hants

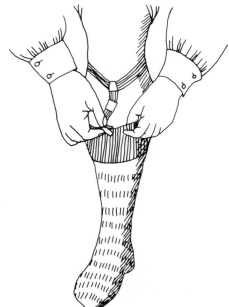

5 Sock suspenders formed of one
length of web adjusted by means
of metal attachments. Alf
Breese, Brewer Street, City,
1884

While many manufacturers incorporated the new elastic webbing into ready-made garments, a lot of elastic was sold over the haberdashery counter. Far more varieties were available to the general public then than now. It came in several widths, in cotton, silk, or mohair; black, white, or coloured; plain, or with a fancy pattern. In February 1848, Christopher Nickells, one time manager of Hancock's Paris showrooms, registered a series of designs for broad patterned elastics, in extraordinary colours. In the 1880s, the largest Leicester elastic manufacturer, Archibald Turner, fought a running battle with his son and rival Luke, across the sample book pages; the two registering remarkable elastics, patterned, striped, or with pretty pictures, in colours such as yellow, scarlet and magenta.

Even then, elastic was a difficult substance for the shopkeeper to cope with. In *The Draper and Haberdasher* of 1878, J. W. Hayes mentioned problems still encountered with this 'very important and useful article' the demand for which was 'fast increasing'. Because it was sold in seventy-two yard lengths:

Care should be exercised in dealing out cut lengths to customers, as the pieces are frequently in very short measure. The assistant having cut off a piece of elastic, should be careful to wrap the end round the centre of the card ... it would be a good plan for manufacturers to send out every card provided with a small metallic clip to secure the end ... these goods require plenty of air: the reserve stock should be stored in drawers or boxes. If kept too long in air-tight parcels, the India rubber will lose its elasticity and become perfectly useless.

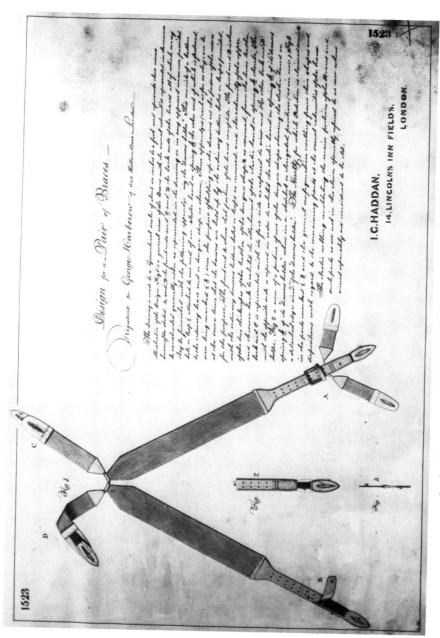

6   A pair of braces. George Harborrow, Holborn Bar, London, 1848

Although vulcanised rubber was a vast improvement, it still perished with time, as it does today. For this reason, very few nineteenth-century garments incorporating rubber survive. This makes the evidence of the registered designs extremely useful.

Many women bought elastic to make garters, but as early as 1834, they could be bought ready made, since they are listed by Perkins. Ladies rarely cherish their old garters; and so the actual samples registered and still surviving are rare finds indeed –

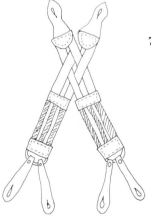

7 The last word in braces. Samuel Taylor, belt and brace manufacturer, 56 Lever Street, Manchester, 1885

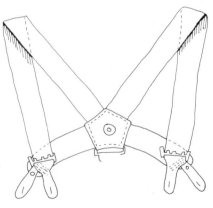

8 'Shoulders back and chest out' with the combined braces and chest expander. Richard Kew, Shudehill, Manchester, 1884. (Shudehill is still the centre of the Manchester rag trade)

with taffeta ends and engraved yellow metal buckles, they came in inch wide bright pink or red elastic. Such garters may have been beneficial to health. Tilt complained that ordinary garters were worn so tight that they impeded the blood and caused varicose veins. (*Elements of Health and Principles of Female Hygiene*). By the 1890s it was:

> Only in out of the way parts that . . . cords, tapes and bits of string are sometimes used. The most humble servant maid who is a little civilised buys elastic garters with buckles. (Baroness Stoffa, *The Lady's Dressing Room*.)

Stocking suspenders sometimes attached to the corset can be seen in the designs from 1882. Many versions, both male and female, were registered by Alf Breese, of 34 Brewer Street in the West End. The author of *Progress and Commerce* of 1893 sang his praises:

> Mr Breese, though young, has displayed a capacity for business which entitles him to rank among the pioneers of the mercantile world . . . take for instance, the 'ladies' shaped band stocking suspender'; by the aid of these ingenious and comfortable contrivances, garters are entirely dispensed with, and ladies fond of athletic and outdoor exercises have found them a boon which no persuasion would bring them to relinquish. This daintily got up suspender is made in different forms, and of a variety of suitable materials, and is fitted with the Hoven Clip, whose grip is of bull-dog tenacity . . . Turning to the requirements of the other sex, we find Mr Breese provides a 'Sock Suspender', an ingenious and simple arrangement, which, being worn below the knee, does not impede the motions of the joint, and therefore is a special favourite with dancers . . . Mr Breese, being a manufacturer, deals with wholesale houses only, but the public will find no difficulty in procuring his specialities from any retailer of standing.

Elastic came to have one other major function in the masculine wardrobe, for it fairly soon came to be used in the manufacture of suspenders in the American meaning, or braces in English usage. Throughout the nineteenth century, trousers were held up by braces. At first these consisted of two separate straps but by the 1840s, a connection began to be made at the centre back, and two tongues were introduced at the front. Small lengths of elastic were inserted to make them more flexible. Although Victorian men had a comparatively restricted choice of outerwear, this was partially compensated for by the vast array of braces available. Even Charles Goodyear was at a loss to recommend the best:

> This is one of those articles with which fashion has much to do, and the choice among the different kinds depends so much upon the fancy of the wearer, as well as upon the real utility of the article, that it may be considered presumptuous in anyone to assert absolutely what kind is best. (*Gum Elastic and Its Varieties*).

Many different kinds of braces can be seen among the registered designs, usually with their own ingenious elastic insertions. Perhaps my favourite was the 'combined braces and chest expander', registered by a Manchester firm in 1884. Few pairs of braces were entirely composed of elastic in the early years. This may have been because they would have stretched too much, particularly as they became old, or because of their expense. Towards the end of the century, all-elastic braces became more common.

Although some designs were registered for elastic topped drawers, these were rarely worn before the twentieth century. This may have been for the same reasons that all-elastic braces were uncommon, and also because elastic would not have withstood the more vigorous laundering of the time.

7
Shirts, Collars and Blouses

With fingers weary and worn,
With eyelids heavy and red,
A woman sat, in unwomanly rags,
Plying her needle and thread –
Stitch! Stitch! Stitch!
In poverty, hunger and dirt,
And still with a voice of dolorous pitch
She sang the 'Song of the Shirt!' (Thomas Hood, 'The Song of the Shirt').

AS THE population grew, so too did the demand for shirts. Moreover, the demand for ready-made shirts increased as more people had clerical jobs, spending power rose, overseas markets were opened up and women felt less inclined to make their menfolk's linen.

Cotton shirts certainly helped to raise the living standards of ordinary people. The shirt was vitally important. Worn next to the skin, it protected outer garments, which were hard to clean, from being soiled by the body. Until the Industrial Revolution, linen was generally worn but it was expensive. With the introduction of cotton, people could afford more shirts, and so were able to keep cleaner. This further encouraged the cotton trade, but its expansion was at the expense of linen. While real gentlemen continued to wear linen shirts, and would-be gentlemen wore cotton shirts, with linen fronts and cuffs, the decline in linen production brought widespread hardship.

In *Lights and Shadows of London Life* published in 1842, James Grant described the London shirtmaking trade, which employed between four and five thousand women:

Will it be believed, that there are several houses in London which only give four shillings and sixpence for making a dozen shirts, which is at the rate of fourpence halfpenny each! Of course these are what are called plain made shirts. And yet, with all their plainness, the best and most industrious hands are not able to make more than two per day: in other words, can only earn ninepence a day, or four shillings and sixpence per week. I leave my readers to form the best idea their imaginations can enable them, of what must be the privations and misery of the poor creatures who are doomed to toil from morning to night for these wretched wages.

While, as in other parts of the clothing industry, conditions improved as production shifted from outworking to the factory system, shirtmaking was always poorly paid and attracted those most desperate for work. The present author's great-grandmother, a single parent, worked in a Macclesfield shirt factory by day and took

"A SHROUD AS WELL AS A SHIRT."

MESSRS. MOSES AND SON have disclaimed the disgrace of being the employers of the unfortunate shirt-maker EMMA MOUNSER.

We are glad to find that kind-hearted THOMAS HOOD did not write the "Song of the Shirt" altogether in vain, since some of the taskmasters of the poor needlewomen are alive to the discredit of paying $2\frac{1}{2}d$. for ten hours' labour.

By the kindness of the pawnbroker we are enabled to furnish a pattern of the "Twopenny-ha'penny Shirt," which can be had ONLY (it is to be hoped) of MESSRS. HENRY EDWARD AND MORRIS MOSES of the Minories.

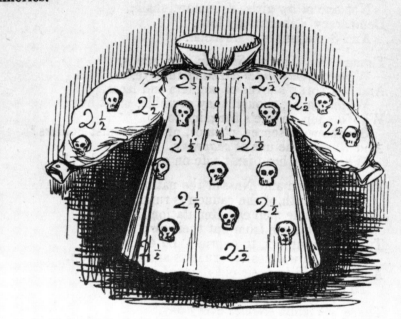

1   *Punch* 1848

shirts home to make by night. The author's grandmother remembered how as a seven year old at the turn of the century, she would help her mother by making all the button holes in two shirts each evening.

Ready-made shirts were traditionally made near ports. For instance, the London docklands, Southwark and Bermondsey, Portsmouth and Bristol all had thriving shirt trades. The great cotton towns Manchester and Glasgow supported important

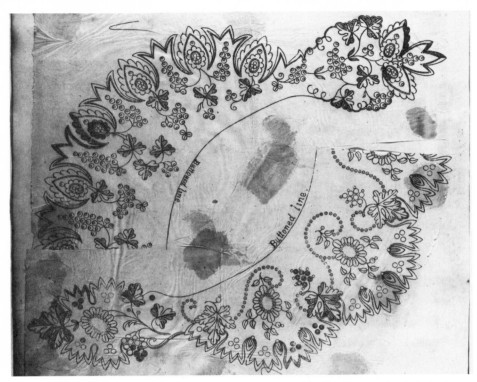

2   Pattern for exquisite embroidered collar to be worked by a cottager. G. L. Behrens & Co., Glasgow, 1853

industries devoted to making up cotton goods, including shirts. From the 1850s, mainland British firms often had outposts in Northern Ireland, where a good supply of cheap labour meant that huge quantities of shirts could be turned out very profitably.

Shirtmaking in Northern Ireland was an extension of the activities of Scottish manufacturers in the province. Since the 1840s they had employed Irish women on sewed muslin work. Until then this had largely been carried out in Scotland. It was white embroidery on white cotton, done by hand, or by a chain stitch made by a fine hook passed through taut fabric in a technique known as tambour work. Whole pieces were tamboured ready to cut out and make into dresses. Accessories such as collars were embroidered. The patterns were printed on fabric and sent out to remote cottages. Sometimes instructions for payment were also given; a collar registered by Behrens & Co. of Glasgow in 1853 bears the message 'six days allowed for this piece'.

Shirtmaking was introduced into Ireland in the late 1840s. The unsophisticated workforce accepted factory production on a massive scale, and by the end of the next decade, 15,000 people were involved in it. The Glasgow firm Tillie & Henderson installed 200 sewing machines at their branch in Northern Ireland in 1855. The Children's Employment Commission of 1863 heard that they employed a thousand people in a custom built factory, capable of turning out 500 dozen shirts, fifty gross collars, and cutting up two to three thousand yards of cloth daily. The scale of this

50

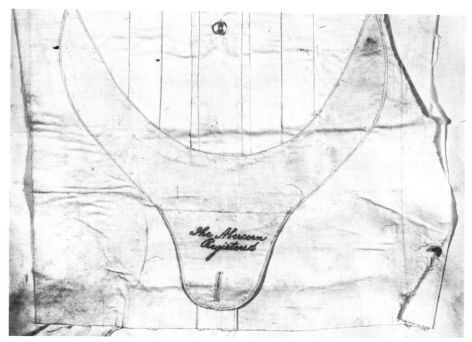

3 'The Abercorn Regd' Shirt. Tillie & Henderson, Glasgow and Northern Ireland, 1866. Note the minute machine stitching on this actual sample

enterprise was quite unprecedented on the mainland. Moreover, Tillie & Henderson were among only a handful of clothing manufacturers to work all their sewing machines successfully by one steam engine turning a central shaft, before 1860.

Tillie & Henderson registered several designs, including this actual front piece from a shirt of 1866. One of the trials of the hand shirtmaker was that the garment had to be very strong, to withstand heavy washing and wear. Minute back stitches were used, and all the seams were felled. This example is completely machine lock-stitched, and it shows that this was a perfect substitute for laborious hand work, effortlessly producing yards of tiny stitches. The machine was even used to embroider 'The Abercorn Regd' in red on the front tab, which fastened to the undergarment. It was evidently intended to use the registration as a selling point.

Tillie & Henderson were strict employers. They took on no one under eleven, nor would they accept married women with children. Tillie told the commission: 'Though they often beg to be admitted saying that it would be a charity to take them on, I refuse, telling them that I would almost sooner pay to keep them at home.' Moral standards were important: 'We endeavour to raise these as much as we can by insisting on all coming in bonnets with shoes and stockings.' The factory workers cut out and machined the main parts, which were then sent to outworkers in the country-side to be made up. Including these cottagers, Tillie & Henderson in the early 1860s employed as many as ten thousand people. The vast majority were women, working under male supervisors. This was usually the case in Northern Ireland. Another firm

4 'The Aptandum Shirt', William Westlow, Wood Street, City, 1848. The collar is cut so that no band is required for setting in of the back part of the collar and a much better fit is thereby obtained about the upper part of the body. The sleeves are cut in one piece so that no gusset, side pieces or gathers are required in connecting them to the body. The strings regulate the fit about the shoulders

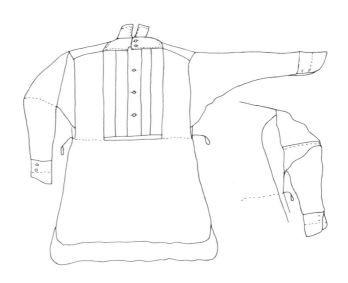

told the commission that they would prefer female overseers, but since virtually no women could write it was impossible.

The time-honoured way to make shirts was to have rectangular pieces for body and sleeves, square underarm gussets, and the neck gathered into a band. More and more of the shirt front was visible from the early nineteenth century, and this came to be

5 Embroidered shirts were popular with dashing young men. John Edward Ford, Addle Street, City, 1856

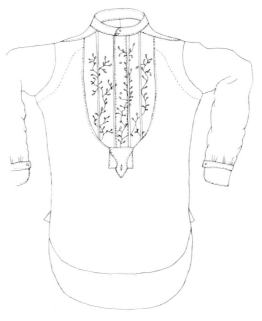

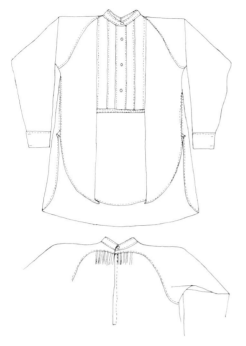

6 Dawson and MacNicol's
economical raglan sleeved
shirt, 50 Buchanan Street,
Glasgow, 1859

pleated and starched. The fullness at the neck was replaced by a shoulder yoke. The new shirt manufacturers were always looking for cost cutting dodges, and sometimes registered them. The 'Aptandum Shirt', made by a Wood Street firm in 1848, has sleeve and gusset cut in one, and also the collar and yoke. A drawstring at the waist held the front nicely in place. The Aptandum still followed traditional lines, being very bulky and square-cut. Within the next decade, shirts were to undergo a rapid transformation. This was perhaps because of the consideration of large scale manufacturers who were coming to dominate the market, as much as through changes in fashion.

An embroidered shirt registered by John Edward Ford of Addle Street in 1856 is cut from considerably less material. The smaller armholes are reinforced and the curved laps have little gussets. Very few shirts had attached collars from the 1850s, when collar making had become a specialised trade. The embroidery might seem unexpected, but in fact it was quite usual. The hero of Surtees's *Ask Mama* of 1858 not only had magnificently embroidered dress shirts, but also several dozen with horses, dogs, birds and foxes on them. Shirts of this type were never generally considered to be in the best of taste, but they had a distinct and dedicated following ever since Dickens had satirically described a shady character in *Pickwick Papers* of 1837 as 'a gentleman in a shirt emblazoned with pink anchors'.

The Raglan sleeve was one of the fashion successes of the 1850s, named after Lord Raglan, the Crimean War hero. It was used on all kinds of garments, but shirtmakers

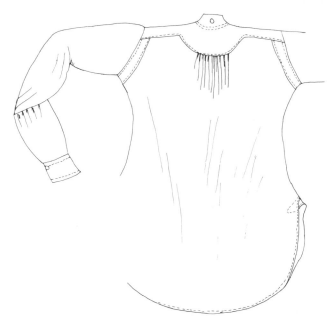

7 'The Volkommen
Shirt', Alexander
Grant and Bros.,
St Clement's
Court, City, 1855

found it particularly useful, since it did not need shaped armholes. Dawson &
MacNicol of Buchanan Street, Glasgow, registered their version in 1859 for its
'simplicity of construction and the better fitting of the shirt to the human body with
ease and comfort'. Like a good number of mid-century shirts, it fastens at the back.
This may have called for fewer button holes. The front, being stiffly starched, would
have been hard to fasten, and it would have looked smarter with its pretend buttons.

Many of the designs for shirts indicate elaborate top stitching. Once established,

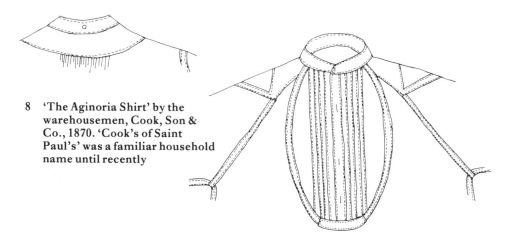

8 'The Aginoria Shirt' by the
warehousemen, Cook, Son &
Co., 1870. 'Cook's of Saint
Paul's' was a familiar household
name until recently

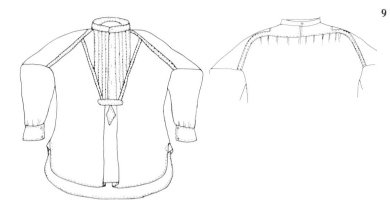

9 'The Lorne Shirt', Foster, Porter & Co., Wood Street warehousemen, 1871. 'The sleeve and armhole being formed of one piece of material gives a free action to the arm without disarranging the front, and the front being small at the bottom allows the full play of the shirt without creasing'

the sewing machine was used to create feats of virtuosity. Cooks of St Paul's Church Yard made full use of it in their 1870 design for a shirt with extensive strapwork.

The constant search for novelties led firms to think up all sorts of ways to fasten shirts, some more practicable than others. Foster Porter & Co., Welch Margetson and McIntyre Hogg & Co. all registered ideas for them, but it was Brown, Davis & Co. of Aldermanbury who registered in 1871 the first shirt to open all the way up the front. This seems an obvious development, but it is only in recent years that they have been generally adopted.

The quality and presentation of ready-made shirts improved as manufacturers aimed at an ever widening cross-section of the community. By the end of the century they were seriously affecting the trade of the old bespoke shirtmakers. The 'Major of Today', author of *Clothes and the Man* (1900), complained:

> It is unfortunate that most hosiers do not make their own shirts . . . It is quite possible that a hosier will take your measurements, attend carefully – as far as you can tell – to all

10 'The Figurate Shirt', Brown, Davis & Co., Love Lane, Aldermanbury, 1871. 'Does away with the old and objectional way of putting on the shirt by putting it over the head. It allows of the shirt being made to fit the person both in width of the body and in the armholes, which cannot be done if the shirt is to be put on over the head. Shirts made according to this design are for this reason more comfortable than shirts of ordinary construction'

55

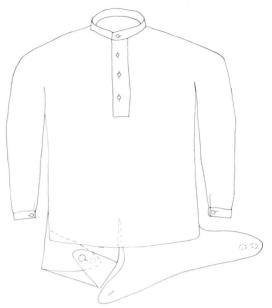

11 'The Leg Fitting Shirt',
Richard Copley, Liverpool,
1877. 'To cause the shirt to fit
better by retaining the said
shirt in position so as to
prevent the action of the body
from causing the said shirt to
be wrinkled or puckered'

that you say, and then when the business of measuring is over he may write to a factory and ask them to send down a certain number of shirts to a stock size nearest to that corresponding to your size.

The Major was vehemently opposed to all ready-made garments, and was well aware of the distinction conferred by good quality linen. Ever since Brummell's day, a gentleman could be recognised by the crispness, whiteness and purity of his shirt. Its maintenance was a considerable expense. The rigours of boilding and starching to give the right effect, and ironing the cuffs into a polished surface, soon made it frayed and shabby. A man's shirt was observed and its condition noted. Writers often used it as a guide to character. The linen of the monstrous dwarf Quilp in *The Old Curiosity Shop* was 'always of a particulour colour, for such was his whim and fancy'. Arnold

12 1891 shirt with attached collar
and possibly an elasticated
hem. Edward Robinson Buck,
Salford. Soft collared shirts
were becoming very popular
for sports at this time

13   Striped shirt, Edmund Potter & Co. Ltd., Manchester, 1900. This formula was to remain virtually unchanged for the next 60 years

Bennett used the state of a man's linen more than once as an omen. In *The Old Wives' Tale*, Gerald Scales

> was dressed with some distinction; good clothes, when put to the test, survived a change of fortune. Only his collar, large shaped front, and wristbands, which bore the ineffaceable signs of cheap laundering, reflected the shadow of impending disaster.

And the reader knew Willie Price was doomed in *Anna of the Five Towns* from the moment Bennett mentioned his dirty collar.

For some people the problem was not so much a clean shirt as any shirt at all. This was why the Major warned in *Clothes and the Man* that: 'The waistcoat neck should show a small margin of shirt front on both sides. Even an Ascot tie should not cover the shirt front completely.'

The separate shirt front or dicky filled a gap, so to speak, in many a wardrobe. Nearly all shirt manufacturers made them, and proportionately more were registered than shirts. It was evidently quite a problem getting them to stay in place. The designs registered tried out different combinations of tapes and loops which passed over the braces. Shirt fronts were cheaper to buy and maintain than shirts. They could hide a dirty shirt, transform a daytime shirt into evening dress, or hide a shirt made in fabrics or colours other than white linen or cotton. The man shown here is wearing his over a striped shirt. These were common, but not socially acceptable until the 1890s. An 1876 etiquette book (*How to Dress, or Etiquette of the Toilette*) gave the reason why: 'Never wear, if possible, a coloured shirt. Figures and stripes do not conceal impurity, nor should this be a desideratum in any decent man.'

Striped shirts were generally cheaper, probably because they were preferred by poorer customers. The Manchester wholesalers Rylands & Sons included striped shirts in a catalogue of the 1870s: known as 'regatta' shirts, they were 9s 6d per dozen, while their best white shirts were sold dressed and boxed at £5 per dozen. By 1900, striped shirts were beginning to be accepted by the upper classes. It is interesting, however, that an element of status display remained: for wear in the city they had white collars and cuffs.

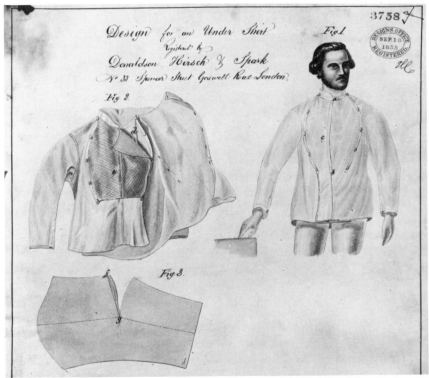

14 Undershirt to keep out the cold: detachable layers of red flannel for an extra warm chest. Donaldson, Hirsch & Spark, Goswell Road, City, 1855. The shirt developed originally to protect the outer garments from bodily dirt, and so it was worn next to the skin. Two were commonly worn for warmth: Samuel Pepys referred to this practice in his diary from the 1660s. In the 19th century the habit was gradually superseded by the wearing of woollen vests.

15 'The New Uniform Shirt Front', Thomas Richard Barlow, 143 Tooley Street, Southwark, 1858. For 'easy adjustment to the figure and its close resemblance to the shirt and also the impossibility of its becoming disarranged through exertion'

Grey flannel was a popular shirt fabric, among working men, and also as sportswear. It was hardwearing, absorbent, warm and it did not show the dirt. Several examples were registered, including one by Adams Fryer & Co. of Bristol in 1873, which was provided with an example of its purple and black tartan front band.

Collars

When H. G. Wells' shop assistant, Kipps, got the sack from Shalford's drapery bazaar in Folkestone in the 1890s, his friend Buggins gave him a word of advice as he was preparing to look for work in Wood Street:

'Whatever you do,' said Buggins, 'keep hold of your collars and cuffs – shirts if you can, but collars anyhow. Spout them last.'
(He remembered his appearance when last unemployed): 'Boots been inked in some reading rooms ... tailcoat buttoned up, black chest plaster tie – spread out. Shirt, you know, gone.'
Buggins pointed upward with a pious expression
'No shirt I expect?'
'Ate it,' said Buggins.

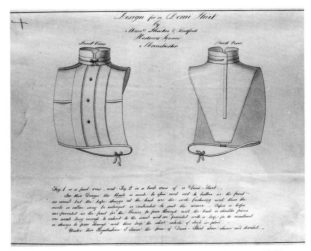

16   Design for a demi-shirt, Thacker & Radford, Manchester, 1847

One of the greatest expenses for those with small incomes who wished to appear respectable was the maintenance of clean starched collars and cuffs. H. G. Wells himself experienced this problem, which afflicted many of his characters. The science student Lewisham saved threepence out of his income of one guinea a week by wearing a patent waterproof collar and thus avoiding laundry bills: The collar was: 'one of those you wash overnight with a toothbrush, and hang on the back of your chair to dry, and there you have it, next morning, rejuvenesced. It was the only collar he had in the world . . .' (*Love and Mr Lewisham*).

Perhaps more popular than rubber collars were celluloid ones, like those described by Robert Roberts in Salford at the turn of the century: 'All boys save the poorest wore celluloid Eton collars that curled with age, turned yellow and exuded a peculiar smell.' (*The Classic Slum*).

17   A simpler shirt
      front, A. K. Cook
      & Co., Taunton,
      Somerset, 1891.
      The Bristol
      clothing trade
      took in much of
      the West Country

60

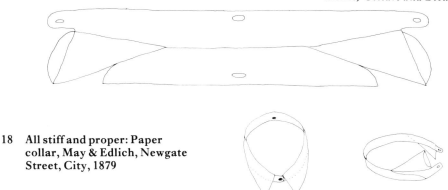

18   All stiff and proper: Paper
     collar, May & Edlich, Newgate
     Street, City, 1879

The other poor man's alternative to cloth was paper. Paper collars and cuffs were
worn by people such as Mr Povey, the draper's assistant in Bennett's *The Old Wives'
Tale*. Rylands & Sons' catalogue gives an idea of the comparative costs in the 1870s.
'Gentlemen's linen collars' were 2s 6d to 7s per dozen wholesale, while paper collars
cost 3s to 8s 6d per gross wholesale. The cheapest paper collar therefore cost a
farthing and the dearest three farthings. If these retailed at a halfpenny and a penny
halfpenny this was still cheaper than Lewisham's threepence a week laundry bills. In
1870 the Bermondsey firm Newland & Potter registered a cardboard shirt front with a
fabric effect finish, which simply hooked on over the buttons of a real shirt. It was

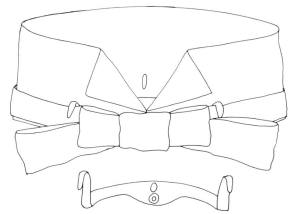

19   Tie holders were
     needed with
     slippery celluloid
     collars. Albert
     Wacker, Nurem-
     berg, 1900

carefully indented to represent stitched lines, and printed all over to look like fine blue
striped cotton.
     All types of collars formed a solid band round the neck. It was anchored to the shirt
by studs front and back, which had to be forced through stiff button holes and were
liable to burst out at any time. Compounding the difficulties, with a stand-up collar,
the necktie would slide around unless hooked down. Collars were at their highest in
the 1880s, and a spate of designs for necktie retainers were registered. In the end, a
loop attached to the shirt at the back was found to be as good as anything for this
purpose.

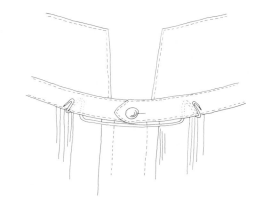

20 Welch Margetson
    supplied nearly
    every sartorial
    need: necktie and
    scarf retainer,
    1883

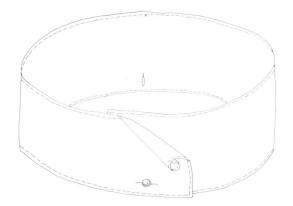

21 Stylish design for
    1896: George
    Longland, 26
    Beech Road,
    Sale, Cheshire,
    'furniture
    salesman'

The collar was quite a sensitive fashion item. The examples registered often had splendid names. In the 1850s, Dent Allcroft registered the 'Devonshire', the 'United Service', and 'Dent's Perfected', while Welch Margetson included in their range the 'West End', the 'Oriental', and the 'Corded Leopold'. Most collars were more or less uncomfortable. The most fashionable tended to be the most excruciating (except for a brief spell in the 1860s when the turn down collar was first introduced).

Poor Kipps, who as an apprentice was provided with clothing, and wishing to look grown-up,

> purchased at his own expense three stand-up collars to replace his former turn-down ones. They were nearly three inches high, higher than those Pierce wore, and they made his neck quite sore and left a red mark under his ears ... (H. G. Wells *Kipps*).

A well-designed collar could be a major feat of engineering in fabric. The special requirements of collar making soon made it into a distinct trade from shirt manufacture, although it was carried out in the same areas.

While each firm produced a steady stream of new collar designs, many are virtually indistinguishable. It seems surprising that firms should have gone to the trouble of taking their rivals to court for piracy. Yet on 18 January 1846, the *Manchester Guardian* reported a case:

> Yesterday, Messrs Flusheim and Hesse, Stock and Shirt Makers, Back Piccadilly, were summoned to the Borough Court to answer an information laid against them by Messrs Welch and Margetson, a firm in the same trade, for infringing the design for a shirt collar, which the complainants had registered ... The defendants had also registered a design for a shirt collar, about twelve months after the complainants had registered theirs, and that was the design complained of as a piracy ... Mr Green, contended upon behalf of the defendants ... that the collar differed from that of the complainants in being made all in one piece, and in having a horizontal line at the band part of the neck, whereas the complainants appeared to have registered their collar in consequence of the novelty which a curvature at that part produced. He then called three witnesses – Mr and Mrs Rowland, and Mr William Sells, all of whom were practically acquainted with the making of collars, and who gave it as their opinion that the two designs were perfectly dissimilar ... Mr Mander said that the Magistrates had come to the conclusion that the defendant's design was not a piracy. The case occupied the court about two hours.

However scrupulous Hesse may have been in registering his design, he had no compunction about advertising it in the same paper as 'Flusheim and Hesse's Imperial Patent Shirt Collars Registered March 29th 1845'. In using the term patent he was not doing anything unusual. Many manufacturers liked to foster public confusion in this area.

David Hesse was an example of a new type of entrepreneur. The son of a Cologne rabbi, he came to England in the 1830s. He started a small drapery business which was transformed into a shirt and collar manufacturing empire with the aid of a succession of partners. By the 1850s he had a factory in Ireland and was importing goods from France and Germany. As his commercial status grew, so too did his position in the Jewish community. He was a radical, and he supported Manchester's reformed synagogue.

Collar makers quickly realised the potential importance of the sewing machine. Its small tough stitch was ideal for giving collars the required strength. The first, and for a time, the only, registered designs incorporating machine stitching were for collars. These were registered from late 1857 by Richard Adams Ford & Co. of 38 Poultry, a lane off Gresham Street, and John Crawley & Son of 82 Wood Street, closely followed by several Glasgow makers – all were for women's collars. They were made along the same lines as men's, but had fancy scalloped edges, top stitching and inserted panels. These could be done most effectively by machine.

This type of collar harmonised well with the perky, rather masculine fashions of the late 1850s and early 1860s, with their bright colours, military looking boots, coarse

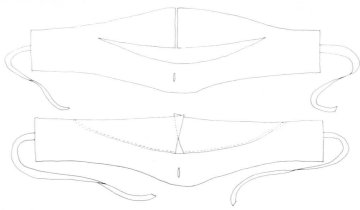

22 David Hesse's controversial collar, 1845: 'Both top and bottom being formed of one piece of cloth. The shape shown is cut out of the centre of it . . . to give greater stiffness to the collar at the top and to prevent it falling down in the wear a cord is stitched in along the line of the junction of the two cheek pieces with the under part'

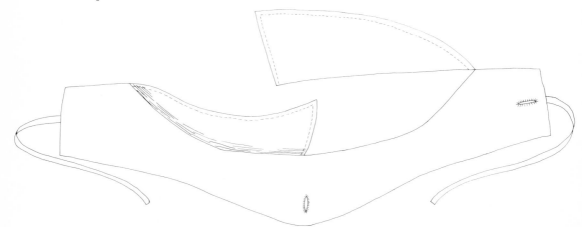

23   The plaintif's version: Welch Margetson, 1844

broderie anglaise flounces, Garibaldi blouses and bold little hats. It made a complete contrast to the delicately pretty embroidered muslin collars which had predominated until around 1850. Neat, starched collars continued to be registered throughout the period. The main alternative was a little frill stitched inside the dress. These came into the realm of the milliners, since they were often composed of gauze and lace. Most of these registrations came from Nottingham, which had long been known for its wholesale millinery, such as caps, decorative aprons and different frills for trimmings.

The development of more practical clothing for women in the late nineteenth century was of great significance, reflecting as it did their gradual emancipation. The

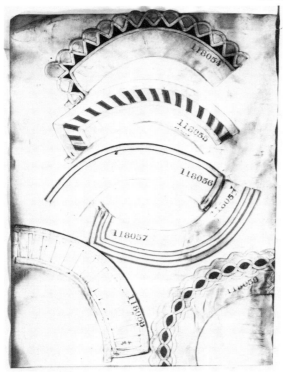

24 **Women's machine stitched collars. John King & Co., Buchanan Street, Glasgow, 1859**

bright red blouse and sturdy skirt worn by some young women in the 1850s was the first outfit that allowed really vigorous activity. It was not until the 1890s, however, that the blouse and skirt was generally adopted for daytime wear. It had many advantages over conventional dress. The skirt, usually wool, was hard wearing and not easily damaged. The top might be washable – perhaps of knitted jersey fabric or of cotton. In either case it would be comfortable to wear, and cheap to renew, so it could always look smart and fresh and suitable for the 'new woman' to wear at work in offices and schools. The more masculine styles were often made by men's shirt and collar makers but frillier versions were produced by wholesale milliners, who were beginning to call themselves ladies' outfitters, and to be based in the cotton clothing areas.

The names which crop up most frequently among the registrations of the 1890s were E. & H. Tideswell of Wood Street, James Carter of Belfast, Hancock & Leighton of Houndsgate, Nottingham.

I. & R. Pritchard of Madeira Court, Glasgow, made delightful children's cotton clothing. This was another era in which cheap ready-made clothing was rapidly becoming available.

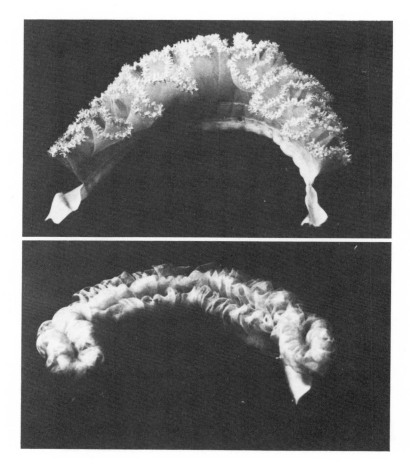

25   Elegant confections from C. G. Hill & Co., Plantagenet Street, Nottingham, 1893

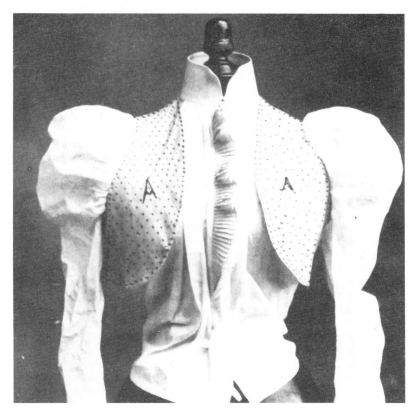

26 By the 1890s the blouse was a firm favourite. E. & H. Tideswell, Wood Street, City,
1892

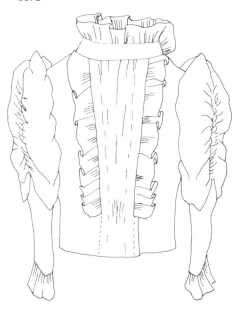

27 Blouse by Dorothy Taylor,
manufacturer, John Street,
Manchester, 1896

28 Blouse by Adolphe Rosenthal &
    Co. Ltd., London Wall, City,
    1897

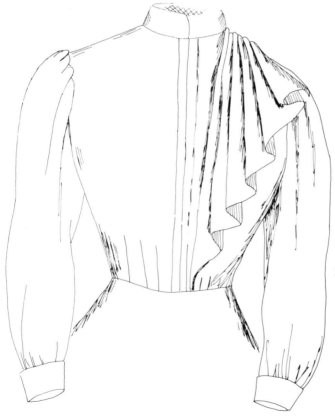

29 Blouse by Hancock &
    Leighton, Nottingham,
    1898

30 Serviceable
    frocks for
    growing girls
    were made by I. &
    R. Pritchard &
    Co., Madeira
    Court, Argyle
    Street, Glasgow,
    1890

8
Mantles and Dresses

COMPARED WITH the male ready-to-wear trade, the women's clothing industry lagged behind. This was firstly because female clothes were usually made from lighter fabrics than male dress, and they could be easily worked at home by amateurs. Secondly, while men's clothing was tending towards greater standardisation, women still sought to make a highly individual statement through their clothes. The diversity of decoration on surviving early Victorian dresses would have been impossible to produce commercially before the introduction of the sewing machine. Most important, the bodice and, in the 1840s, the sleeves, were expected to fit like a second skin. Bodices were often boned and padded. Careful fitting was needed to achieve the desired 'upholstered' effect. Added to this, there was a great deal of prejudice against ready-made clothing, which was thought to be of poor quality. At many levels of society, openly patronising ready-made clothing would be tantamount to committing social suicide.

Moreover, the restricted lifestyles of many women gave them a great deal of spare time. The planning and creation of the wardrobe was a welcome and ladylike occupation. Those who did not make their own clothes could hire a dressmaker very cheaply, since the limited employment opportunities for respectable women meant that too many were forced into this overcrowded trade.

There were some garments, however, which gave scope for selling ready made since they could be as good as individually made ones, and so the prejudice against them was less acute. Cloaks and mantles were simple to make and, being worn loose, would fit a variety of figure types. Drapers' shops and travelling salesmen had stocked them ever since the days of the red flannel hooded cloak which was the typical country dress of the eighteenth century. In *The Lady's Shopping Manual and Mercery Album* of 1834, E. E. Perkins listed 'lady's silk and merino cloaks'.

In the 1840s the most popular outergarment for women was the huge rectangular shawl, which swept well down behind and was worn clutched to the body in front. The best came from Kashmir, but cheaper versions could be had, chiefly woven in Paisley and Norwich, in designs which followed, more or less, the oriental prototype, or in simpler styles. The shawl's popularity in 1842 when the classes for registered designs were drawn up is evinced by the fact that a whole category was given over to shawls alone. They remained popular for many years, perhaps because of their snob value:

Fig:1. *Oxford London* *Fig:2.*

1   Mantle. Walley & Hardwick, Oxford Street, London, 1848

they were hard to wear, especially when carrying things, and could be exorbitantly expensive. As the author of *How to Dress Well* wrote in 1868:

> Every servant girl, every maid of work has her Sunday cloak. None but the rich can sport an Indian shawl. It requires falling shoulders and a tall and graceful figure.

The mantle, a semi-fitting garment with wide sleeves arranged so that they left the arms free, was in the ascendant in the 1850s. The Oxford Street silk mercers Walley & Hardwick registered the first design for one in 1848. The text explained how 'a greater superiority of fit' was attained by using a 'gored construction'. It seems to have been made in a light, crisp silk with pinked and scalloped edges left unhemmed, as was the fashion for dress flounces. It was a quick and effective finish for a mass-produced garment.

Private dressmakers and tailors did not as a rule move into the early women's outerwear market. They had as much work as they could cope with making commissioned clothing, without having to maintain a stock of ready-made goods. Nor were there as yet shops specialising in women's ready-made clothes as well known chainstores do today. Instead, silk merchants and linen drapers, such as Walley & Hardwick, who sold fabrics by the piece, were first to take the logical step of having

2 'The Duchess'. A
   ready-made cloak
   from Vyse & Sons,
   76 Wood Street, City,
   1862

their materials made up, or buying from wholesale mantle manufacturers, such as
Donald Nicholson of St Paul's Church Yard.

   Mantles were often supplied to shops by millinery wholesalers, used to dealing with
ready-made headwear, fancy trimmings and small items such as collars and cuffs.
They were thus geared up to making and selling them. One millinery firm which came
to manufacture mantles was Thomas Vyse & Sons of Wood Street. The gradual
extension of their activities makes an interesting story. They were founded in 1794,
and ladies' magazines in the 1820s frequently carried advertisements for their straw
hats. By the 1850s they described themselves in post office directories as 'wholesale

3 Billhead, Jay's
   Mourning
   Warehouse,
   Regent Street,
   London, late
   1840s

72

milliners' – implying they dealt in more than just straw goods. By then they were large and important enough to be included in Daniel Puseley's *Commercial Companion* of 1858, in which they were an 'extensive and eminent straw hat and bonnet establishment', with a New York branch, and manufactories at Luton, St Albans and Redbourn in Hertfordshire, and Prato in Italy, as well as a factory at the rear of their London premises 'for the manufacture of the richer description of fancy goods for which the house is celebrated'. A significant development had taken place by 1863, when they were included in the post office directory under the headings wholesale milliners, straw hat dealers, ladies' outfitters, and mantle and cloak warehouses. Vyse's were obviously proud of this new enterprise. In the early 1860s they registered a succession of designs for cloaks by means of rather nice engravings. These illustrate how simple such garments were, requiring a minimum of construction and decoration. The firm continued to make women's clothing, and constantly expanded their lines, until well into the twentieth century.

One of the first areas where mass-produced clothing became widely accepted was mourning dress. Mourning was almost a national pastime in the nineteenth century: with the demise of the most distant relative, black was worn for a considerable time then replaced by semi-mourning of grey, mauve and white. After a bereavement, there was a special need to buy clothes quickly which conformed to rigidly set rules. Black crape was the most extensively used mourning fabric (through which Courtaulds first made their fortune). Widows' weeds were complete swathes of the stuff. Ordinary mourning dress involved not only deep bands of it on the skirt, but crape collars and cuffs. These were the province of the milliner, as were widows' caps. As early as 1842 they were chiefly mass produced:

> Widows' caps are all much alike, whether the wearer be young or old, rich or poor. The making of widows' caps has therefore naturally become a sort of manufacture, with which the (private) milliner has commonly nothing to do. (*The Guide to the Trade: The Dressmaker and Milliner.*)

That mourning millinery was a highly developed wholesale trade by the 1840s is shown by the many examples registered. Mourning dress was worn intensively for a limited period, and then thrown away, it being considered unlucky to have black crape in the house between deaths. Surviving specimens are therefore unusual. Most of the registered designs were for collars and cuffs, with elaborate pleated and twisted crape loosely stitched on black net. In February 1845 Lyons & Co. of West Square, Lambeth, registered a deep collar with a V-shaped bodice piece attached composed of a series of tucks. This was the first design to be registered which could be described as a recognisable part of a dress. Other designs included a variety of trimmings, caps, and bonnet veils. Papers for lining boxes registered by Wellington Williams had splendid patterns of hearses, tombstones, angels and such like, to put purchasers in the right mood. All were manufactured by London firms except some of the bonnet veils, which were registered by George Bayless Yates of St Mary's Gate, Nottingham.

These were black tulle with beautifully appliquéd flowers in attractively transluscent puffs of crape.

Life was hard for most dressmakers but making complete mourning outfits was a particularly severe trial for them. Dresses had to be made at short notice and stitching black fabric tired the eyes. At times of general mourning they had to work for long stretches. The 1843 Children's and Young Person's Employment Commission heard how following the general mourning for William IV, a girl was made to work from 4 a.m. on a Thursday to 10.30 p.m. on the Saturday following without stop, and as a result her eyesight was permanently damaged. To meet this demand, entire shops were set up which sold nothing but mourning requisites. Of these, the biggest and best known was Jay's Mourning Warehouse on Regent Street, founded by William Chickall Jay in 1841. In 1865, Henry Mayhew described this emporium in *Shops and Companies of London*:

> Bright eyed fair damsels clad in black silk . . . will, in a few minutes, lay before us every description of mourning we may require . . . Mantles all a bristle with bugles and beads, and trimmed with every variety of gimp ornamentation – marvels of design and work-manship. White Zouave jackets, whose sheen is dazzling, and whose braiding is a mathematical puzzle . . . Bonnets of the most subtle design and most ornate specimens of floriculture nod at us from every table; and should you wish to purchase a cloak, one of the aforesaid young ladies will immediately put it on to show you the fit thereof and the young lady will look so nice also that you purchase it without asking another word . . . Are collars and cuffs your weakness? . . . Boxes taken from shelves reveal collars of white crape, of black crape, of tulle, and of muslin, collars dotted with black and edged with black.

Jay maintained a staff of several hundred in his shop and workrooms and he had a good reputation as an employer. His efforts to alleviate the working conditions of his dressmakers and milliners were recounted to the 1863–7 Commission. It appears his main obstacle in this were the women themselves. Although they worked from 8.30 a.m. to 9 p.m., this was not considered excessive. Jay's progressive attitude is also shown by the fact that he frequently registered designs from 1857 onwards. His first design made history because it was registered by means of a photograph, using the wet plate method to create a paper print. It was the first of many photographs on paper used to register costume, and is probably the earliest surviving photograph taken by a manufacturer to record a garment. Fashion houses have used such pictures ever since. The mantle was presumably intended to be half-mourning because of its pale colour. The rather wooden pose of the figure suggests it was a dummy rather than a person.

A further step towards manufacturing ready-made dresses was taken in the early 1850s when decorated fabrics ready to be incorporated in dresses began to be registered. Nicholson's rival silk mercers in St Paul's Church Yard, George Hitchcock & Co., registered two 'Ladies' Dress Fronts', triangular panels for skirts embroidered and appliquéd with flowers, swags and scallops. In September of that year, Moses & Son, branching out into women's wear, registered a similar one with an

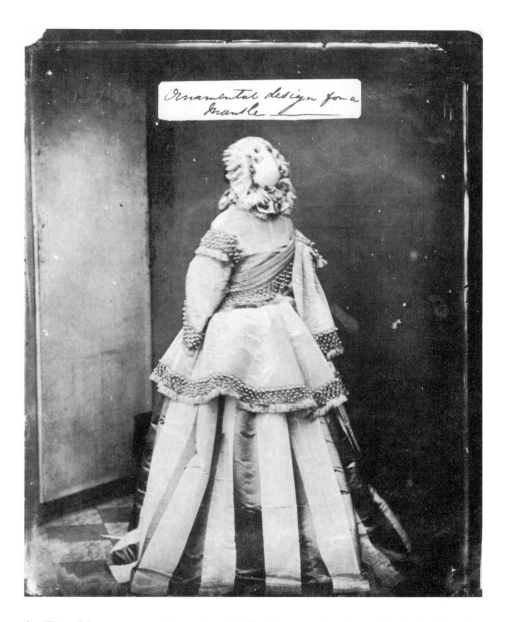

Ornamental design for a mantle

4 'The slightest nuance of regret', embodied in a mantle registered by Jay's Mourning Warehouse in 1857 by means of an unusual photograph. Pale shades like this were worn for 'half' or 'slight' mourning

actual example. It was made from black cloth with rather tattered embossed velvet leaves stuck on to a loosely embroidered stem. James Houldsworth & Co., of Portland Street Mill, Manchester, had registered professional looking appliquéd serge skirt fronts the year before. Although Houldsworth had pioneered machine embroidery in the 1840s, another Manchester firm, Roberts & Heaven, of Back Piccadilly, registered a machine embroidered skirt front, with an inserted ribbon panel and decorative buttons. Evening dress pieces were also made. The London firms Brickley & Lodge, James Collett and Jay's all registered fabulous confections of gauze puffs, ribbon bows and artificial flowers ready to be run up into dresses at a moment's notice. These would have been a boon indeed for the hard pressed dressmaker, whose main source of trouble were customers who demanded quick service yet left everything to the last minute.

Ready-decorated fabrics were a good compromise. They were clearly a success, and were soon being sold as complete skirts. The problem of making the bodice fit remained, however. The 1874 edition of Perkins' *Treatise on Haberdashery and Hosiery* explained that costumes needed:

> more than ordinary discrimination and care in selection, from their variety and fluctuation. They are most frequently sold in a made-up skirt, with a piece of stuff to match, from which the body is made.

The term 'costume' was coined in the 1860s to distinguish this early type of ready-made clothing from a 'dress'. 'Buying a dress' in those days implied buying the fabric to be made into a dress.

Attempts were made to get round the bodice problem, notably by William Chickall Jay, who registered his 'Eutheima Bodice' in December 1865 and brazenly advertised it in *The Illustrated London News* the following year as 'Jay's Patent Eutheima Bodice':

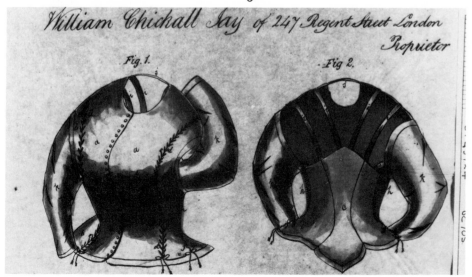

5   Jay's Patent 'Eutheima Bodice', 1865. 'The same bodice is capable of being adapted to fit different figures and . . . allows freedom of movement to the wearer'

'A self expanding bodice, recommended to ladies in cases of sudden bereavement or any less painful emergency, when a ready-made and stylish dress is required at a moment's notice.' From the design specification it seems to have been an awkward garment with laces, straps and elastic at the back which would need to be covered somehow.

It may have been possible to buy a complete ready-made dress as early as the late 1850s. E. Moses & Son's *Spring and Summer Manual* for 1857 advertised a 'Lady's Emigration Outfit'. These were entire wardrobes which could be bought on the spot ready made. Included in a long list of garments, mainly underwear, were two merino Union dresses. These cost 7s to 11s 6d and so cannot have been of very good quality. Perhaps ladies bound for the wild west did not feel the need for superbly fitting bodices. The 'complete dress to be sold as one' registered by Andrews & Williams, commission agents, in 1861 may be the earliest known picture of a fully ready-made

6 'Complete dress to be sold as one', 1861. Andrews & Williams, 3 Old Fish Street, City

dress. Its wide skirt and sleeves posed no problems, although the bodice may have presented a difficulty. It is possible that the registration was for the loud Acanthus leaf decoration which could have been sold as an appliqué or stitched onto the unmade fabric.

> The rapid development of the costume trade is entirely owing to sewing machines, and ought to convince drapers of the necessity of combatting with ready-made goods ... during the past few years they have wonderfully developed the drapery business. The demand for ready-made goods having more than doubled, and is still increasing. The reason for this vast increase is obvious – sewing machines have so conveniently put the ready-made article within the reach of all, that where one handkerchief was used, there are now two or three. So with gentlemen's shirts, ladies' and children's underclothing, costumes, fancy dresses, neckties, collarettes, sleeves and various other fancy articles. (J. W. Hayes, *The Draper and Haberdasher*.)

7 Costume by Henry Robinson of 12 Watling Street, City, 1869, one of the first large manufacturers of women's ready-made clothing

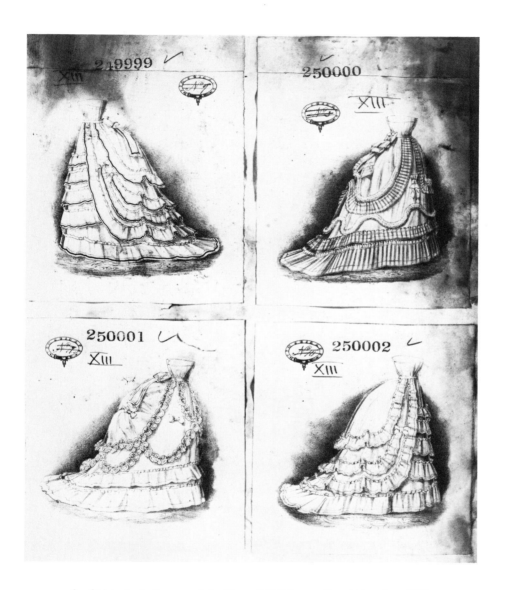

8   Skirts for ballgowns. John Hunt, 349 Edgware Road, London, 1871

9   The Princess costume by Henry Robinson, 1875

Without the sewing machine, ready-made dresses could not have been produced on any scale. Its marvellous ability to tuck, braid and create all sorts of decorative effects compensated for the difficulty of fitting them. Moreover, once its potential had been understood, it provided an incentive for the development of proper sizing systems. In *How to Dress Well on a Shilling a Day* of c. 1875, 'Sylvia' considered that 'Dresses bought ready made in shops are apt to exhibit a distressing similarity'. But losing the personal touch was a small price to pay when mass production brought a high quality of decoration into the reach of more women than was previously possible.

10 High fashion interpreted in the East End as crumpled fabrics and shabby trimmings. Rosa Salter, 2 Crombie Row, Commercial Road, London, 1873

While some registrations for dresses, like those put forward in 1873 by Rosa Salter of Crombie Row, Commercial Road in the East End, were obviously of poor quality, ready-made dresses were not necessarily cheap and nasty. Paradoxically, at the top end of the market women had long been willing to sacrifice fit to decoration. Exclusive French-made dresses had been bought at a distance ever since the Napoleonic era, either by private customers or as models for dressmakers. As a logical development, some firms commissioned French firms to design dresses for mass production. In 1883, George Henry Lee & Co. of Liverpool registered some elaborate dresses which were actually designed by Pingot & Poullier of 28 Rue des Bons Enfants, Paris. This enterprise, which also started out in millinery, was by the 1880s one of the largest of its kind in Liverpool, supplying a professional rather than an aristocratic clientele. Two French firms who exported ready-made goods to England and registered them were Felix d'Alsace & Co., who registered dresses and jackets in the 1890s, and Alfonso Boccardo who dealt in jersey bodices. Many of the registrations were illustrated by very high quality drawings and lithographs, implying that the end product was of an equal standard.

In the late nineteenth century a new attitude towards dressing was evident in women. Boned and swathed dresses began to give way to skirts and blouses. Both garments were simple and cheap to mass produce. Being worn loose, a limited size

11   Shawl-style mantle by Scott & Son, 8 Cannon Street, City, 1876

12   Exclusive French design registered in 1883 by the large Liverpool costumiers G. H. Lee & Co., a firm which is still trading today

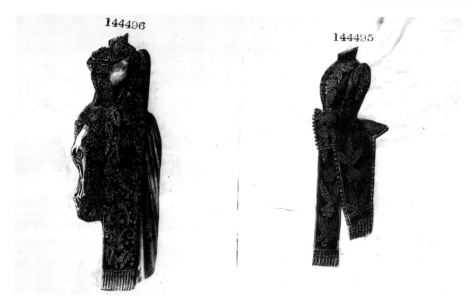

13 Heavily beaded mantles like these were a popular status symbol in the 1880s and 90s. Spencer Wicks & Co., 4–6 Watling Street, City, 1890

range could accommodate most figure types, especially since the skirt and blouse could be of different sizes. Manufacturing considerations may thus have been as important a factor in their rise to popularity as the increasingly active lives of women. Tailored jackets and suits could be easily made by the male wholesale tailors with their highly developed mass-production techniques. Once introduced, the popularity of these smart, hardwearing garments was assured. The wholesale tailors also made versions of sailor suits for women, like the one registered by George Macbeth & Son of King Street, Manchester, in 1891.

By 1900, women's ready-made clothing still had a long way to go before it was universally accepted. The changing emphasis detectable in the 1890s was only the first step towards the transformation of women's clothing to cater for their new lifestyles, which had taken place more fully by the 1920s. However, by the turn of the century, writers on dress had a great deal that was good to say about the new mass-produced clothing. In 1903 *How to Dress* states:

It would be foolish to imagine that because a garment is ready made it must necessarily be bad! In many instances ready-made garments are particularly excellent, especially in the case of coats, cloaks, jackets, and of course, MacIntoshes of all kinds. Indeed, it is impossible for the amateur tailor or dressmaker to make at home a coat or jacket which shall own anything like the smart appearance of those turned out by even quite inexpensive shops ... so far as actual costumes are concerned, except in the case of purchasing French models ... the hang of a cheap ready-made skirt generally leaves

14　Sketch for an evening dress by
　　Felix d'Alsace & Co. of Paris,
　　1898

much to be desired, while we can see at a glance the invariably unsatisfactory results obtained by the cheap blouse or bodice.

Everyday, however, ready-made clothes of all kinds are improving, and now that fashions change so frequently, and that many women have not the time to work at home, nor the money at hand to spend on a first rate dressmaker, there is an ever increasing demand for, and consequently, supply of, ready-made garments of fairly good and reliable quality.

9
Millinery

FROM THE beginning of the nineteenth century, a large proportion of millinery sold was ready made and the wholesale trade was highly developed. Completely decorated items could be bought, or else elaborately made-up trimmings such as artificial flowers, fancy ribbon knots and straw decorations, or plain untrimmed bonnets. These could be of fine leghorn straw from Tuscany, imported as a basic shape which was tucked and cut into the latest fashion, or English straw, made up in the cottages of Bedford, Luton and St Albans areas. Straw hat dealers like Welch & Son of Gutter Lane, Cheapside, registered straw plaits, showing that this was a competitive field. Sometimes great feats of virtuosity were attained. Around 1840 a process of twisting split straws into a continuous strand by machine was developed. This could be mechanically braided into a continuous filigree pattern, as on the bonnet shown here, which incorporates silk thread. It was probably registered by G. Long of Loudwater near High Wycombe, Buckinghamshire, who registered similar bonnets by means of an actual section. In this case, not unusually for the time, the clerk forgot to give it a number. Such bonnets, although extremely delicate, survive in some quantity, perhaps because they were particularly treasured possessions.

Paper had been used as a cheap alternative to straw since the eighteenth century. Coloured and embossed with a plait-like texture, from a distance it looked convincing. It could be used most effectively when simple flat styles were worn, such as the saucer shapes of around 1870. Several paper hats were registered at this time, in bright yellow card with coarse pinked cotton ribbons.

Fabric bonnets made on wire frames covered in tulle could be had wholesale. John Farmer of St Mary Gate, Nottingham, registered a number in the 1850s. Nottingham developed its millinery industry as an ancillary to the machine lace and hosiery trades. It specialised in pleated muslin and lace ruffles and bonnet fronts. These were used when caps ceased to be worn under bonnets, to represent their decorative frill.

Country milliners and dressmakers came to London as the centre of the fashion world to see new styles and buy in new stocks, while country ladies came to shop and rub shoulders with London society. It was thus inevitable that London should be the natural home of wholesale millinery as well as of hundreds of private milliners. The latter could be found in the West End, but the addresses accompanying registered designs for decorated ribbons, frills and tulle caps in the 1840s and 50s tended to come from Islington, Hoxton and the City. It would seem that the wholesale trade was centred here. This tulle cap, with pink silk ribbons and blonde lace was registered by

1 Intricate machine plaited straw
bonnet. Probably by G. Long,
Loudwater, near High Wycombe,
1849

Fisher & Watson of 20 Milk Street in August 1849, by a sample which, though squashed, still appears fresh and attractive. It was meant for afternoon or evening wear and its clusters of ribbon and blonde would have been the perfect foil for drooping ringlets.

The milliner's art lay in accurately folding ribbon loops and rouleaux like these so that they looked effective rather than messy. The successful milliner needed great skill and a natural flair, as well as light, cool and dry fingers, and the ability to work quickly so that the product remained clean and fresh. In return for her labours, she was usually more highly esteemed and better paid than the average dressmaker.

The early Victorian period was the heyday of the cap. The idea of surrounding the face of an adult woman with a frilly haze seems to go well with the contemporary female ideal of 'The Angel in the House'. This incongruity did not go unnoticed. In a book on etiquette F. Talbot wrote:

> We dislike exceedingly many of those untidy ornaments which ladies in this country wear
> in the shape of headdresses. They destroy the symmetry of the human figure, and call off
> the eye from real beauties to childish gewgaws, ribbons and lace.

2 Jaunty paper hat for an outing
on a dry day. Simeon Miles, 89
Bunhill Row, City, 1870

3 Drawing room
delight: Fisher &
Watson, Milk
Street, City, 1849

It is significant that this was written in 1857, when women's dress was developing a more assertive image. The deep bonnet brim which blinkered out the world had already gone, and bonnets were being worn far back on the head. By the late 1850s, the more intrepid were casting off their bonnets altogether in favour of hats. When Sophia Baines eloped with Gerald Scales, a travelling salesman in Arnold Bennett's *The Old Wives' Tale*, she wore 'a hard Amazonian hat, with a lifted veil, the final word of fashion in the Five Towns'. Such a hat, usually of dark coloured straw, had a wide brim which dipped seductively in front. The equally pert alternative was a close fitting pork pie hat which could hide no secrets. These examples were both registered by Robert Heath, who owned a high class retail establishment specialising in riding hats near Hyde Park Corner. As at all periods of dramatic change in fashion, an outburst of designs was registered by firms anxious to protect their versions of the new style.

4 Plush trimmed winter bonnet by
George Smith & Co., Borough,
1853

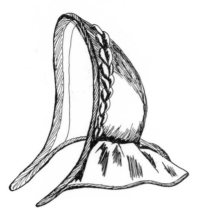

5 The women of the 1850s began
   to look out beyond their bonnets.
   This is a simple style in the new
   shape by Charles Clark,
   Hackney, 1858

6 'Amazon' hat for the new woman
   by Robert Heath, St George's
   Place, London, 1859

7 Another new design by the same firm, 1860

8   Straw hats by Munt Brown & Co., Wood Street, City, 1860

From the 1860s onwards, however, a sharp decline in the number of hats, bonnets and other millinery items registered is evident. Why this should be so is difficult to say, given the increase in registrations for other ready-made articles. There must always have been a fine balance to be achieved between making a product in sufficient quantity for registration to be worthwhile, and making too many so that people kept bumping into others wearing the same thing. The quest for individuality was possibly more important in millinery than in any other area of the wardrobe. In the 1840s, there were comparatively few alternative bonnet shapes, and this situation hardly changed

9   Cloth hat for a young woman by Sadok Schneiders & Son, owners of a vast Whitechapel manufactory, 1888

10 For many, a death was followed by a
    new hat: Jay's Mourning Warehouse, 1873

over the years. Manufacturers could launch a new style confident that it would not go out of fashion and that it would be widely patronised. It was thus a good idea to register it. By the 1860s, women's headdresses had not only diminished and retreated into the recesses of elaborate coiffures, but were also far more decorated. Variations in shape were important, and fashions changed more quickly. Milliners had to create more styles, each in very small numbers, and it may not have been worth the effort of registering them. Exceptions to this were the new tweed hats registered from the late 1880s by men's hat manufacturers and knitted Tam O'Shanters. Both were practical styles with a long lifespan. They developed along with tailor made suits, serviceable walking skirts and weatherproof outerwear, as a response to the growing interest in outdoor pursuits, and the changing female image. Apart from styles which were less susceptible to fashion, the few hat registrations from the 1870s onwards tended to be made by large firms assured of their market, such as the retail shops Jay's Mourning Warehouse and Henry Heath of Oxford Street. Otherwise, they were designs for which commercial success seemed assured. This must have been the case with the superbly elegant straw sailor hat manufactured by White & Auborn of 57 Upper Princess Street, Luton.

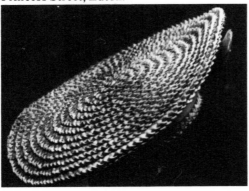

11 Elegant simplicity: White &
    Auborn, Luton, 1896

10
Men's Coats and Boys' Suits

FROM THE mid-eighteenth century, the simple woollen frockcoats originally worn by gentlemen around their estates had been accepted as informal wear in Britain. When they began to be adopted as fashionable European dress in the 1790s, English tailors were sought out: they alone could cut cloth and mould it to the body, so that it fitted like a second skin. Science and art were bought together as studies of anatomy were used to develop complex measuring and cutting systems. A logical progression was the introduction of the tape measure in the early nineteenth century. Each tailor was naturally anxious to prove the supremacy of his own particular system, and many did so, either by publishing a book, or by perfecting a measuring or pattern cutting device, which could be marketed. This practice was still popular in the 1840s, and many scientific measures were registered in that decade, such as the one made by the well-known tailor George Doudney of 17 Old Bond Street in 1844.

These developments benefited many who would never have dreamt of patronising a bespoke tailor. They were among several factors which led to improved standards and increasing availability of ready-made male outerwear in the 1840s. Other factors were developments in textile production such as the power loom which lowered the cost of cloth, and new cheaper fabrics, such as coarse tweeds. In addition, ready-made men's wear supplied a long felt need of many who wished to buy new clothes on a limited income. Given the will, it was quite easy to produce passable men's clothing on a large scale. Although, of course, a good fit was sought for coats and trousers, a good fit did not necessarily mean a close fit. These garments were essentially of a loose, tubular construction, and the heavy, dark woollen cloth could hide many deficiencies of cut and workmanship. Most important of all were the changes in retailing and manufacturing processes by which the old slop sellers raised themselves up to the status of 'clothiers and outfitters', and had their products made up cheaply by sweated labour. The new clothiers emerging in the 1820s and 1830s were to be found particularly in the East End of London. They attracted custom by vigorous advertising campaigns and price slashing. Production costs were kept to a minimum, and many traditional tailors were forced to adopt the same methods in order to survive. The twin practices of sweated labour and price cutting spelt disaster for the

H. J. & D. NICOLLS' ESTABLISHMENT, REGENT STREET.

1   H. J. & D. Nicoll's Establishment, Regent Street, London, 1860

industrious workman. One vividly described to Henry Mayhew how H. J. & D. Nicolls, Regent Street clothiers, began the practices:

It is now five years since my master began to make any reduction upon the price for making any garment whatsoever. Before that, every article was paid for at the rate of 6d per hour. But between the years 1844 and 1845 – I cannot call to mind the exact date – my master had a consultation with his captain as to making up the new cheap tweed wrappers, which were coming into general fashion at that time; and he decided upon paying for them at a rate which, considering the time they took to make, was less than the regular 6d per hour. He said that the show shops at the East End were daily advertising tweed wrappers at such a low figure that his customers, seeing the prices in the newspapers, were continually telling him that if he could not do them, they must go elsewhere. Since then cheap overcoats, or wrappers have been generally made in our shop ... Amongst all the best and oldest houses in the trade at the West End they are gradually introducing the making of cheap paletôts, Oxonions, Brighton coats, Chesterfields, etc., etc., and even the first-rate houses are gradually subsiding into the cheap advertising slop tailors. (*The Unknown Mayhew*.)

A variety of outergarments were available to the Victorian male. The most popular of which was the paletôt, a loose hip length coat. While the fit of ready-made clothing was improving, it still had a long way to go and firms tended to specialise in outerwear requiring a minimum of fitting. Not surprisingly, registered designs for these far outnumber those for other tailored clothing like trousers and jackets. The proliferation of fanciful new names for outerwear in the mid-century was almost certainly a product of the clothiers' incessant search for sales gimmicks. In *Gaslight*

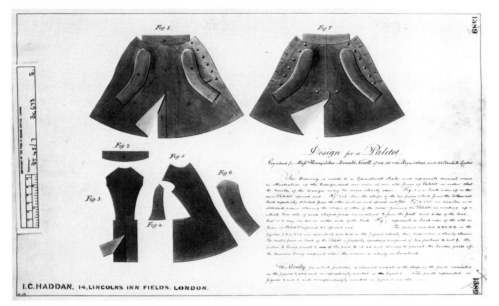

2 Version of H. J. & D. Nicoll's celebrated Paletôt, 1848

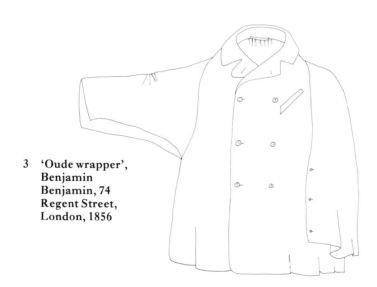

3 'Oude wrapper',
Benjamin
Benjamin, 74
Regent Street,
London, 1856

and Daylight of 1859 George Augustus Sala bemoaned the death of the old greatcoat, caused by this rash of interlopers:

> We have paletôts (the name of which many have assumed), ponchos, Burnous's, Sylphides, Zephyr wrappers, Chesterfields, Llamas, Pilot wrappers, Wrap-rascals, Bisuniques and a host of other garments, more or less answering the purpose of an overcoat. But where is the greatcoat? The long-voluminous, wide-skirted garment of brown or drab broad cloth, reaching to the ankle, possessing innumerable pockets . . . Your father wore it before you, and you hoped to leave it to your eldest son.

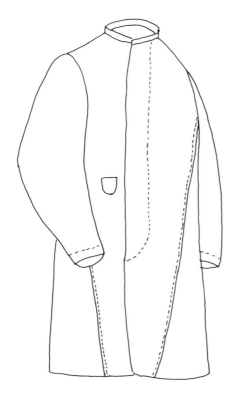

4 'Dustcoat to be called "The Traveller's Friend" ' featuring ticket and map pockets, 1867. An early product of Lewis & Co. of Ranelagh Street, Liverpool, now better known as the chain store Lewis's. The coat was considered both beautiful and useful, and so it was registered in two classes.

Elias Moses & Son were one of the largest of the ready-made clothiers, and perhaps the best known because of their constant stream of self-aggrandising literature. *The Past, the Present and the Future* of 1846 ostensibly commemorated the opening of new premises, but was in fact a price list. Ready-made waistcoats could be had for 1s 6d to 14s, and dress coats from £1 8s. Prices were also given for made-to-measure waistcoats, from 6s 6d, and dress coats from two guineas. Many clothiers offered a made-to-measure service, since it helped to upgrade them in the public eye. The firm sold every article of masculine dress as well as many female garments. They also

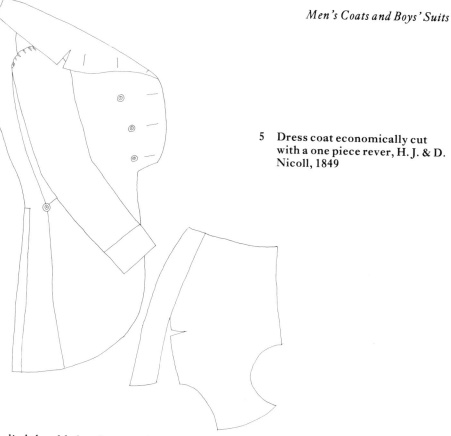

5 **Dress coat economically cut with a one piece rever, H. J. & D. Nicoll, 1849**

supplied the old slopshop staples of emigration outfits, seamen's and captains' attire, liveries, mourning wear and work clothes. Like all high class tailors, they made ladies' riding habits. In *The Past, the Present and the Future*, they assured the fair sex of the respectability of their fitting room:

> Its distinct character and general seclusion are such as cannot fail to give the utmost satisfaction to the fair visitors at Moses & Son's establishment. Ladies will suffer no annoyance while being waited upon, as the habit room is a separate and private apartment devoted exclusively to the purpose alluded to.

Their 1857 handbook noted an important feature of their firm, a revolutionary step then being taken by many British drapers and clothiers:

> Important! All goods are marked in plain figures the lowest price, from which no abatement can be made, should any article not give satisfaction, it will be exchanged (if desired) or, if preferred, the money will be refunded without hesitation.

H. J. & D. Nicholl operated on a grander level but by the same principles. Daniel Puseley's *Commercial Companion* of 1860 described them thus:

6 Coat for all contingencies, Sam
Shirley, Market Street,
Manchester, 1884

The house was founded in Conduit Street and Old Jewry, rather more than half a century
since by the father of the brothers now conducting the most extensive business ever
known in the Metropolis in their branch of trade, that is to say, merchant clothiers and
dealers in first-class goods only. There are, and always have been, large houses in what is
commonly known as the slop trade, but H. J. and D. Nicoll were the first to establish on
an extensive scale, one for the sale of made-up garments adapted to supply the wants of
the middle and wealthier classes. It has been calculated that from the date their well-
known registered paletôt was introduced, namely, about fifteen years since, that this
firm has sold more than twenty millions of that popular garment, which perhaps, more
than anything else, tended to do away with the tight and unhealthy male costume
formerly in general use.

The astonishing sale of paletôts may be an overstatement, but the firm was
certainly very profitable. One of its employees told Henry Mayhew that the Nicoll
brothers were 'said to have amassed £80,000 each, in a few years, simply by reducing
the wages of the 1,000 workmen they employ to one third below that of the honourable
trade'. (*The Unknown Mayhew*).

Moses & Son registered only one or two articles of clothing, but H. J. & D. Nicoll
took a different view, perhaps believing in the advertising value of registration. They
registered a succession of improvements to their paletôt in the late 1840s and early
1850s, and liked to describe themselves, confusingly, as 'patentees of the registered
paletôt'. The brothers regularly registered garments (and patented different ones)
until the break-up of the partnership around 1869. Two companies were then formed,
both of which continued to register designs.

Nicolls' original paletôt was a fairly narrow garment in comparison with the 1850s
version, a raglan sleeved 'A' line in keeping with current fashion. Other designs
included capes, cloaks, overcoats, a tailcoat and knickerbockers.

Both brothers registered garments with more than one use. For instance, in 1871
Donald sought protection for a 'Military Groundsheet and Waterproof Garment'
which could be 'buttoned or laced to form a *Tente d'Abri*' or made into a sleeping bag.

7 Loud tweed overcoat: Stone & Forster, St James's, 1874

8   Overcoat with velvet collar: John H. Wilson & Co., Love Street, Liverpool, 1876

In 1869 Henry had registered a ladies' mantle which could be worn as a skirt. Such garments combining several functions frequently cropped up among the registered designs. They must have been novel sales gimmicks, presenting obvious economies for the less affluent – providing of course, that they actually worked. Most of the combination garments registered featured ingenious methods of buttoning and hooking and rearranging, and they were probably more trouble than they were worth.

9   Little boy's outfit. Donald Nicoll & Co., St Paul's Church Yard, City, 1870

98

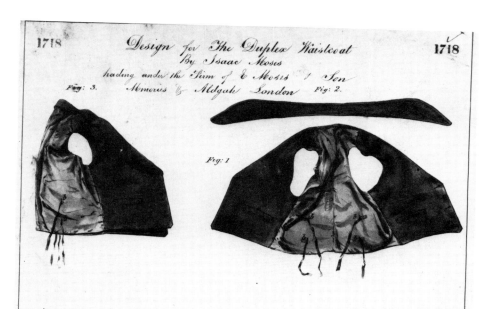

Design for The Duplex Waistcoat
By Isaac Moses
trading under the Firm of E. Moses & Son
Minories & Aldgate London

Fig: 3   Fig: 2

Fig: 1

This Design consists in a novel configuration of Waistcoat which is capable of being turned and worn either side upwards at pleasure, and has the effect as regards variety of apparel, of combining several different appearances. Fig: 1 is a view of the Waistcoat laid out nearly flat. Fig: 2 is a similar view of the collar of the Waistcoat, it being removable at pleasure, and Fig: 3 is a view of the Waistcoat with the collar attached. This waistcoat is provided with pockets or indications thereof as shown at a. a. on both faces of the waistcoat, so that whether it be the pleasure of the wearer to have the face as represented by the red color or that represented by the own color outwards, there will be apparently an ordinary waistcoat presented to the eye. The collar is composed of colored stuffs corresponding to those of which the waistcoat is composed, and it is made separate as shown at Fig: 2 for the purpose of being turned to bring that color or fabric uppermost which corresponds to that face of the Waistcoat which is intended to be worn outermost. b.b. are small openings made in the back and to an edge of each opening a string is sewn, the object being to draw the strings through so as to make them tie on either side of the back according to which side is worn outwards. The Waistcoat may if thought desirable, be worn without the invertible collar.

Under this Registration I desire to claim the invertible collar as shown detached at Fig: 2 and in place at Fig: 3 and also the pockets or indications thereof as at a. a. viz on each face of the waistcoat as shown in the drawing & further the openings b. The waistcoat is of the ordinary configuration in other respects.

10   The notorious Moses & Son's appropriately named 'Duplex Waistcoat', 1849

11 Detail from a surviving boy's
suit made by the firm towards
the end of the 19th century.
Note its work tag. Armley Mills
Industrial Museum, Leeds

Many designs involved transforming a light coat or jacket into a heavy winter
overcoat by buttoning on skirts and hoods, thus saving the expense of a complete coat.

Others were supposed to create the illusion of an extensive wardrobe. Moses &
Son's 'Duplex' waistcoat of 1849 was:

> a novel configuration of waistcoat which is capable of being turned and worn either side
> upwards as desired, and has the effect as regards variety of apparel, of combining several
> different appearances . . . The collar of the waistcoat . . . being removable at pleasure . . .
> This waistcoat is provided with pockets or indications thereof as shewn . . . on both faces
> of the waistcoat so that whether it be the pleasure of the wearer to have the face as
> represented by the red color or that represented by the green color outwards, there will be
> apparently an ordinary waistcoat presented to the eye.

'Clothing for Juveniles' was one of the earliest and most successful branches of the
ready-made tailoring trade. In *Dombey and Son*, Dickens described how, in the 1840s,
Captain Cuttle went out to buy a ready-made outfit for his little assistant. For many
people, ready-made clothing became synonymous with boyhood and the acquisition
of one's first made-to-measure suit was a triumphant declaration of manliness. In the
1890s, Kipps's boyish attire placed him firmly at the bottom of the Shalford's Drapery
Bazaar hierarchy. On his Sunday walks:

> Sometimes the apprentice next above him would condescend to go with him; but when
> the apprentice next but one above him condescended to go with the apprentice next

above him, then Kipps, being habited as yet in ready-made clothes without tails, and unsuitable therefore to appear in such company, went alone. (H. G. Wells, *Kipps*.)

People who would never have considered buying their own clothes off the peg did not hesitate to clothe their offspring in this way. Obviously, style and a glove-like fit were less important than cheapness and durability. Anything that was too big could always be grown into.

It is a curious paradox that the Victorian attitude to children combined strict discipline, sometimes to the point of brutality, with genuine affection, indulgence and a sentimental preoccupation with childish innocence. An interesting feature of boys' clothing from the 1840s onwards was the prevalence, for everyday wear, of styles which today would be relegated to the fancy dress box. As soon as they were out of petticoats, little boys were often dressed as miniature soldiers, sailors with whistles,

12   Boy's jacket with cloth bands, by Barrans of Chorley Lane, Leeds, 1884

or Scotsmen, complete with dirks. Under the stern guidance of the paterfamilias, children's dress reached heights of imaginative invention never subsequently attained. Whether this was because of an idealised view of children whereby they were seen as mindless doll-like miniatures to be dressed according to a parent's whim, or through a genuine understanding of a child's need to fantasise would be hard to establish.

Ready-made clothing manufacturers found these styles particularly lucrative. They could compensate for deficiencies in fit by using sewing machines to produce wonderfully decorated outfits, incorporating yards and yards of braiding and frogging. The design for a boy's suit registered by Donald Nicoll's new company in 1870 illustrates not only the usefulness of such trimmings, but also how a manufacturer could sell matching accessories too, such as a lanyard and satchel.

Many children must have enjoyed dressing up as soldiers and sailors, but the same could not be said for the 'Little Lord Fauntleroy' suit, worn by the hero of Frances Hodgson Burnett's book of that name, an immediate success when it was published in 1886. The suit was popularised by John Everett Millais's painting 'Bubbles'. Compton Mackenzie remembered the agony this caused his six year old self in 1889:

> That confounded Little Lord Fauntleroy craze which had led to my being given as a party dress the Little Lord Fauntleroy costume of black velvet and Vandyke collar was a curse. The other boys at the dancing class were all in white tops. Does this require explanation as a white top to one's sailor suit instead of the blue of daily use or the pale blue of summer?
>
> Naturally the other boys were inclined to giggle at my black velvet, and after protesting in vain against being made to wear it I decided to make it unwearable by flinging myself down in the gutter on the way to dancing class and cutting the breeches, and incidentally severely grazing my own knees. I also managed to tear the Vandyke collar. Thus not only did I avoid the dancing class, but I also avoided being

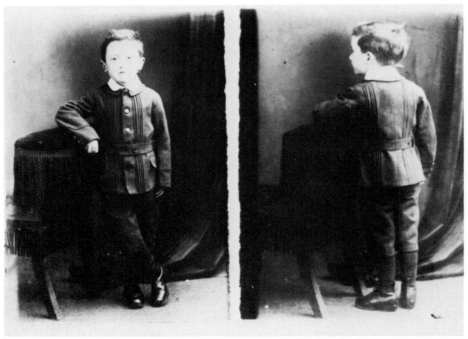

13   An early example of a Hepworth's suit. Wellington Street, Leeds, 1884

102

14 The seventeenth century interpreted in sturdy cloth. Macbeth & Co., King Street, Manchester, 1879

photographed in that infernal get-up, for a sitting to Faulkner in Baker Street had been arranged. (*My Life and Times, Octave One.*)

An early version shown here, registered by the large Manchester clothiers, Macbeth & Co., was clearly intended for more mundane occasions.

By far the majority of designs for boys' suits were registered by the Leeds wholesale clothiers John Barran & Sons. These begin in 1872, represented either by drawings, or impressions taken by rubbings with crayon over paper, showing intricate spiral braiding patterns for jackets or trousers. Such braided suits, loosely based on military frogging, were tremendously popular. Soon Barran and other manufacturers were registering their designs by means of photographs of little boys, which sometimes had actual fabric samples appended.

When John Barran came to Leeds from Surrey in 1842 the town had thriving engineering and woollen industries but no links with tailoring. Barran apprenticed himself to a pawnbroker and second-hand clothier. Then, although he had no training, he set up on his own as a tailor and clothes dealer. He continued in a steady way, until the early 1850s, when his accounts, which survive today, suddenly showed

15   Girl's coat. John Barran & Sons, Chorley Lane, Leeds, 1884

an increase in his stock of ready-made clothes. It marked the beginning of Barran's development into one of the largest wholesale ready-made clothing manufacturers in the country and founder of this major Leeds industry. From the start it is likely that his staple product was boys' clothing. By the mid-1850s his small factory with its sewing machines was operating efficiently on a divisional system with the different processes shared among the workers. Barran's firm had many advantages: It was close to the producers of woollen cloth and 'shoddy', made from re-cycled wool; it was in an engineering town where mechanics understood the new sewing machines; it was in the centre of the communications network of railways and roads, but above all, neither he nor his workforce had had any experience of the traditional tailoring system, and so they were willing to try out new processes such as the band-knife, which Barran invented in 1858, for cutting many thicknesses of cloth.

By the end of the century Barran's employed three thousand people, and over twenty other large wholesale clothing firms had started up in Leeds, as well as innumerable small workshops. Ever since Herman Friend, an early collaborator with John Barran, had employed skilled Jewish tailors alongside unskilled female machinists, Jewish labour had contributed to the success of the Leeds clothing industry. In the 1880s and 1890s, Leeds was one of the most popular destinations for immigrant Jews escaping from Russian pogroms.

Two of Barran's rivals, W. Blackburn & Sons and J. Hepworth & Sons, both claimed credit for a new idea in wholesale tailoring. This was to set up their own shops instead of competing with other firms to supply independent drapers and outfitters. Of the two, Hepworths are today the best known; the results of their early enterprise still being evident on many British high streets. The company had been founded by Joseph Hepworth in 1867, although he had been in business for some time, he began his commercial career at the age of ten in a Huddersfield mill. His son, Norris,

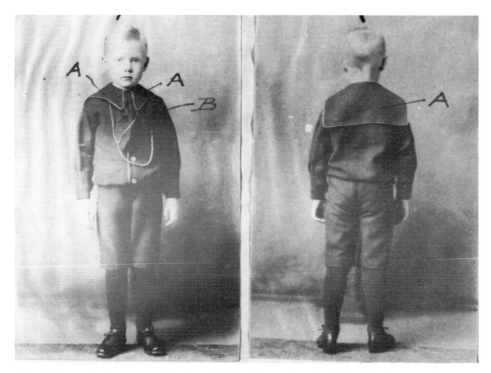

16   Sailor suit. Stewart & Macdonald, Park Lane, Leeds, 1891. The letters refer to an explanation which was omitted

pioneered the direct retailing scheme from 1884. By 1905 they had 143 branches and their profits were £33,323 per year. In contrast Blackburns stayed small, having twenty-eight outlets by the time of the First World War. (The scheme was adopted later by other tailors including Montague Burton selling made to measure suits.)

The staple product of all these firms remained boys' clothing, but some men's wear, women's tailored suits and tweed hats were made. The practice of registering designs by means of photographs like these has enabled a record of many firms' products to survive in a very clear form when otherwise they would certainly have been lost.

11
Men's Hats

FOR GENERATIONS, the Englishman and his hat had been inseparable. Foreigners, like Frederick Engels, writing in the 1840s, often commented on this fact, which is verified by the many photographs of crowds taken up to the last war. For both sexes, and all classes, covering the head was considered essential for decency. Of his childhood in a Salford slum at the turn of the century, Robert Roberts (*The Classic Slum*) wrote: 'A man or woman, walking the streets hatless, struck one as either "low", wretchedly poor, just plain eccentric or even faintly obscene.'

The small boys Roberts recalled, running after the bare-headed shouting 'The no 'at brigade!', would perhaps have been surprised to know that such a brigade actually existed, dedicated to breaking down this social convention. An editorial in *The Dress Review* 1904, the journal of the Healthy and Artistic Dress Union, hailed the 'new hatless league' which included the Manchester Physical Health Culture Society, with their motto 'Less Hat More Hair'.

At the beginning of the nineteenth century, felt hats were generally worn; they were made from fur, such as beaver or rabbit, wool, or a combination of both. Silk and silk plush became popular in the mid-century, stretched over a stiffened cotton support. Straw could be worn informally, as could the stitched tweed hats and caps which appeared later on.

The early Victorian top hat was heavy, and the atmosphere inside it could become a hot mixture of steam, sweat and hair oil. Manufacturers constantly sought to make their products more comfortable. This was the aim of many registered designs, and by 1900, hats were indeed much lighter, and more carefully shaped.

All kinds of ventilators were concocted to air the head. Although the problem was simply, and most frequently, solved by a little hole in the centre of the crown, a special device made a good selling point, particularly if endowed with the added cachet of being a registered design. They tended at first to be made as a simple grill, mounted on a metal or bone ring, like John Fuller of Southwark's 'Bonafide Ventilating Hat' of 1849. Later on, adjustable air flow ventilators were made, with movable shutters, such as those registered by James Marlor & Sons and Daniel Lever of Denton, Cheshire, in the 1880s.

Another solution was to reduce the weight of the hat. Fuller's 'Neoteric Ventilating Hat' of 1851 had a loosely woven frame of light manila grass or willow, which supported the fabric. Alternatively, the hat could be suspended away from the head. This had the added advantage that it not only kept the head cool, but also kept the hat clean. Flanagan & Company of Liverpool perfected their 'Aeolian Hat' in 1853, with its airpocket moulded into the crown:

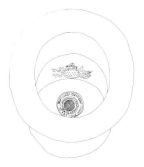

1 The Bonafide
ventilating hat for
hot heads: John
Fuller & Co.,
Southwark, 1849

In this way a completely encircling air chamber is formed to embrace the head, and making an easy pleasant fit and also preventing the natural grease from the hair penetrating to the exterior of the hat.

Variations on this theme became very popular. The 'Corrugated Ventilating Hat Antimacassar Pad' registered by S. & J. Carrington of Stockport in 1863 was held away from the head by fluted stiffened calico. One of the earliest uses of corrugated cardboard was for ventilated hat bands.

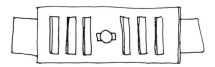

2 Adjustable airflow hat ventilation by James Marlor & Sons, 1885, of Denton, Cheshire

Christy's, the well-known hat manufacturers, tackled the problem from a different angle: their registered Gutta Percha hat of 1848 had a rubbery lining impervious to rain and perspiration.

Since the late eighteenth century, Christy's had traded in Gracechurch Street in the City of London. They prospered and in 1826 opened a manufactory in Canal Street, Stockport. At least since the seventeenth century, Manchester and its neighbouring towns, including Stockport, Denton and Dukinfield, had been renowned for their felt hat making.

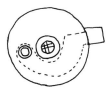  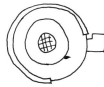

3 Adjustable airflow hat ventilation by Daniel Lever, 1885, of Denton, Cheshire

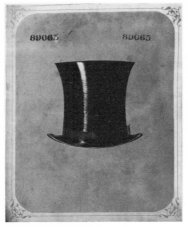

4 The subtle curves and shining surface of top hats, like this example by Christys, 1853, made them perennial favourites

The early Victorian top hat was not only uncomfortable, but also unmanageable when removed. For this reason, collapsible hats were invented. The best known of these was the Gibus. Designed in the late 1830s by a Frenchman of that name, it had a system of springs and wires activated by a deft flick. A similar top hat was registered by James Bickerton Junior, a hat manufacturer from Blackfriars in the City. The explanation stated that it worked without the use of springs and that 'the elasticity particularly depends upon the shape of the tip which is oval'.

The top hat was a nuisance particularly in crowded omnibuses and railway carriages, unless its owner happened to have a hat suspender and could clip it to a convenient beam. In 1849 Edward Newman Fourdrinier of 9 College Place, Camden Town, registered a device 'to suspend a hat in second class railway carriages where there are rails as shown'. It was made from a strip of sprung steel. When not in use, it was restrained by a screw. This was a serious proposition. That hats were hung upside down in railway carriages by some means or other is shown occasionally in contemporary pictures, and other hat suspenders were registered apart from this one. Railway carriage design changed in the 1860s and no longer featured a convenient beam. Undaunted, in April 1870, James Butt of Stroud registered a hat suspender intended for the new vehicle which had 'a foundation plate screwed to the new railway

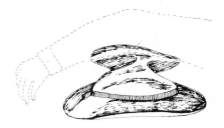

5 James Wickerton Junior of Blackfriars' 'Elastic dress and opera hat', 1844: 'The novelty of the design sought to be protected consists in making a hat that will assume various forms or configurations which are essential when required to put the hat in a small place, as for instance a dress or opera hat'

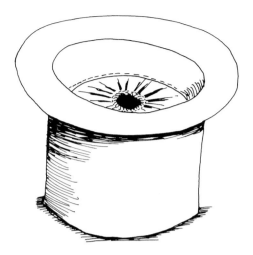

6 'Ventilating, expanding and contracting hat lining', Charles F. A. Rider, 61 Red Cross Street, Borough, London, 1847

carriage or other article to which the bracket is to be affixed'. He did not specify whether the screwing on of the plates was to be the responsibility of the individual passenger or left to the railway company concerned.

Hats may have been inconvenient, but they had their uses. For example, they could be used for carrying things. Several of Dickens's characters from the 1840s and 50s did this: Daniel Doyce in *Little Dorrit* 'had an old workmanlike habit of carrying his pocket handkerchief in his hat'. In *The Old Curiosity Shop* Kit was arrested because a five pound note had been planted in his hat. The Reverend Francis Kilvert told the tale in the 1870s of how a real thief had been caught when a stolen pat of butter melted and the fat trickled from under his hat. Given this widespread habit, it is not surprising that in 1847 Charles Rider of 61 Red Cross Street, Borough, registered a design which incorporated 'a ring of India rubber or other material inserted therein' so that:

> In constructing the lining it will afford facility for placing the handkerchief or light parcels in the hat while at the same time it will support the handkerchief or parcel so placed free from the head of the wearer.

At about the same time, devices of this sort must have appeared in the United States since Charles Goodyear gave them short shrift in *Gum Elastic and Its Varieties* of 1855:

> Hat pockets are a recent invention among hatters, made by shirring the double lining of the hat, near the bottom, with an elastic ring, so that a convenient receptacle is formed for gloves, letters, etcetera. This appendage, of however doubtful utility, is more safe than carrying the same articles loose in the hat.

Presumably, hat pockets were not favoured by gentlemen, but doctors were evidently intended to use a spring clip registered in 1876 which surmounted a hat ventilator. It was described as a ticket, stethoscope or pencil holder. Other hat accessories registered included a hat brush and a smoking cap to be carried inside the

7   Sometimes hats contained hidden treasures like this colour print of a courting couple by Wareham & Hollingworth, Hyde, 1878

hat, a compass set into it, and of course, a number of the perennially popular hat guards; lengths of string or elastic attached to the headgear by a clip or screw and looped onto the clothing, to stop it blowing away.

The diversity of shapes to be seen among the registered designs confound the widespread belief that Victorian men's hats hardly changed. Moreover, parts hidden in use were equally capable of fashionable variations to seduce the buyer. The hat tip, an oval lining inside the crown, often bore the manufacturer's name in an attractive motif, but the registered designs show that many had decorative printed pictures. The wearer of one of Wareham & Hollingworth's hats, of Hyde, Cheshire, could take subtle pleasure in knowing that it contained a picture of the 1878 Paris Exhibition, or of a military hero such as Hardy, Napier, or Worsley, or a coy portrayal of a courting couple. Such a hat could be used to great effect on meeting a pretty girl! In the 1880s the firm, then Samuel Wareham & Co., was making hat tips with scenes from eighteenth-century life, and of soldiers in Africa.

Fashionable mileage could also be gained from the hat leather. In the 1880s and 90s, William Ruttenau of Audenshaw, Cheshire, and T. W. Bracher & Co. of Stockport were particularly assiduous in registering leather bands decorated with embossed, punched and gilt patterns. *The Hatters' Gazette* of 1886 claimed that Brachers 'Belted the globe' with their 'top edging leathers' (vol. XI, 1.12.86, p. 697). They survive today as a subsidiary of a New York firm.

An early alternative to the top hat for youth was the high crowned peaked cap. Originally a naval style, by 1830 the cavalry officer author of *The Whole Art of Dress* bemoaned its adoption by 'boys and the lower orders generally':

110

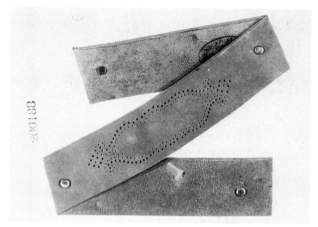

8   Hat leathers also gave scope for splendour, T. W. Bracher & Co., Stockport, 1895

More especially, the last winter, it was really amusing to perceive groups of low apprentice-lads with cloaks and naval caps, with chin pieces down, shuffling about in diverse holiday-places, to the utmost indignation, doubtless, of the youthful aspirants in either gallant service. For the above reason, it has grown almost degrading to wear a cap in public, however comfortable and convenient at times.

The 'Wideawake', a flat brimmed felt hat with a shallow round crown, and straw hats both came into general use in the 1850s. The straw hat was ideal informal summer wear, and the boater and helmet styles derived from safari hats were always popular. Straw hat manufacture formed a cottage industry in the Luton area. They were made of British straw, then later of Chinese and Japanese varieties. For some reason, while registered designs abound from the felt hat makers of London and the Stockport area, designs for straw hats are few.

The Bowler was an innovation of the 1850s, supposedly first commissioned by William Coke as headgear for his gamekeepers, and so nicknamed the Billycock. It was widely worn from the 1860s, and by 1900 was threatening the popularity of the top hat among certain sections of society. Made from felt stiffened with shellac, a fine lacquer, it was hardwearing, conferred a pompous dignity on the would-be important, while its narrow curled brim lent itself to fashionable novelty when required. So many were its varieties that great care was needed when purchasing a new hat, in order to avoid the trap fallen into by staid Mr Benshaw in H. G. Wells's *Bealby*:

9   The ever popular flat cap with a
    Japanned peak, here improved
    by a hidden elastic, David
    Nyman, Bristol, 1851

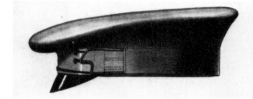

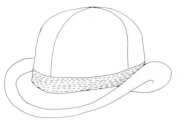

10 'The perfection roll curl for top hats', Sadok Schneiders & Son, Whitechapel, 1870: a cloth version of the felt bowler

He went into the nearest shop and just bought the cheapest hat he could, and so he got hats designed for the youthful and giddy, hats with flighty crowns and flippant bows, and amorous brims that undulated attractively to set off foolish and flippant young faces.

11 Many bowler hats in the 1880s had extraordinarily shaped brims. James Hague, Hooley Hill, Nr Manchester, 1886

The Bowler's universal appeal survived into this century. It was to form part of the typical dress of the City gent and the artisan of standing on each side of the Atlantic. As such it has been immortalised in the films of Laurel and Hardy.

Felt hat making was an unpleasant business, since it involved working with substances like shellac, vitriol and nitrate of mercury (which caused madness in hatters) and manipulating saturated felt in vats of boiling water. In the Stockport area, it was at one time carried out in small workshops adjoining private houses, but firms such as Christy's had large manufactories where the processes could be done in bulk. After the hat was formed and blocked, there was still the trimming to be done by

12 'Planking' at Battersby's Hat Works, Stockport, 1911. By this process the soft felt shape was hardened and shrunk: while immersed in boiling water and sulphuric acid, it was rolled around by hand. Battersby's is now part of Christy's hat manufacturing group. The photographs were first published in *The Gentleman's Journal* 23 September 1911. Stockport Museums and Art Gallery Service

women, which was also heavy work, as an employee of Christy's in the 1890s remembered:

> I had loved working at Christie's (sic) because of the work room, but the hats were very hard. If your wrist was not very strong you could not push the needle through or pull it out ... Just think of the binding on men's hat brims; if they were a quarter of an inch or even less crooked, back they came, and you had to take them off and do them over again. And the fine leathers – a crooked stitch in those and you had to take them out ... We were working hard all day, bringing work home and working until eight or nine o'clock at nights for 13s and 15s per week ... (Cooperative Working Women, *Life as We Have Known It.*)

Another hat which will be remembered as belonging to the twentieth century, the flat tweed cap, first crops up in the registered designs in the 1890s, when it was worn for sport. Fabric hats such as these and Deerstalkers called for tailoring rather than hatting skills and their popularity posed a serious threat to the old manufacturers. They could be made anywhere that cheap labour could be found, with great profits.

Sadok Schneiders & Son's Whitechapel factory was well situated to take advantage of the immigrant labour of the East End clothing trade. Theirs was a new type of firm, run on a vast scale, which concentrated on every type of stitched headgear for men,

13　The flat cap of the
twentieth century:
Andrew & Watson,
Glasgow, 1899

women and children. They registered quite a few of their styles. Their commercial achievements were expounded in *Modern London* around 1890:

> There are few firms in London that employ so many hands in any branch of manufacture as Messrs S. Schneider & Son, the well-known cap and cloth hat manufacturers, who are by far the largest makers in this special branch in the Metropolis. The business was formed in 1847 . . . There are no less than 500 sewing machines, all driven by steam, and in the majority of instances these are superintended by women. The cutting machines will cut out the various sizes and shapes of the cloth, linings, etc., and some of them will cut out nearly 100 pieces at one stroke . . . As many as 4000 dozen caps are manufactured per week. The proprietors command a most extensive trade not only in the United Kingdom, but also with the leading shipping firms. They also carry on a very extensive and important direct export trade to Melbourne, where they have a spacious depot.

It would be nice to picture one of the Schneiders as Mr Murray Posh, Lupin Pooter's friend, benefactor and rival in love, and felt hat manufacturer:

> On being introduced, Gowing with his usual want of tact said 'Any relation to Posh's three shilling hats?' Mr Posh replied 'Yes, but please understand I don't try on hats myself. I take no *active* part in the business.' I replied, 'I wish *I* had a business like it.' Mr Posh seemed pleased, and gave a long but most interesting history of the extraordinary difficulties in the manufacture of cheap hats . . . Lupin said Mr Posh was worth thousands. 'Posh's One Price Hat' was a household word in Birmingham, Manchester, Liverpool and all the big towns throughout England. Lupin further informed me that Mr Posh was opening branch establishments in New York, Sydney and Melbourne, and negotiating for Kimberly and Johannesburg. (G. and W. Grossmith, *Diary of a Nobody*.)

12
Hosiery

EVER SINCE the knitting frame was invented by the Reverend William Lee of Calverton, Nottinghamshire, in 1589, that county, along with Leicestershire and Derbyshire, has been a centre of the British hosiery industry. The stocking frame, with two thousand separate parts, was one of the most complex pieces of machinery known to the pre-industrial world. It did not fall into disuse until the later nineteenth century when it was superseded by steam-powered rotary frames and the Cotton's patent machines, and the simultaneous development of the automatic seamless hose machines. Traditionally, the three counties avoided direct competition by specialising in different materials: Nottingham cotton, Derby silk and Leicester wool.

Frame knitting was a cottage industry. A man owned his frame, or rented it. While he worked his family wound the thread and finished the goods. A hosier would supply the materials and buy the finished product, which was taken to a warehouse to be made ready for sale.

Stockings were among the first ready-made garments to be widely available. Ever since Lee presented Elizabeth I with a pair, it had been socially acceptable to wear frame knitted ones. Knitted stockings presented few sizing problems. Their elasticity gave a smooth fit, and they could be either exquisitely fully fashioned or simply seamed tubes. When men wore breeches and women saw nothing immodest in a show of ankle, leg coverings were a subject of fashionable concern. High prices were commanded for good workmanship. The new retail drapers represented an insatiable market, supplied by big hosiers who were among the first to open wholesale warehouses in London. I. & R. Morley of Nottingham had an establishment in Russia Row from 1791, while Brettles of Belper came to Wood Street in 1810. Everyone either wore stockings, or aspired to that condition. It seemed as if the industry was unassailable, and yet it failed. By the time Victoria's reign began it was undergoing a terrible recession. Wages having stood still for thirty years, 'stockingers' were reduced to breaking stones to obtain parish relief.

Conditions became so bad that a Parliamentary Commission looked into the trade. Its findings, published in 1845, gave several reasons for the decline. Changes in fashion were largely to blame, as John Withers Taylor from Ward Sturt & Sharp pointed out:

When the ladies' garments were worn shorter and the instep was seen, they used to take pride in having a handsome and well-made stocking: But since the introduction of long petticoats, there has been no inducement for any lady to put on a pair of well-fashioned stockings. (As for men) . . . having taken to wearing boots almost universally, it does not

1 The hosier at work on a
traditional knitting frame,
from *Ure's Useful Arts and
Manufactures 1850*

matter to them, perhaps, how the stocking is made, if it will wear as well. All these things
have a tendency to drive the manufacture into a lower grade altogether, for an article that
is purely invisible in the wear.

Fully fashioned stockings were giving way to cheap 'cut-ups', straight pieces of
knitting cut and sewn to shape. Moreover, with a general depression in trade, many
impoverished workers could no longer afford good stockings. Yet what they could not
wear, they sought to manufacture. Thousands flocked to the hosiery districts, where it
was easy to rent a frame and at least have the possibility of employment.

The warehouse owners usually rented out the knitting frames and found the
assured income from them a convenient buffer against the vicissitudes of business.
Stockingers paid rent for their idle machines because refusal to do so would risk the
hosier denying them materials when the work was available. Even people with their
own frames not infrequently paid a sum in lieu of rent, to ensure their share of raw
materials.

A generation later, life was still hard. The 1863 Children's Employment
Commission heard about conditions in this cottage industry. In Nottingham:

As a rule the small shops as well as the houses are unfit as places of work for the young.
Such a shop is generally just as long and broad enough to hold the number of frames
placed in it in a single or double row, with bare passing room, often not more than six or
seven feet high, and without means of ventilation, and with dirt from accumulated
rubbish and dust ... In the country cottages ... many of these rooms are squalid far
beyond what is usual in the country dwellings of the poor, and of necessity in these,

2 Technical developments in the 1840s enabled stripey stockings to be manufactured more simply, and there followed a vogue for them lasting many years. Child's stocking, Billson & Haines, Leicester, 1855

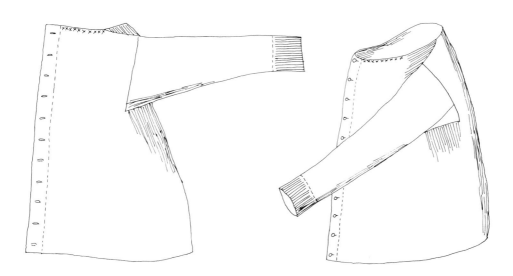

3 'The configuration of shirts made of lambswool without the usual two seams extending from the armpit to the hips'. John Biggs & Sons, Leicester, 1843

117

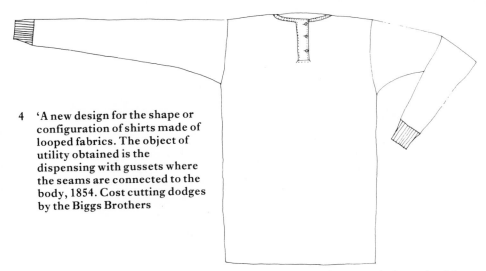

4 'A new design for the shape or
configuration of shirts made of
looped fabrics. The object of
utility obtained is the
dispensing with gussets where
the seams are connected to the
body, 1854. Cost cutting dodges
by the Biggs Brothers

crowded as they are with frames, furniture and inmates, and noisy with the rattle of the
frames, meals such as can be had are cooked and eaten, infants nursed or put to sleep,
and other housework done, of which, however, cleaning seems to form but a rare part.

Happily, some employers were generous and enlightened men. The Leicester non-
conformists John and William Biggs combined active careers in radical and liberal
politics with the running of their family firm, John Biggs & Sons. A memorial to the
elder brother, John, acclaimed him as 'one of the best employers the framework
knitters ever had'. (Reverend C. Coe, *The Friend of the Poor in His Prosperity and
Affliction*). The firm made stockings, gloves and men's vests, or undershirts. The
firm's collapse in 1861 has been blamed on the brothers' preference for political rather
than business activities, but they were interested enough to register designs
throughout the 1840s and up to 1858. Their stand at the Great Exhibition was
awarded a prize medal for 'general excellence of the specimens of hosiery, adapted to
every market, where worsted and low priced cotton stockings, gloves, and woollen
shirts are in demand'. (Great Exhibition, *Report of the Juries*).

This undershirt's cunning abolition of seams was a recipe for cheapness. (Men
wore woollen undershirts and drawers years before Dr Jaeger invented his Sanitary
Woollen System in the 1880s. They remained substantially unchanged throughout
the period and are worn by old men to this day.)

Richard Harris, born in 1777 to a family of Leicester stockingers, was also a
committed nonconformist who held several public offices. After his death in 1855 he
was remembered for his kindness to the poor and great personal integrity. Harris went
as a youth to Nottingham to learn about new types of knitting frames which were
being developed there alongside lace-making machinery. These could produce
intricate patterns, and were especially useful in what was known as the fancy hosiery

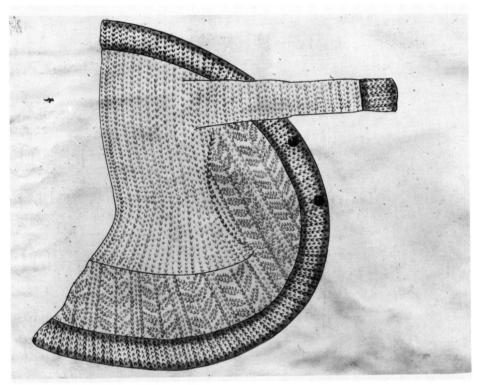

5 The humble knitted polka in pale pink with a blue border. Richard Harris & Sons, 1850

branch of the trade. This meant all types of knitted garments other than the purely utilitarian: Harris adapted the machinery, which was intended for cotton, so that woollen goods could be made, and set up business in Leicester knitting shawls and scarves.

Diversification into fancy hosiery was a stroke of genius. If people were not prepared to pay for quality in garments that were hidden, there was always a ready market for novelties. Fancy hosiery was already being imported from Germany, where all kinds of garments were made out of new soft wools in bright colours. Harris has been called the father of the fancy hosiery business in Leicester, and for many years he was the only manufacturer in the field. In the 1830s, he maintained two hundred different lines. The 1843 Children's Employment Commission heard that he employed, in addition to many country outworkers, 'five hundred women in Leicester and their children and neighbours. Each woman may have six under her'. He also kept one hundred females on his premises aged between fourteen and twenty, working 8 a.m. to 8 p.m. with 2½ hours break.

119

February 1853 THE WORLD OF FASHION. Plate 4

6 *The World of Fashion*, **February 1853**

7   Cheerful crocheted undersleeves; the left example has a gold thread incorporated.
Sarah Nathan, Southwark, 1851

Like stockings, larger garments were enabled to fit well through the elasticity of
knitting. Ladies' 'polka' jackets, with tight bodies and wide skirts, were highly
popular in the late 1840s and 50s. As fashion plate manifestations, they were typically
of some dark rich fabric with a fur trimming, but their more frequent appearance on
the streets may have been as knitted jackets, with looped borders instead of fur.
Harris is said to have made women's knitted jackets from the 1830s, but polkas,
including some by Harris, first occur in the design sample books from 1849, when
they were the height of fashion, and were registered until the late 1850s. These cheap
serviceable garments were sold for years: the Manchester wholesalers John Rylands &
Sons included 'children's polka jackets' in their catalogue from the early 1870s.
Despite their popularity, it is unlikely that any survive today, nor do these humble
woollies often appear in contemporary art or literature. Platt Hall Gallery of English
Costume in Manchester has a three-inch version, however, forming part of the stock
in trade of a pedlar doll.

   The same sort of women who patronised knitted polkas undoubtedly bought the

8 The impressive main entrance of Corah's Saint Margaret's Works, built in 1865 (reproduced by permission of Corah PLC)

decorative knitted and crocheted undersleeves which were registered as often as the jackets. Squashed and grubby examples, surviving in the books, made by all the big firms, are frequently striped in soft, bright wools, with elasticated cuffs. A snug substitute for the starched white muslin version worn under the bell-shaped sleeves of the fashion plates, these were obviously intended for women with work to do.

Specialised goods like these would have been hand made as a cottage industry. But while firms like Biggs & Sons were still firmly in the tradition of employing outworkers and renting frames to them, the fancy hosiery trade was increasingly centred on factories. This was because the frames were more sophisticated, and manufacturers preferred to keep them under one roof for fear of industrial espionage. The 1845 report into the condition of the framework knitters noted that Richard Harris housed 'a considerable number of hand frames' on his premises. His employees, benefiting from his farsightedness, were all earning a good wage, for the time, of a pound a week.

9 Registered trademark of Cooper, Corah & Sons, St Margaret's Works, Leicester

Steam engines were an important factor in the move from cottage to factory production in the 1850s. By 1855, the outlook over Leicester had been transformed by the chimneys of eighty steam engines. The Leicester firm Nathaniel Corah & Sons installed one about this time. Ever since Nathanial Corah had gone into business in 1815 with the idea of buying stockings in Leicester and selling them in Birmingham, Corah's had been an innovative set-up. By 1824, it had so prospered that a warehouse was purchased, with enough space to enable goods to be manufactured on the premises; a revolutionary step for the time. The firm's adoption of steam power was thus a natural development. So too was the building in 1865 of St Margaret's Works, with its beam engine and gigantic 140-foot chimney.

Factory production brought with it an ever increasing range of goods. Knitting machines now made larger pieces that could be cut up and sewn into cheap comfortable clothing which required the minimum of shaping to produce a good fit. The 1860s

10 One of several
jersey bodies
registered by
Parisian manufac-
turer, Alfonso
Boccardo, 1888

and 70s saw a dramatic increase in the use of hosiery. Traditional staples such as
stockings and underwear were joined by jackets and cardigans, elaborate hats,
mantles and tippets, then later, bathing suits, football and yachting jerseys, while the
new knitted fabrics were extensively used for working class clothing at this time. The
jersey came into its own in the late 1870s as a fashionable lady's bodice, popularised
by Lily Langtry. It showed off to perfection a woman's curves, and was equally useful
for clothing growing girls and boys.

Significantly, nearly all the designs registered by Corah date from the early 1880s
when the jersey vogue was at its height, and new patterns were at a premium. They
include a fringed cape, hats, a waistcoat, a pair of knitted trousers and a cycling

An Ornamental Design

for

A Jersey Dress to be called the "St. Margaret's Gem"

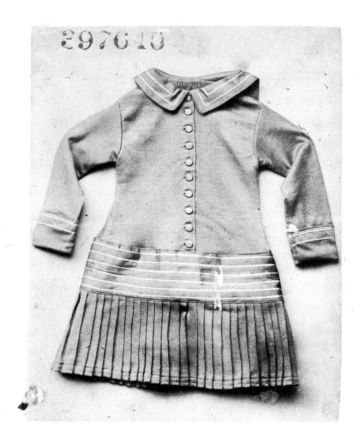

11 'The Saint Margaret's Gem' as shown in Corah's registration 1883

12   'The Saint Margaret's Gem' as advertised in *The Queen,* 1885

costume, as well as a variety of jersey bodices, with names such as the 'Fedora', the 'Princess', the 'Louise', the 'Iolanthe', the 'Empress', the 'Windermere' and the 'Scarborough'. The original 'St Margaret's' jerseys were worn in the highest circles: Corah's have a photograph taken on the royal yacht in 1878 showing Princess Alexandra and her children wearing them. The 'St Margaret's Gem' was another profitable line, registered in late 1882. This children's dress was being sold by Debenham & Freebody in 1885, who advertised it in *The Queen*. 'St Margaret's' was Corah's trademark, one of the first to be registered when the scheme began in 1875. The advertisement shows how useful brand names were for manufacturers since customers could recognise their goods.

Corah's were always good employers. In the 1890s, they took the unprecedented step of giving all their staff an annual paid holiday. An article in *Leicester in 1891*

13 Although this photograph of Corah's making-up room was taken around 1920, the scene would have been substantially the same in the late 19th century (reproduced by permission of Corah PLC)

14   **Hurst & Cane of 14 Friday Street, City registered this disconcertingly modern-looking pullover in 1986. Its wiggly pocket and hem betrays its cheap manufacture.**

about the firm outlined their good working conditions and also their progressive methods:

> . . . We saw the yarn brought in on spools, in cops and bundles, and after being wound on bobbins, it was placed on top of the machines, and there apparently left to itself – half a dozen stockings or jerseys seeming to grow like magic upon each machine, whilst the men stood idly by, watching the process. This seeming idleness, however, was, in reality, the strictest vigilance, each pair of eyes watching hundreds of threads of yarn closely, and if by accident, as sometimes happens, a thread breaks, the mischief is remedied, and a knot tied before the uninitiated would know that anything had occurred. Down each side of the room rotary machines are whirling round with great rapidity, and though we

make no pretensions to describe their work with technical accuracy, some idea of what they were accomplishing may be gathered from our remarks. One machine was turning out jerseys to be worn by the men on Her Majesty's yachts; it made them six at a time, converting the yarn into fabric and narrowing it to the form of the body . . .

15   **Long knitted drawers by Fraser & Fraser & Co., Kilmarnock, 1888**

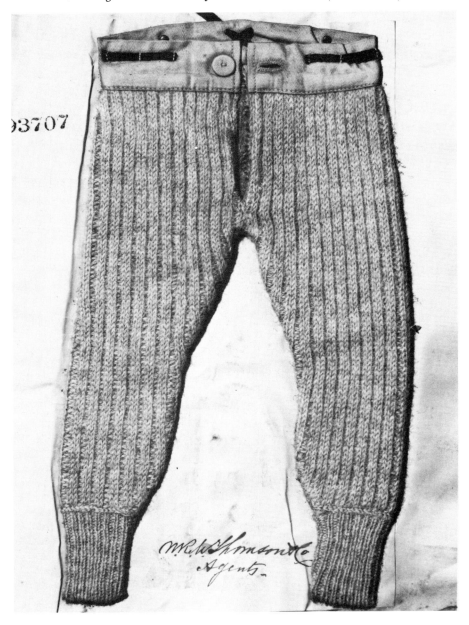

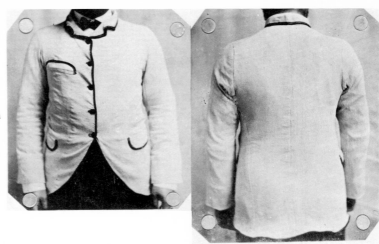

16 Many working men
in the late 19th
century wore
knitted jackets like
this crudely made
'coat shaped
wrapper' by
Robertson,
Higginson
& Lowe, 1885

The milling and finishing rooms came next, and it was wonderful to see the transformation that took place in the goods during the time that they remained in this
department. They enter rough and unfinished, but they are soon taken in hand; the wool
is raised on the face of the hose, they are placed on shapes, pressed, dried by centrifugal
action, and turned out most exquisitely finished . . . while here we also looked into the
bleaching department, but the sulphurous exhalations were too powerful to be stood
longer than was absolutely necessary.

With all this technological achievement, it must be remembered that many
processes, such as finishing and seaming stockings, still had to be carried out by
hand. They continued to be done in the homes of outworkers for what were often
miserable rates of pay. In fact, as mechanisation increased productivity, so too did the
demand for outworkers increase. D. H. Lawrence paints a vivid picture of their life in a
scene in *Sons and Lovers* set around 1885:

At the end of the Bottoms a man stood in a sort of old-fashioned trap, bending over
bundles of cream coloured stuff; while a cluster of women held up their arms to him,
some with bundles. Mrs Anthony herself had a heap of creamy, undyed stockings
hanging over her arm.
  'I've done ten dozen this week,' she said proudly to Mrs Morel.
  'T.t.t,' went the other, 'I don't know how you can make time.'
  'Eh!' said Mrs Anthony. 'You can find time if you make time.'
  'I don't know how you do it,' said Mrs Morel. 'And how much shall you get for those
many?'
  'Tuppence-ha'penny a dozen,' replied the other.
  'Well,' said Mrs Morel, 'I'd starve before I'd sit down and seam twenty four stockings
for twopence-ha'penny.'
  'Oh, I don't know,' said Mrs Anthony, 'you can rip along on 'em.'
  Hose was coming along, ringing his bell. Women were waiting at the yard ends with
their seamed stockings hanging over their arms. The man, a common fellow, made jokes
with them, tried to swindle them, and bullied them. Mrs Morel went up her yard
disdainfully.

13
Gloves

The texture and colour of the skin, and the appearance of the nails, show how much care and culture the possessor has bestowed upon them, and consequently, may be regarded as evidence of his or her taste . . . a soft white hand . . . the palm and the tips of the fingers should be of the colour of the inner leaves of a moss rose, with the blue veins distinctly visible . . . gloves should always be worn on exposure to the atmosphere, and are graceful at all times for a lady in the house, except at meals. (*How to Dress or the Etiquette of the Toilette*, 1876.)

GLOVE WEARING was immensely important in the last century, delineating the boundary between those who worked and those who did not, or who wished to look as if they did not. They protected the hand from wear and tear, while preventing it from carrying out many activities since they were commonly worn extremely tight. Social barriers were enforced by the complex code of etiquette surrounding glove wearing. Etiquette books were full of advice for the parvenu. One warned:

Whether in town or country always wear gloves, those for town wear should be of a light delicate tint as such a glove has an air of elegance and finish. Gloves for the country may be stouter, but the material must be kid and the fit perfection. A gentleman is known by his gloves. (*Etiquette for Gentlemen*, 1866.)

Gloves were an expensive item: The author of *How to Dress Neatly and Prettily on £10 a Year* of 1881 estimated that the minimum quantity for a lady was four pairs of kid gloves at 2s to 2s 6d each in winter, and a pair of black cotton gloves at 8d or 9d every six weeks in summer, as well as a pair of black silk ones for best at 1s 3d. She considered that dark gloves wore better; her inepecunious readers were fortunate to live at a time when they were briefly in fashion. Even so, gloves took up a substantial proportion of the allowance.

Cotton or silk could be acceptable alternatives to kid. They were stronger and easier to clean, as well as cooler in summer. Glove making formed one of the staples of the hosiery trade in Britain. They were traditionally made by outworkers, and brought from a wide area into the town warehouses, to be bleached, and then glazed in a gas oven, or over hot sulphur. They were then pressed, and packed in paper envelopes, ready for sending away.

Ladies' silk gloves and fingerless mittens of delicate lace-like fabrics were in vogue throughout the 1840s and 50s when glove wearing had reached its zenith. These gloves, made by Topham & Fawcett of Derby in 1843, have an entirely elasticated hand. The advantage of such an elasticated glove will be apparent to anyone who has

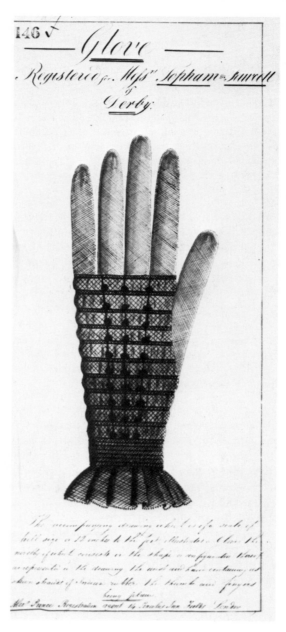

1   Dainty elasticated glove. Topham & Fawcett, Derby, 1843

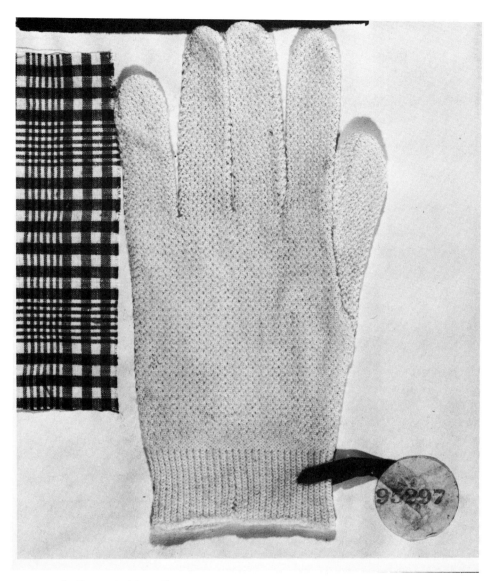

2   Remarkably ordinary cream knitted glove by the Biggs brothers, 1854

experienced the gradual loosening of an ordinary knitted cotton or silk glove which occurs with a few hours' wear.

In *The Lady's Shopping Manual and Mercery Album* of 1834, E. E. Perkins described

133

3   Advertisement card for Ward Sturt & Sharp's Ringwood gloves, late 19th century.
This shows how trademarks and registered designs were exploited as sales features
(Leicester Museum and Art Gallery)

a new type of knitted glove: Berlin gloves, originally from Prussia, but now made in
England. They were:

> An improvement on cotton, but it is to be lamented both as a matter of taste, and for the
> sake of the industrious poor, that their introduction has nearly superseded the manly
> buckskin as well as the elegant kid.

This was an overstatement. But the soft brightly coloured new type of wool was
certainly supplanting the traditional crewels for many other purposes. These cheap,
hardwearing gloves were the first of many knitted products to be imported from
Germany, representing formidable competition for the English manufacturers, who
imitated them out of self-protection. Berlin gloves were much too sensible for the
taste of gentlemen, and were soon seen as a sure indication of poverty. Thackeray
warned in 1847 in *The Book of Snobs*, 'My son, it is you who are the snob if you lightly
despise a man for doing his duty, and refuse to shake an honest man's hand because it
wears a Berlin glove.'

This Biggs glove of 1854 could have been the type referred to. Its ordinariness
makes it interesting; only a particularly narrow thumb gusset distinguishes it from a
modern glove, and betrays its cheap manufacture.

Woolly gloves have been worn for generations by ordinary people. The traditional

134

4 'The National Rifle Glove' registered by Ward Sturt & Sharp in 1860 from their warehouse at 98 Wood Street, City

Ringwood style of brightly patterned knitted gloves for everyday wear, named after the area in Hampshire where it originated, was as popular in the nineteenth century as it is today, and large manufacturers included them in their ranges from the 1870s.

135

Many Ringwood gloves were registered, in a range of patterns and colours which in many cases are so indistinguishable that it is hard to know why anyone bothered to register them at all.

Ward Sturt & Sharp made other kinds of stout winter gloves as well as the Ringwood style illustrated here. The 'National Rifle Glove' was registered by means of a photograph in 1860. Made from flannel with red braiding, it was presumably intended for use by members of the National Rifle Association, one of the volunteer regiments set up in 1859 during a bout of francophobia: Napoleon III's new battleship had frightened the government into thinking that he intended to invade Britain. It would be expected that a rifle glove would be modified in some way to facilitate pulling the trigger, but Ward Sturt & Sharp seem only to have been registering the attractive braiding touched in on the photograph.

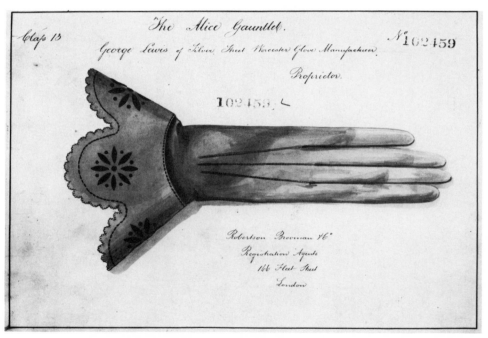

5 'The Alice Gauntlet' named after one of Queen Victoria's daughters. George Lewis, Silver Street, Worcester, 1853

Since gloves were widely worn and quickly worn out, their frequent renewal gave scope for fashionable novelties. In contrast to the homely Ringwood, registered designs for leather gloves follow with elegance and exquisite workmanship the latest trends. Since time immemorial Worcestershire, Warwickshire and the West Country have been the centres of leather glove making in Britain. Not surprisingly, most

136

6   The bright machine embroidery on this kid glove takes advantage of the fashionable long length. Dent Allcroft & Co., 97 Wood Street, City, 1880

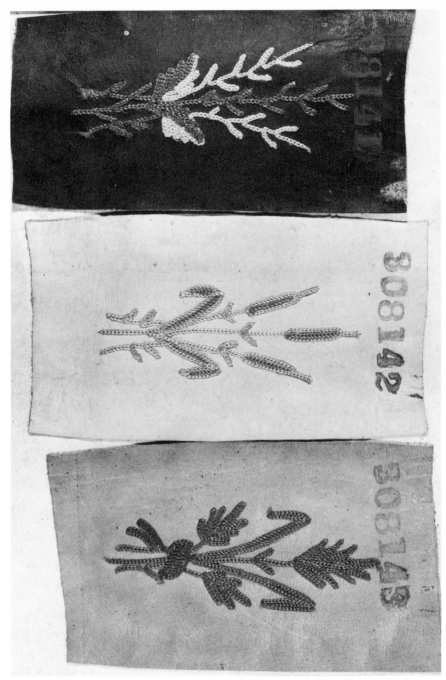

7 Machine-embroidered glove back in floral design, Whitby Bros., Yeovil, 1877

8   The elegant image of Fowne's gloves as advertised in *Modern London*, c.1885

leather gloves were registered by firms from these parts of the country or their London warehouses.

The 'Alice Gauntlet' was registered by George Lewis, of Silver Street, Worcester, in 1853. It follows the contemporary fashionable line of the undersleeve with its wide cuff, and the pinked border echoes the stamped patterns often used to edge silk dress flounces at that time. The aniline dyes derived from coal tar which made such an impression on fashionable costume of the 1860s are seen in bright purple and blue glove trimmings. As women's sleeves were worn shorter from the mid-1870s, the glove lengthened, often coming to the elbow. Even Ringwood gloves from the 1880s tend to come well over the wrist. Long gloves beautifully exhibited fine soft leather and good workmanship. Those registered at this time were often in dark colours with beading or embroidery. The same embroidery machines which were being developed for the corsetry trade were used by glovers.

While French gloves were considered, like everything French, to be innately superior to their British counterparts, home workmanship gradually gained ground. In 1878, J. W. Hayes in *The Draper and Haberdasher* considered that:

> The French have excelled in glove making, but English makes are now considered equal in every respect, in fact ... gloves are also shipped to France and imported to England to accommodate the prejudice of buyers.

Without going to these extremes, some British glovers achieved a worldwide reputation. The two largest, Fownes Brothers and Dent Allcroft & Co., vied for the credit of being the oldest glovers in the country. Both had London warehouses, and in *Modern London* of c. 1891, Fownes claimed to have been 'founded by John Fownes of Worcester in 1777' while Dent Allcroft said they were 'the oldest and largest firm of glove manufacturers in the world'.

Fownes's new factory in Clare Street, Worcester, was described in *Modern London*, in an article which noted:

> the attention given to the health and comfort of the work people which is altogether praiseworthy. Here are ventilators securing a plentiful supply of fresh air, while any downward draught is prevented; separate staircases for men and women employed ... completely fitted lavatories are on every floor, and one room, in which are benches and forms, and a delightfully mixed collection of tea-pots, proves to be a tea room for the women employed at the sewing machines ... some of the work is still done at the homes of the workers, and one room here is set apart as a waiting room for those who come to fetch work or bring it back – generally wrapped in a clean white handkerchief.

In other parts of the factory, the leather was sorted, and treated, by being steeped in egg yolk. No substitute had been found for 'this expensive material', although, 'Messrs Fownes have improved on the old-established usage and replaced by a mixture of chemicals, the urine which was, and still is, used to cleanse all grease from the skins before dying.' The glove shapes were then punched out and tied into bundles to be sewn.

Both Fownes's and Dents made specialised gloves in different localities. Dents had 800 workers in Worcester, branches in London, Devon and Somerset, and hosiery factories in Nottingham and Leicester. They had agents the world over, with depots at Paris and New York, and factories at Grenoble, Brussels, Prague and Halberstadt, as well as skin dressing yards at Grenoble and Ottignes.

This Fownes glove of 1898 illustrates one of the most important developments to affect the glove industry: the press-stud. A French firm called Raymond has been credited with the invention in 1880 of the first workable snap-fastener, designed for gloves. The registered designs show that the idea was also 'in the air' in Britain – at least two Worcester glovers, John Nicol and Robert Black, had developed press-stud type fastenings in 1879 and 1880. Raymond's fastener had a solid head which was gripped in a hollow with four petal-like sections. Another early press-stud, known as the 'bird cage', had a slit dome which was forced into a ring. About 1900 a German firm devised a more successful snap-fastener with an internal spring. It was never patented, and before long, it was universally copied and marketed.

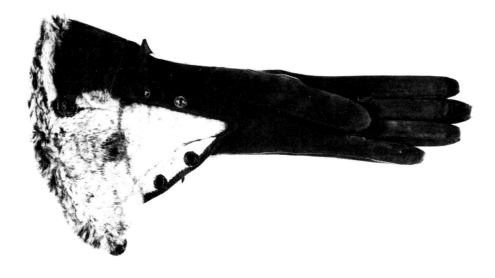

9   Early press studs on a Fownes glove, 1898

14
Neckwear

IN THE Victorian period, a man's neck was one of the few areas which gave him scope for sartorial individuality. Introverts and exhibitionists alike could find patterns and colours to suit them, and far more styles of knot than are customary today.

In the 1840s, the high black satin stock, a military style introduced into the civilian wardrobe by George IV in 1822, was as popular as ever. Several inches deep, stiffened with buckram and fastened with a large buckle, it gave the wearer a stately, if pained, demeanour. Dickens described Mr Turveydrop, the aged beau in *Bleak House*, thus:

> He had such a neckcloth on (puffing his eyes out of their natural shape) and his chin and even his ears sunk into it, that it seemed as though he must inevitably double up, if it were cast loose . . . As he bowed to me in that state, I almost believe I saw creases come into the whites of his eyes.

These contraptions were usually registered in the useful class. Their design was evidently a serious matter of great import. Welch Margetson registered several stocks in the 1840s, including the 'Aerial Stock' of 1847 and an improved version of 1849. These featured a steel spring which wrapped itself around the neck, and saved the weaver from having to wrestle with a buckle at the back. Other new inventions were incorporated. Mrs Hannah Smith of Halifax registered a stock stiffener with 'a small piece of Indian rubber forming a connection' between gores.

The example made by Welch Margetson shown here illustrates the subtle shaping which necessitated their being professionally made, usually by female outworkers in the back streets of the cities.

In *Lights and Shadows of London Life* of 1842, James Grant estimated the scale of production there:

> That the numbers so employed must be very large, may be inferred from the fact, that the highly respectable and rapidly rising house of Messrs Alexander Grant & Bros, of Clement's Court, Cheapside, employs no fewer than 400–500 young women in the making of this article. Their weekly earnings, as they work by the piece, vary from eight to eighteen shillings. The above number of young women are employed direct by Messrs Grant, and get their materials from their warehouse; but several of those so employed, after taking the material to their respective homes, 'sub-engage' (if that be a proper phrase) a number of girls, and pay them so much for their labour. Of course, as the females who are engaged by the stock merchant must have their profit on the work done

1   Severe black satin stock with the name 'Welch Margetson' just visible, printed in copperplate script on the lining, 1840s. Museum of London

by the girls whom they employ in their turn, the earnings of the young women who receive their employment at second hand ... must necessarily be very small. Their earnings are in many cases as low as five shillings per week: in no instance do they exceed half a guinea.

Being black, many stocks were particularly unpleasant to sew all day. One of the Grants told the 1843 Children's Employment Commission that 'some of the work tries the eyes' but the hours were in general very moderate, being 8 a.m. to 7 p.m. with 1½

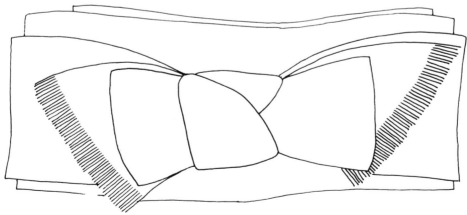

2   'Ornamental stock', Alex Grant & Bros., 2 Clement's Court, Wood Street, 1848

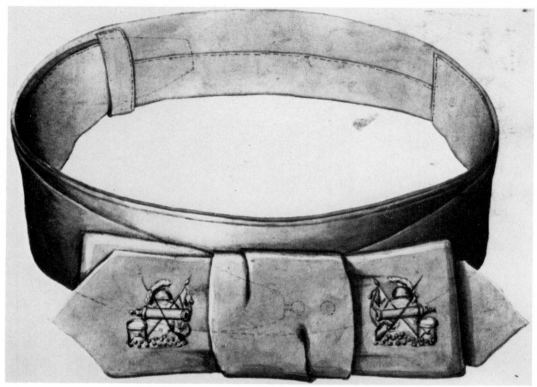

3   This stock by John Ford, 15 Addle Street, City shows the bows tendency towards
increasing splendour, 1853. The motifs are crossed out because they were not being
registered

hours off for meals. The designs registered by Alexander Grant show what the
subjects of these discussions actually looked like and so complete the picture. The
firm went from strength to strength, registering designs not only for neckwear, but
also for shirts and parasols. In 1863, they had branches in Londonderry, Portsmouth
and Salisbury. As is so often the fate of a prosperous enterprise, they were eventually
taken over, in this case by Welch Margetson.

John Edward Ford's splendid ornamental design for a stock of 1853 shows the next
evolutionary stage. With more emphasis being placed on the bow, it was becoming a
necktie proper. At the same time, its alarming height and rigidity were diminishing.
According to a lady quoted by *Punch* in 1854: 'As for your scarfs I have seen young
gentlemen wear neck handkerchieves no thicker than the ribbon we put around the
neck of a kitten.'

Stocks gave way to ties and scarves, as the neck decoration continued to shrink.
Collars were also worn narrower and frequently turned down. A variety of styles of

144

4 Fancy scarf rings from the 1860s:

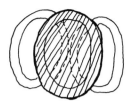

(a) Ebenezer Baines

(b) Moss Levi Jacob & Lewis Woolf

(c) Hall & Dutson

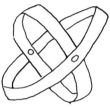

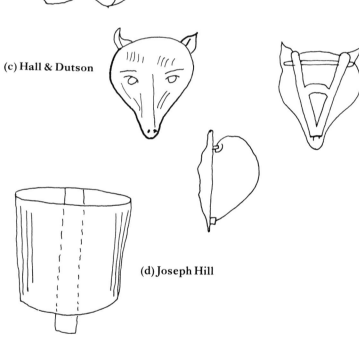

(d) Joseph Hill

(e) Henry Jagg

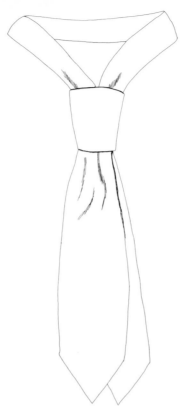

5 'The Duke of Edinburgh cravat',
one of many registrations by
Slater Buckingham & Co.,
35 Wood Street, City, 1886

scarf vied for popularity with the front bow. When Bertie Stanhope shocked Barchester by wearing, for the bishop's ball, a blue neckerchief fastened beneath the throat with a coral ring, he was wearing the *dernier cri* in daytime neckwear for 1857. (Anthony Trollope, *Barchester Towers*). Scarf rings continued to be popular; many designs were registered for them right into the 1890s. Cowboys in the American Wild West took to wearing scarf rings at this time, perhaps because of their attractive designs and the fact that they were less trouble to put on than knotted ties. They are now an essential ingredient of traditional cowboy dress, holding bootlace ties round their necks and those of their emulators – the British Teddy Boys, who emerged in the 1950s.

Another style first seen around 1860, the 'four-in-hand', was a prototype for the predominant twentieth-century style. Being long, thin and flat, they were often registered by means of a sample. A beautiful sky-blue silk tie, the first to be machine stitched, was registered by Lloyd & Attree in 1862.

George Attree had joined John Lloyd as a partner in his warehouse at 29 Wood Street only months before. The firm, known as Lloyd Attree & Smith from 1865, were

146

6   This unknown young man's necktie is probably one of the ready made variety; note the narrow neckband and its apparent independence from the front piece, late 19th century. Private collection

to publish a booklet in 1957 celebrating a hundred years in Wood Street. This described their first bestseller, the 'Octagon Scarf'. Not only was it made up ready for use, but the separate front piece could be revolved to fit the neck band of each of its eight sides, thus equalising the wear. It was an extreme example, but by no means unusual. A large proportion of Victorian manhood was well acquainted with the made-up tie, and they are often detectable in old photographs. Because these were more complicated than ordinary ones, they predominate in the registered designs. The made-up tie typically had a cardboard front with broad silk bands folded over it, and a neck piece. This could fasten with a buckle, or have a stiffened end which passed through a loop on the back of the cardboard. The effect was solid to say the least. In 1900, *Clothes and the Man* offered a word of advice:

If you fasten both ends of the tie to the shirt you don't make it any more secure, and you give the tie a stiff appearance: It will then look very much like a made-up tie. Of course no gentleman ever does wear a made-up tie, and doesn't want the credit (?) of wearing one.

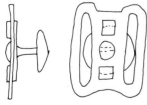

7   Bow tie fastener. John Compton Weeks Jeffereys, London, 1887

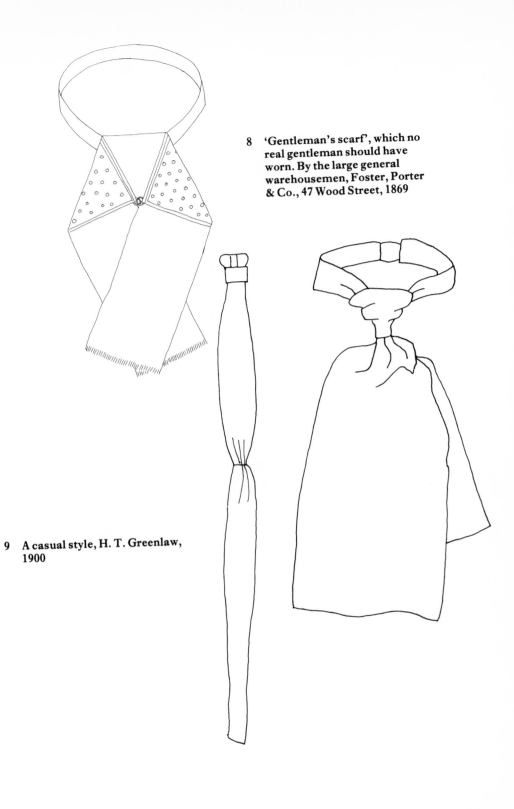

8 'Gentleman's scarf', which no real gentleman should have worn. By the large general warehousemen, Foster, Porter & Co., 47 Wood Street, 1869

9 A casual style, H. T. Greenlaw, 1900

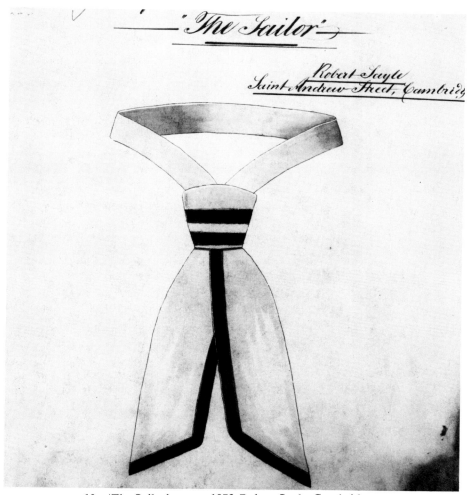

10   'The Sailor' cravat, 1873. Robert Sayle, Cambridge

Those privileged enough to have time and perhaps a valet to tie their tie heartily despised the ready-made version. But the thousands who were not prepared to stand in front of a mirror every morning creating difficult arrangements continued to patronise them, with only a few doubts as to their respectability. Mr Pooter, hero of the Grossmiths' *Diary of a Nobody* of the late 1880s, was dining with an important American businessman:

> That sort of thing, continued Mr Huttle, belongs to a soft man, with a soft beard, with a soft head, with a made-up tie that hooks on.
>   This seemed rather personal, and twice I caught myself looking in the glass of the chiffonier. For *I* had a tie that hooked on – and why not?

149

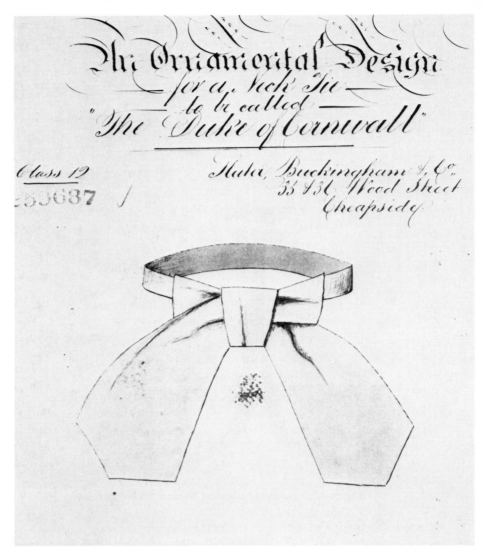

The Ornamental Design
for a Neck Tie
to be called
"The Duke of Cornwall"

Class 19
253687

Slater, Buckingham & Co.
55 & 56 Wood Street
Cheapside

11 'The Duke of Cornwall' necktie. Slater Buckingham & Co., Wood Street, City, 1871

Mr Pooter would have been wearing an evening dress bow tie, which may have fastened on like the one registered in 1887 (see p. 147).

Made-up ties had an important advantage, which must have outweighed all other considerations for some dashing young men: all kinds of extravagant, impossible looking effects could be created, destined to win the admiration of all who saw them. The design registered in 1886 for a tie like a lady's leg has already been mentioned.

150

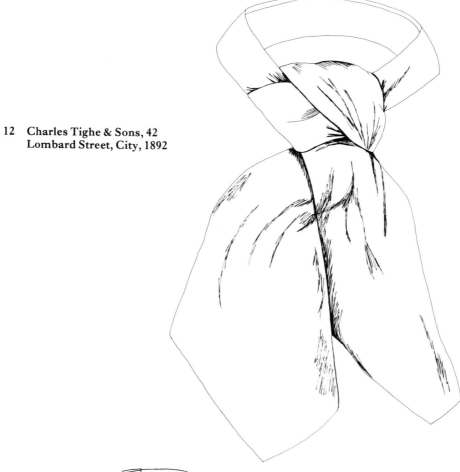

12 Charles Tighe & Sons, 42
    Lombard Street, City, 1892

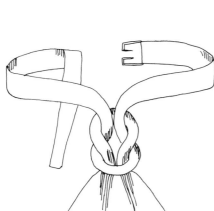

13 Robert Evans, Stoke
    Newington, 1900

14 Scenes from Greenlaw's Golden Lane premises, c1905. Men in the cutting room use a rule to achieve the perfect bias. In the finishing room, women turn the stitched tubes. These are from an album which also shows the factory canteen and rest room, complete with piano. Private collection.

15   H. T. Greenlaw's finishing room, where women turned the stitched tie tubes.

The 1860s and 70s were particularly fruitful for made-up ties: designs include scarves folded so that their woven pattern exactly formed a circular motif, such as a firework or a cobweb. One tie formed a gigantic ace of clubs, and one had a white mouse peeping round its folds. Some, like that registered by Henry Tucker Greenlaw in 1888, had an arrangement of folds with no knot, which must have depended on being stitched to a board.

16   Cunning arrangement by Henry Tucker Greenlaw, 83 Golden Lane, City, 1888

Kipps's friend Buggins would have appreciated a novel alternative to the false shirt front, which seems to have greatly excited the trade in 1869 and 70, since several firms registered versions in rapid succession. This was a made-up tie, with the front part extending over the whole chest, cunningly made to represent an imitation waistcoat, in rich satin, complete with V-neck and buttons.

Neckwear continued to be made in the workers' homes rather than in factories until the turn of the century. This could have been because of the large amounts of hand sewing involved; even large wholesale warehousemen like Welch Margetson, Foster Porter & Co., or Lloyd Attree & Smith would give out the silk to women who came to their premises. Henry Tucker Greenlaw was one of the first specialist manufacturers in the modern sense. He started out not as a shopkeeper or a warehouseman, but as simply a wholesale manufacturer. After being a shipboy, a bookbinder and a wine merchant's porter, H. T. Greenlaw fell in love with the girl next door, who was a tiemaker. He learned the trade from her, and after their marriage in 1870, they set up a workroom employing other tiemakers, fulfilling wholesalers' orders. This was not a sweatshop, but a factory with employer and employees. Soon they were buying up remnants and off-cuts, and making bow ties speculatively for sale at 4s 6d a dozen. Greenlaw used to say, 'There is no fun like hard work,' and he lived up to his dictum. Despite a major fire, by 1886 his turnover was £5000 and by 1895, it was £50,000. Greenlaw was a great believer in the importance of novelties, and this may explain why he was keen to register designs. He wrote in his unpublished memoirs:

> There is always a demand for new and original goods. To procure new goods and novelties means constant application and self-reliance, but the hard work to find novelties is amply repaid by the production from time to time of goods such as our house has had the good fortune to place on the market.

15
Footwear

THE VERY first registered design to feature elastic was a boot with side gores, submitted on 14 May 1840 by Joseph Sparkes Hall, owner of the cloth shoe warehouse at 308 Regent Street. Hall had been making galoshes with rubber supplied by Thomas Hancock since 1830, and he is said to have actually invented the elastic sided boot, of which he patented a version in 1837.

In 1846, he wrote *The Book of the Feet* which, as well as describing their history from ancient Egyptian times to the present, expounded the virtues of the new boot.

I am of the opinion that the best coverings for the feet are boots: Not only do they look neat and tidy, but the general and gradual support they give all over the feet and ankles induces strength, and gives tone to the veins and muscles . . . the trouble however, of lacing and unlacing, the tag coming off, the button breaking, or the shank hurting, the holes soon wearing out, and many other little annoyances, have all been experienced as *bores* by thousands who have worn that kind of boot . . .

About ten years since I first thought of an elastic boot, that might possibly remedy in a great measure all these minor evils, and combine many advantages never possessed by any former boot . . . My first experiments were a failure . . . (But) subsequent improvements in materials and workmanship have combined to make the elastic boot the most perfect thing of its kind . . .

For many years since I have scarcely made any other kind of boots but the elastic. But I have not made a fortune – I am happy, however, if in any way I have contributed to the comfort of my fellow creatures, or been instrumental in affording employment to my fellow countrymen.

In 1837, Sparkes Hall had presented the new queen with a pair of his boots. She must have liked them, since he noted:

Her Majesty has been pleased to honour the invention with the most marked and continued patronage; it has been my privilege for some years to make her boots . . . and no one who is acquainted with Her Majesty's habits of walking and exercise, in the open air, can doubt the superior claims of elastic over every other kind of boots.

Serving the highest ranks of society from his West End shop, Sparkes Hall was acutely aware of the threat to the existence of traditional craftsmen posed by the rapid growth of the ready-made footwear trade which was 'already being patronised by the bulk of the population'.

1   Sparkes Hall's famous elasticated boot, 1840

There is a large class of persons in London etc. who sell boots and shoes, but do not manufacture them. The greater part of those persons know no more how a boot or shoe is made, than the boots or shoes themselves can be said to possess such knowledge. These articles are principally made in the country, or eastern part of the metropolis, and sent up for sale; perhaps a hundred dozen pairs are made on one pair of lasts ... We see at present, the goods of these places in the shop windows of almost every town in the kingdom, ticketed up at so much the pair; the prices charged being in many cases much less than what some masters pay to the better qualifyed journeyman for the mere making of similar looking articles.

Cyrus & James Clark's manufactory in Street, Somerset, was an example of this type of business. One of their advertisements from about 1850 lists 'respectable dealers' in seventy-six provincial towns, and thirty-two shops in London which stocked their goods, and they were exported, among other places, to Ireland and Australia. Their earliest surviving price list, dating from 1848, gives 334 items.

Cyrus Clark had started on his own originally in 1825 as a fellmonger and woolstapler, dealing in sheepskin rugs. When three years later his brother became his apprentice, they began their shoe trade by selling sheepskin slippers made from waste scraps, and the business grew rapidly from there.

Two of their registered designs are included in a poster issued in 1852, for an elasticated shoe front, and a boot elastic extending around the ankle. They were intended for either sex, and show the comparative flimsiness of shoes. In 1848 *Punch* ridiculed the 'modern fast man', with his delicate boots 'only keeping sole and body together with the aid of Mother-of-Pearl buttons'.

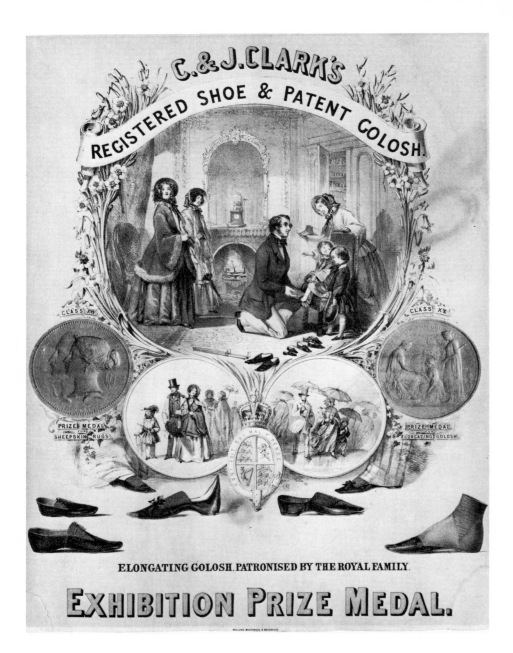

2 Clark's shoes for all the family: a poster from the early 1850s in Clark's Shoe Museum, Street, Somerset

The Osborne Boot,

REGISTERED FOR CYRUS & JAMES CLARK,

STREET, SOMERSET.

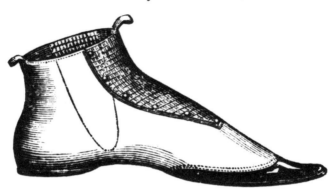

3 'The Osborne Boot', 1856 by C. & J. Clark. Named after one of Queen Victoria's country houses. Clark's Shoe Museum, Street, Somerset

Clarks featured their registered 'Osborne Boot', price 7s 9d or 9s 9d, in their 1858 catalogue, with an extract from the *Practical Mechanic's Journal*:

> The object of this design is to obtain a better fit over the instep of the foot. The dotted line in the engraving indicates an elastic gusset which is inserted in one side only of the boot. A flap of elastic material is brought over the instep, and buttons are inserted, to give the appearance of a buttoned boot, the elastic material being of the peculiar shape shown, for the purpose of securing a good fit.

Clarks added:

> This beautifully-fitting boot has been found to give the greatest satisfaction, lessening the difficulty of securing a good fit either for a high or low instep. For the convenience of those who wish to make to order C. and J. C. will send their Osborne Boot Legs ready-bound, with their registered mark on them. Any parties selling them without their registered mark on each boot, will be liable to a penalty of five pounds.

While firms like Clarks were producing boots and shoes in great quantity, they were mainly doing so by traditional processes. After the 'clickers', a factory élite, had cut out the uppers, they were sent out: first to the 'binders' who stitched them up, then to the shoemaker, who attached the sole, and finally, back in the factory, they were finished and packed.

159

THE
"LORNE" LACE BOOT,

REGISTERED BY

C. & J. CLARK, STREET, SOMERSET,

5   Walking boot with elastic sides and ornamental laces, H. Marshall, Northampton, 1854

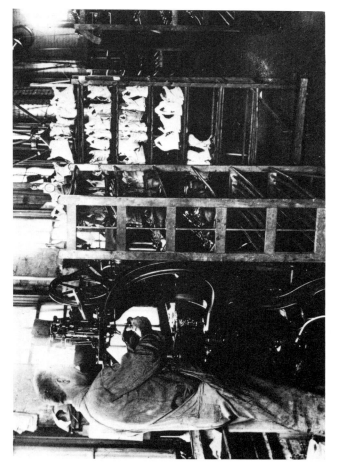

6   Blake's sole sewing machine in use at Lynn, Massachusetts, USA, c1900. Clark's Shoe Museum

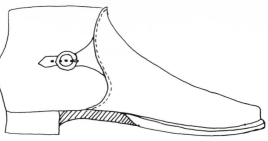

7 'The Wellington Blucher shoe', 'to improve the appearance of the Blucher shoe so that it may appear like a wellington boot': an unusual style by Southall & Hallam, Swan Street, Manchester, 1864

8 Machine-sewn boot 'equals in appearance any hand sewn boot, combining lightness and durability of wear at a great reduction in cost of production and is especially adapted for evening parties, dancing or walking', Jesse Harrison, Broad Street, Northampton, 1884

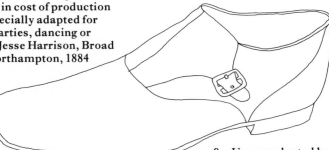

9 Unprecedented buckled style. Fred Bostock, Northampton, 1899

10 Women's walking boot, in dramatic silhouette, Brightman Bros, Bristol, 1869

is the side-lacing arrangement
The other portions
of the boot do not require
Registration

DERHAM BROTHERS
BRISTOL and NORTHAMPTON

11 Shapely ankle boot with complex lacing by Derham Bros. of Bristol and Northampton, 1891. This firm is said to have founded the Bristol footwear trade when it set up there in the 1840s

Because skilled labour was scarce there, the United States led the way in the development of shoemaking machinery. In 1851, John Brooks Nichols, a Massachusetts shoemaker, perfected a needle for Howe's sewing machine which would enable it to stitch leather uppers. Sewing machines were used for this purpose in both Britain and America, but the breakthrough came after 1858 when another Massachusetts shoemaker, Lyman R. Blake, patented the 'Blake Sole Sewer'. This chain-stitch machine was to be further improved in the next decade, and remained in use for many years.

Sewing machines spelt trouble in towns like Northampton where shoemaking had been a major industry since the seventeenth century. The workers protested and trade was lost. Many shoemakers migrated to nearby Leicester. Here, with little tradition of

12 A version of the fashionable
    'Cromwell shoe' with its cut
    steel buckle supposedly based
    on seventeenth century styles.
    Barkers of Kensington, 1890

13 A nautical novelty from
    William Ashby & Sons,
    Leicester, 1894

the craft, entrepreneurs had been busily setting up an entirely new industry for a decade or more, concentrating on cheap ready-made shoes. Leicester was the ideal place. Conveniently situated for railways and roads, it had a labour surplus, and already produced elastic webbing, an essential ingredient of footwear. Leicester rapidly became a centre of the industry: by 1871, its trade had outstripped that of Northampton. Mechanisation had started in Leicester in the late 1840s, when a shoemaker called Thomas Crick began to seek a cheap and easy way of attaching soles. He patented a riveting method in 1853, and made his fortune, raising his annual turnover from £3500 in 1853 to £100,000 in 1860. Yet Crick was not a man to rest on his laurels. When the sewing machine was introduced, he was among the first to use it, closely followed by Stead & Simpson. Crick registered no designs, although one or two rivets were registered later on by others. The 'Lorne Lace Boot', registered by Clarks in 1871, was riveted, and sold for 12s 6d.

Over the next two decades, the footwear industry became more and more mechanised, with a succession of inventions being brought across the Atlantic.

However, it was only from the 1890s that most shoes were completely factory made. Until then, town manufacturers sent their goods out to the country, to have them finished by outworkers. Factory working conditions remained poor: in 1884 a twelve year old boy employee of what was to become Mansfield Shoe Company Limited, worked from 8 a.m. to 6.30 p.m. Monday to Friday, and 6 a.m. to 1 p.m. on Saturdays, with an hour's break in the week and half an hour at the weekend, for 4s 6d (Granger).

Mechanisation and the factory system helped to bring prices down. While the wealthy continued to buy hand-made footwear, mass production enabled poorer people to afford, for the first time ever, to cover their feet adequately with new and attractive boots and shoes. Fashion came to the feet of ordinary people. Many firms were operating on such a scale that they would run national advertising campaigns, and nationally distributed shoes brought national fashions, particularly for women. One of the first of these to sweep the country was the Balmoral Boot, introduced in the 1850s and popularised by Queen Victoria with her love of walking. This was strong and sensible, with a little heel, and stitched patterns. Daring young women wore it with short scarlet petticoats and stripy stockings. Many women were becoming more adventurous at this time, even taking up mountaineering. The Balmoral Boot said as much about their lifestyle as the little slipper had done, peeping mouselike from under the voluminous skirts of its restricted owner. The smart boots with little heels worn by women were to be found attractive by both sexes for many years – witness the booted leg-shaped necktie described in Part I. Laced and buttoned boots began to supersede elastic sided ones in the 1870s, their fastenings providing an additional source of fascination.

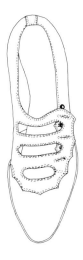

14 Sensible buttoned shoe for use with the new, informal clothes, James Hamilton & Sons, Dundee, 1894

15 Decorative heel plate on a
child's boot featuring the Eiffel
Tower, 1890s. Shown with a
loose heel plate, one of a
surviving bagful, all marked
Rd. 61216, identifiable as the
design of W. H. Staynes &
Smith, Belgrave Gate,
Leicester, 1886. It depicts
flowers, wheat ears, and the
motto 'Plenty', Central
Museum, Northampton

Shoes continued to be worn indoors, and later in the century for some sports. With heels and pointed toes, they were more substantial than their early Victorian ancestors, and far more novelty was allowable. Unusual fabrics and exotic leathers were used – in 1886, a crocodile hide shoe was registered by a firm in Borough High Street, London. From the 1880s too, all kinds of beaded decorations were registered.

Heels continued to be high, sometimes rising to several inches in the 1890s. In order to protect them, iron, steel or brass heel plates were worn. In the case of women and children, even these could be fashionable. By the 1880s, they were a minor art form, their moulded designs leaving exciting footprints behind. Many were registered, from shoemaking towns and engineering areas such as the Black Country and Leeds. The Leeds firm John Blakey & Co. assiduously registered their products. Small metal protectors, known as 'Blakeys', are still made by them and widely used in Britain.

16   A Noah's Ark heel plate for bad weather, John Maddock & Co., Great Western Nail Works, Oakengates, Shropshire, 1890

16
A Nation at Work

N HIS introduction to S. P. Dobbs's *The Clothing Workers of Great Britain*, Sydney Webb, describing the growth of the clothing industry by the late nineteenth century, stated:

> The workman who had hitherto been content to pass his life in corduroy or moleskin now took to buying a new suit of tweeds 'off the peg' once a year or oftener. The new suit was, to start with, only worn on Sundays, but soon it came into everyday wear, until today corduroy has been relegated to the use of navvies and tramps.

The working classes undoubtedly benefited most from the developments in the clothing trade which enabled them to buy cheap new garments often enough to make possible the maintenance of a clean and reasonably smart appearance. The impression of the class as a whole must have been transformed between the 1840s and the First World War. By then, traditional garments like the smock and the old moleskin and corduroy trousers had been supplanted by what was to become the uniform of the twentieth century.

Since work clothes, almost by definition, were intended to be worn until worn out, it is only through chance occurrences such as registration that any record of them survives. Ford Madox Brown's *Work* of 1852–65 gives an unusually detailed picture of a navvy's work clothing. A knitted singlet like those registered by Biggs of Leicester and William Goddard of Nottingham is worn under a heavy check shirt, providing absorbency and warmth. His nightcap was no affectation – it would have kept out the dust nicely. In *The Old Curiosity Shop* a grave digger wore a red one. Geary & Sultzer of Norwich registered a similar nightcap in 1845. It was knitted in stripes with fine cotton thread, and an elastic band round the cuff. The alternative headgear for all workmen was the square paper hat, immortalised in Teniel's illustration of 'The Walrus and the Carpenter' but also seen in illustrations of factory workers.

Women's work clothes are represented in the registrations of stout stockings made by Davies Moore & Co. of Leicester, in 1887 and 1888. These have reinforcements knitted into varying parts of the leg, ankle and foot: reinforced knees for scrubbing steps, or shins for protection against laundry baskets perhaps.

Before the age of the rubber wellington boot, pattens (wooden overshoes with an iron ring on the sole) and clogs were preferred wear for muddy and wet work. Pattens were passing out of use by the 1840s, when clogs became common, made from a wooden sole with a laced or buckled upper. Until well into this century, their clatter was a familiar sound in the cobbled streets of mill towns. They did their job well and they are still preferred by some agricultural and engineering workers. A number of

1   The navvy in his nightcap, woollen undershirt and corduroy trousers, from Ford
Maddox Brown's *Work* 1855–65, Manchester City Art Gallery

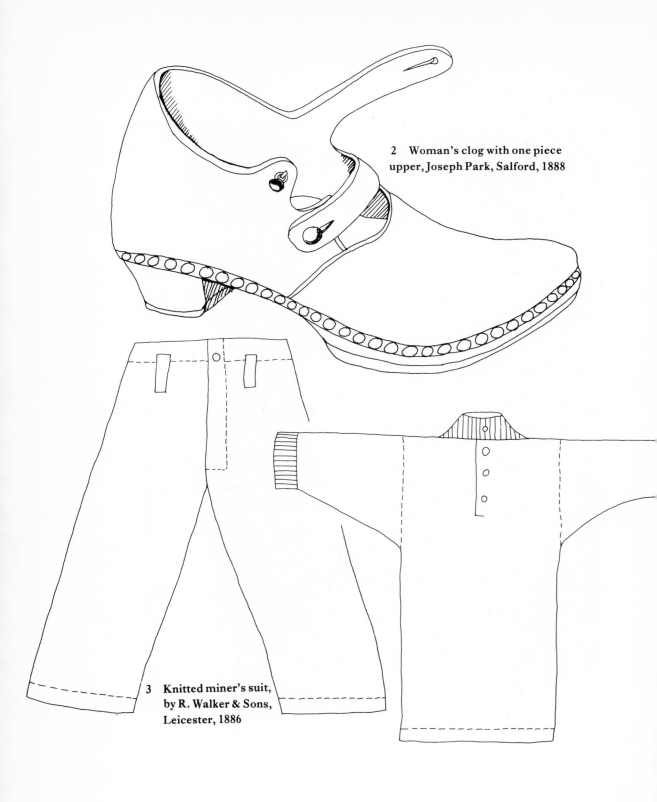

2 Woman's clog with one piece
   upper, Joseph Park, Salford, 1888

3 Knitted miner's suit,
   by R. Walker & Sons,
   Leicester, 1886

4 Baker's outfit with detachable sleeves and apron, both buttoned on, John Blandy, Sloane Terrace, Chelsea, 1889

designs relating to clogs were registered.

Although various trades did wear distinctive dress throughout the century, it was generally an assemblage of ordinary clothes brought together by tradition and

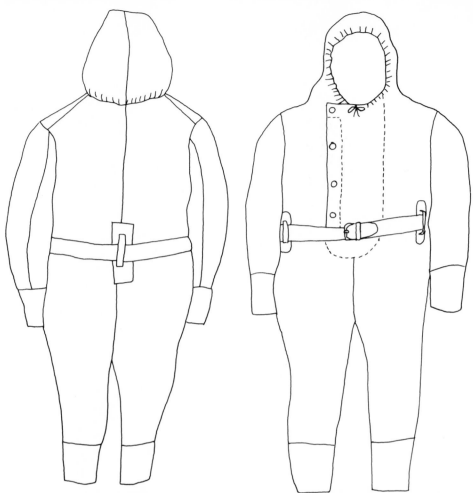

5   **Combination garment by the Irwell India Rubber and Gutta Percha works, 6 Billiter Street, London, 1885**

evolution. It was not until the need for better working conditions was recognised that special clothes were developed for specific tasks. The 1883 Factory Act was the first to mention clothing; owners of white lead factories had to provide overalls and respirators (or air filters), for their workforces. Between 1891 and 1896, sixteen dangerous trades were listed in factory legislation for which protective headgear and respirators had to be worn. This interest is reflected in the registered designs, which from the 1880s include a number of examples of occupational dress.

Knitted singlets were as useful for coalminers as for navvies, being capable of absorbing profuse sweat, helping to prevent chills, and above all, being washable. The Leicester hosiery firm, R. Walker & Sons, registered a 'miner's suit' in 1888, of

172

vest and drawers. This would have been a great improvement on their usual heavy trousers from the point of view of hygiene and they would have been easier to dry out. However, they may not have given much protection against sharp stones. Walter Morel, D. H. Lawrence's miner father in *Sons and Lovers*, wore a pair of moleskin trousers, which he patched himself, 'considering them too dirty, and the stuff too hard for his wife to mend'. On top he wore a low necked, short sleeved flannel pit singlet. Coal mines could be particularly wet places, since subterranean streams often flooded the workings, and in 1890, Charles Hindley of Cleator Moor, Cumberland, registered a miner's watertight clog.

There were new clothes too for the butcher and the baker. An outfit registered in 1889 by a baker, John Blandy of 22 Sloane Terrace, Chelsea, was obviously intended for use in hot conditions. All its parts button loosely together, and it has detachable sleeves. An effective protection from blood, a high necked macintosh was registered by W. E. Sparling, butchers' clothiers of 66 West Smithfield in 1884.

The purpose of 'the combination garment' registered by the Irwell India Rubber Company in 1885 is baffling. It was presumably waterproof. While cotton boiler suits were used in some trades by then, the idea of an all in one hooded suit did not become commonplace for another seventy years, and this illustration from 1885 is without precedent. It may have been intended for a dirty job like sewerage work, or one involving poisonous substances. The Irwell India Rubber Company were a very large firm. It is unlikely that they would waste their time on an idea which they did not know to be viable.

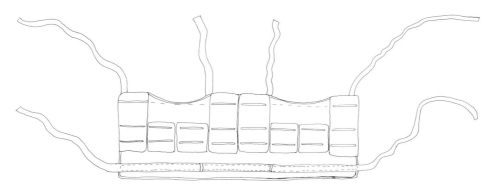

6 A version of the newly adopted cork life jacket. Captain Ward, Royal Navy Inspector of lifeboats to the RNLI, 1865

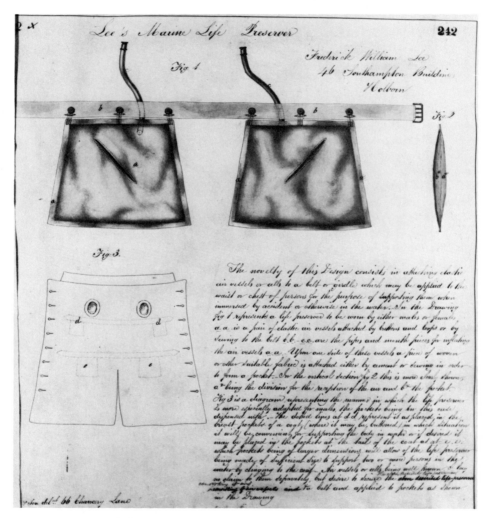

7 'Lee's Marine lifepreserver' for safety with discretion. Fred Lee, 46 Southampton Buildings, Holborn, City, 1844

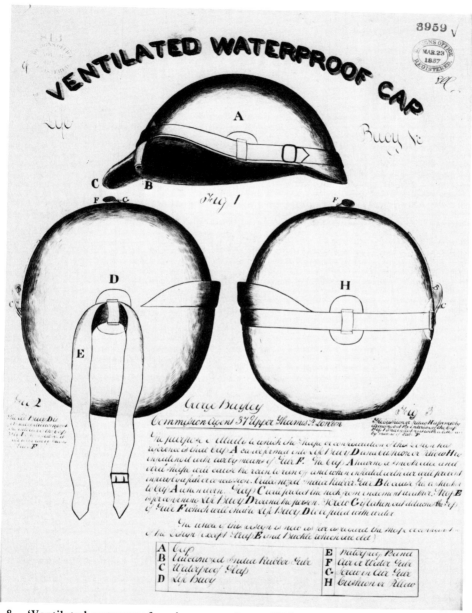

8 'Ventilated waterproof cap' converts into a lifebuoy, George Bayley, 37 Upper
Thames Street, London, 1857

Before efficient lifesaving practices were established, death by drowning was very much more common. Some of Macintosh's first products made from his rubberised cloth in the 1820s were inflatable life preservers. Early models comprised a single bag. Later, a series of linked tubes were adopted, with the idea that they would not sink so rapidly when punctured. Although several life preservers were registered, their obvious drawback could not be overcome. Charles Goodyear did not think much of them. He wrote in the 1850s:

> Although it is twenty years since life preservers were first introduced (in the USA) yet they did not come into favour as we expected, nor as they would have done if they had really been what they are called, life preservers. The price has been reduced by half, yet the demand and sale of them is not half so great as it was fifteen years ago. (*Gum Elastic and Its Varieties*).

The need for inflatable life preservers disappeared when cork life jackets were introduced in the late 1850s. After the Whitby lifeboat disaster of 1861, in which the sole survivor, Henry Freeman, was the only man wearing the new life jacket, they rapidly gained acceptance. Different versions were devised, with fewer cork panels, such as the one registered in 1865 by an official of the Royal National Lifeboat Institution.

Inflatable life preservers did have their uses. One type could be worn under the clothing and was thus undetectable, as for example 'Lee's Marine Life Preserver' registered in 1844. Goodyear made some interesting points about these in *Gum Elastic and Its Varieties*:

> Pocket life preservers, designed to be put in cloth garments such as vests, coats, and cloaks: When the components are inflated by separate tubes they may be considered quite safe, and more so, because they are protected from damage by the garment.
>
> They are always at hand with the garment, and may be worn sufficiently inflated to save a person from drowning when there is any apprehension of danger without attracting the observation of others.
>
> This may be deemed an important recommendation, as many persons, and particularly sailors, would sooner be exposed to drowning than to ridicule from wearing a bag of wind, although in the form of a life preserver.

Perhaps the most futile of all registrations was for the inflatable 'Life Preserver Braces' of 1849. While affording little protection, it would be nice to think they gave their wearer peace of mind.

Macintosh fabric never supplanted oilskin for seamen's dress. Sou'westers, coats and overalls were registered, usually because of their watertight properties. In 1887, Duncan & Black, of Cellardyke, Fyfeshire, registered 'the shape of the guard for preventing ingress of water to fishmen's overalls when the front part is opened out'. In other words, preventing a call of nature from being met with like. The fisherman's ensemble was completed by a heavy knitted Guernsey. These were traditionally knitted to special patterns peculiar to each fishing village or family: But simpler versions were being produced at least from the mid-century by several Leicester hosiery firms.

In 1888, another Scottish firm, Fraser & Fraser & Co. of Kilmarnock, registered a pair of knitted drawers for men of the type known today as long johns. They did so by means of a delightful miniature sample in thick grey wool with red braid trimmings. They may have been intended for fishermen, agricultural or industrial workers; they would certainly have been cosy for any type of work.

While the costume of domestic servants was the most familiar of all occupational outfits, it was atypical in that its appearance was due not simply to practical considerations. Below stairs, servants wore sensible clothes for performing household tasks, but those who appeared above stairs immediately became walking status

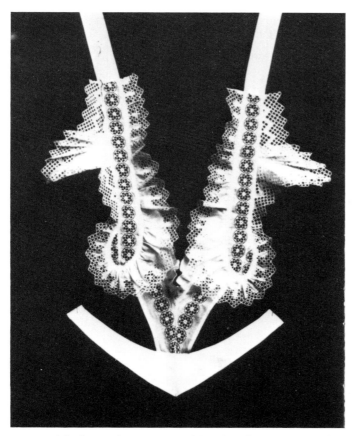

9   The servant maid's finery: Apron top by Ridgard & Thompson, Nottingham, 1896

symbols, displaying their employer's wealth and rank on their backs. As more respectable and clean jobs became available, for example, in offices and schools, the 'servant problem' increasingly worried the leisured classes. The handsome young footman of Olympian proportions, clad in gorgeous archaic livery, moved close to extinction, and in his place came the parlourmaid. In the mid-century, the dress of

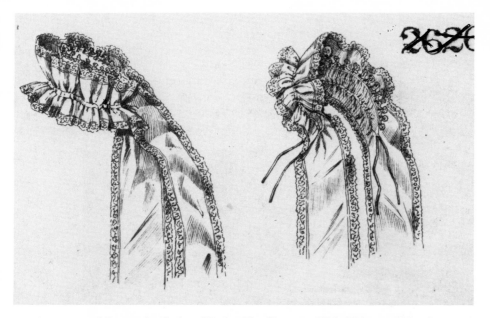

10 Servant maid's cap by Arthur Umfreville, Hoxton, 1895. This could be flattened
for easy laundering.

female servants was not remarkable. *Common Sense for Housemaids*, written in 1850,
did not mention uniforms, but merely indicated that clothing should be clean, neat
and appropriate. The extensive ridicule, in the 1860s and 70s, of maids wearing
crinolines, trains and hairpieces would not have occurred had uniforms been
considered important. In the next decade, with her increasing status, the parlourmaid
emerged as a glorious butterfly, with starched and embroidered white muslin wings
on her head and shoulders and streaming out behind. Her appearance by 1903 was
outlined in *How to Dress and What to Wear*:

> The parlourmaid's apron is a more dressy affair, and is usually made of cambric and
> embroidered muslin. A deep hem with tucks must adorn the skirt, while the bodice is
> made with a pleated bib, or else with a frill of embroidery, arranged to form a 'V' on either
> side of the bodice, starting at the centre of the waist in front, and carried right over the
> shoulders. Her straps must cross at the back and fasten at the waist, while a large
> sash-like bow and ends is usually added . . . The parlourmaid adopts a high fancy shape
> (of cap), usually gauffered and finished with long streamers.

Caps and aprons like these were among the largest single types of clothing
registered in the 1890s. They were submitted by firms such as Ridgard & Thompson
of Nottingham, Carter of Belfast and I. & R. Pritchard of Glasgow, all of whom made
fancy millinery, such as blouses and frills.

178

11   Bell boy's outfit: W. Dixon & Co., Holborn Viaduct, City, 1888

17
Braving the Elements

OF ALL THE garments invented in the nineteenth century, none benefited the working population more than the macintosh. For the first time, outdoor workers could stay warm and dry all day long. Although they had been worn ever since the original double-textured fabric had been patented in 1823, their price was too high for most ordinary people, and until the invention of vulcanisation in 1844, rubber garments were a mixed blessing. Vulcanisation, and the adoption of the sewing machine, paved the way for dynamic companies in Britain and America to make and market macintoshes in such quantities that their benefits could be universally enjoyed. Universally was the word: at the same time, the middle and upper classes were becoming more interested in outdoor pursuits. They were actually choosing to be in the rain, to ride, shoot, fish, or simply enjoy the beauties of the wet British countryside. Although the more elegant waterproofing achieved without rubber of Aquascutum and Burberry coats was to be the preferred choice of the wealthy once they had been introduced, rubber macintoshes were worn by many until recently. Rubber perishes with age, old macintoshes are thrown away, and so virtually no nineteenth century examples survive. Drawings and photographs of registered waterproof garments are among the only records of their appearances and of the once important firms who made them.

Macintosh himself never intended to manufacture coats, but was forced to do so in order to save his reputation and his profits. The fabric was originally sold by the yard but this had to be stopped: against all advice

> the tailors persisted in making the garments to sit close, and were greatly offended when told that they could not sew a watertight seam, and that it was necessary to send the garments to us to have the seams lined to make them proof. Some of them persisted, and actually made a double row of stitches to make sure of it! We tired of all this and opened retail shops, and employed our own tailors, and proofed our seams, and even then, so accustomed were these men to pin their work, that we frequently found pin and needle holes in the body of the cloth. (Thomas Hancock, *A Personal Narrative of the Origin and Progress of the Caoutchouc and India Rubber Manufacture in England.*)

Rubberised coats were uncomfortable if they were not loose, and Macintosh & Co. suffered:

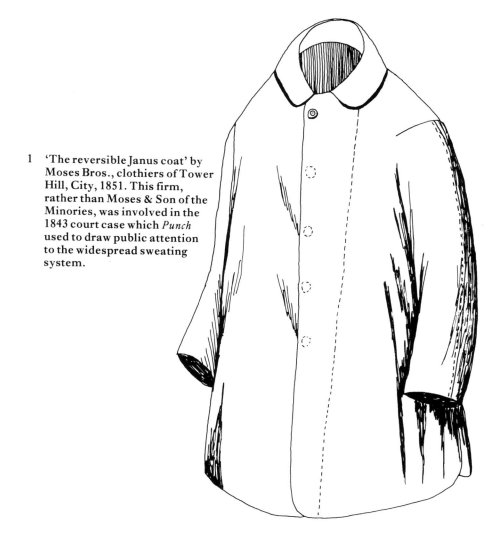

1 'The reversible Janus coat' by Moses Bros., clothiers of Tower Hill, City, 1851. This firm, rather than Moses & Son of the Minories, was involved in the 1843 court case which *Punch* used to draw public attention to the widespread sweating system.

Much trouble and annoyance (from) the persistence of the public for a long time in having garments much too close, which brought the material into some degree of disrepute through want of free escape of insensible perspiration when taking active exercise.

Apart from smelling offensively of sweat and hot rubber, macintoshes were heavy and unwieldy at the best of times, and more or less sticky or brittle depending on their temperature. Despite all this, Hancock states that macintoshes enjoyed quite a vogue

181

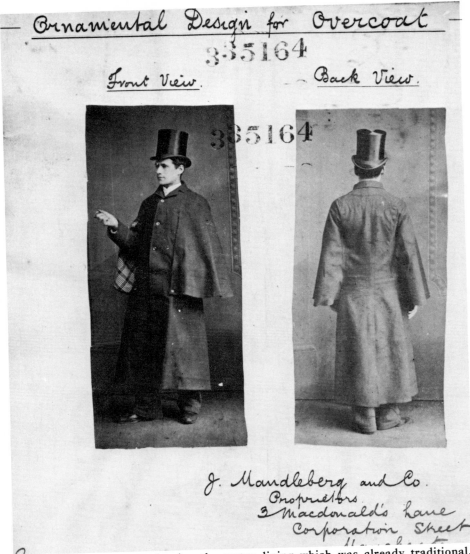

2 Waterproof overcoat showing the tartan lining which was already traditional. Joseph Mandleberg & Co., Manchester, 1879. Mandleberg's were to be in business for many years: after the second world war they traded as 'Valstar'

in the 1830s, especially after 'the officers of the guards began to wear light drab cambric capes on their way to field exercises, and other young men following their example, our material began to take with the public generally'.

'Drab' was a khaki beige colour much worn in the 1830s. The beiges used today for riding macintoshes and trenchcoats are descended from this shade. The traditional

3 'A garment which shall be thoroughly waterproof and at the same time admit a free passage of air round the body of the wearer, to prevent perspiration condensing, which is the only objection to waterproof garments. The two parts are buttoned together, leaving a sufficient fullness to admit the air', A. B. Cow, Hill & Co., 46–7 Cheapside, City, 1871

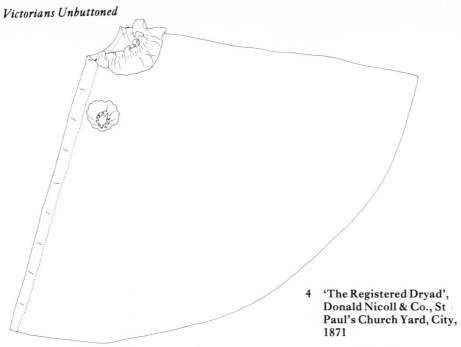

4 'The Registered Dryad',
Donald Nicoll & Co., St
Paul's Church Yard, City,
1871

tartan lining also dates back to this period, when there was a fashion for all things Scottish. They were especially appropriate in view of Macintosh's Caledonian origins.

Eventually, the unfortunate secondary attributes of the macintosh proved too much for fashionable circles. In February 1836 *The Gentleman's Magazine* noted:

> It is impossible to say a word in favour of this freak of fashion, but as it is fast going out, we can only observe that no one can look like a gentleman in such a garb, and it is of a most unpleasant odour.

Three years later, the same journal commented: 'The macintosh is now become a troublesome thing in town from the difficulty of their being admitted into an omnibus on account of the offensive stench they emit.' If one was prepared to travel on top of a stagecoach 'an India rubber cloak' could be very useful, as worn by the young gentleman who smoked cigars all day encountered by Mr Pickwick *en route* to Bath. The demise of the stagecoach seemed to be ending the days of the macintosh. Hancock wrote that in the 1840s:

> Stagecoaches were fast disappearing before the superior speed and accommodation afforded by the railway system . . . In the neighbourhood of large towns, the introduction of omnibuses in a great measure superseded the short stage coaches . . . All these changes occurring almost simultaneously necessarily operated to lessen the demand for water-proof clothing. But last, though perhaps, not least, the doctors spread a universal outcry that these garments were so unhealthy that no one ought to expose himself to the hazards of wearing them.

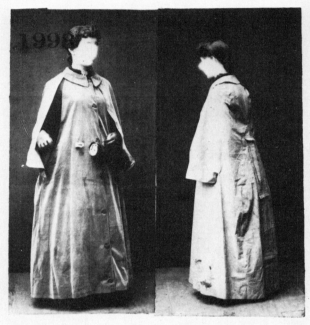

1998

Design
BY
L. Mistorski.
of 94 Shudehill, Manchester.

Front.   Back.

For the Shape of a Lady's Reversible
Waterproof Princess Cloak with reversible
wings.

—— Class 10. ——

5 'Lady's reversible waterproof Princess cloak', L. Mistorski, 94 Shudehill, Manchester, 1884. The model's face has been deliberately obscured

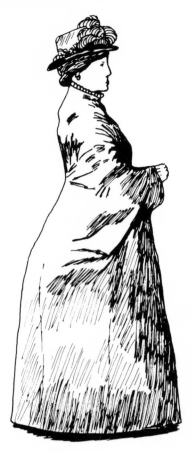

6 'The Lady's waterproof cloak'
with Dolman sleeves and collar
frill. Joseph Mandleberg, 1884

The first signs of a return to favour came at the Great Exhibition of 1851, when both Macintosh & Co. and their American rival Charles Goodyear were awarded medals for their extensive displays. The Jury considered that the Macintosh garments had 'acquired more lightness and less smell and the substitution of vulcanized for the common caoutchouc ensures to them at the present day a permanent suppleness'.

Registrations for rubberised garments reflected their popularity. Hardly any were made until the early 1850s, when a flood of designs were submitted. One of the first, by George Spill, one of the largest London manufacturers, in June 1851, was the 'Thorough Metallic Ventilated Coat'. This featured metal eyelets under the armpits 'forming an outlet for perspiration thus obviating the principle objection against the use of waterproof apparel'. This effective solution is still used today. In December 1851, Maurice and Edward Moses, clothiers of Tower Hill, registered the 'Janus Coat', with the fashionable A-line shape. The trend towards looser coats in the 1850s contributed towards the revival and the popular acceptance of the macintosh, of necessity voluminous, since it could now conform more closely to the fashionable line.

The Moses brothers contracted out their Janus coat to a Manchester firm; a reasonable move since they were not waterproofers themselves and Manchester was by then an important centre of the trade. The 1855 Manchester post office directory carried an advertisement for J. Smith's Original Depot, which sold the 'reversible waterproof Janus coat adapted for fine or wet weather (registered 1851) or two perfect coats in a pocket book – very much superior to all other garments in this style, for their extreme lightness, finish and quality, and unequalled in price'. This would imply that

7 'Arm opening flap in circular macintoshes'. Osmond, Brice & Chidley, 14 Cannon Street, City, 1885

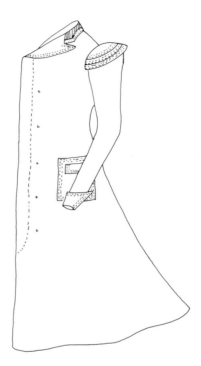

8 'Mantle' by Joseph Mandleberg,
1900. By this time the firm had
moved to Pendleton on the
outskirts of Manchester

some macintosh type garments had been considerably improved. In the same advertisement, the 'Pocket Siphonia' paletôt was described which weighed only ten ounces and could be carried in either pocket or hat. Pocket siphonias were well known, and used by gentlemen on picnics, such as Mr Bunting in R. S. Surtees's *Plain or Ringlets* of 1860.

The Great Exhibition Jury considered that in Charles Goodyear's American waterproofs:

> More strength and greater thickness are to be remarked than in the articles manufactured in Europe, but with less finish in the workmanship and elegance in the forms. It may thus be clearly seen that these articles, which are as yet only used in Europe as objects of luxury or of more refined comfort, have already in America entered into general consumption, and become, by their price, within the reach of the least opulent classes, to the tastes and wants of which, the manufacturer has been compelled to accommodate himself.

As time went by, British manufacturers also began to make garments suitable for working people. The Reverend Francis Kilvert's diary, which he kept in the 1870s, records many macintoshes worn by workmen and gentlemen alike; lent, borrowed

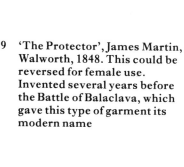

9 'The Protector', James Martin, Walworth, 1848. This could be reversed for female use. Invented several years before the Battle of Balaclava, which gave this type of garment its modern name

and left out in the garden. His own was worn while baptising babies, and while he was preventing a flood one day in 1875 when:

> I found that the cistern was overflowing and deluging the water closet, the tank room, the bathroom and the kitchen. I was obliged to put on a macintosh and stand in the water closet holding up the handle to relieve the cistern while the water ran down upon my head like a shower bath.

Macintoshes may have been practical, but they could never be elegant. On the whole it was not surprising that around the turn of the century the wealthy took to Burberrys and Aquascutums to keep out the rain, as Kipps found out:

> His macintosh flapped about him, the rain stung his cheek. For a time he felt a hardy man. And then, as abruptly, the rain ceased and the wind fell, and before he was through Sandwell High Street it was a bright spring day. And there was Kipps in his macintosh and squeaky leggings looking like a fool! ... A smartly dressed man, in one of those overcoats that look like ordinary cloth and are really most deceitfully and unfairly waterproof passed him and glanced at the stiff folds of his macintosh. 'Demn!' said Kipps. (H. G. Wells, *Kipps*.)

All the waterproof garments registered in the 1850s and 60s were intended for

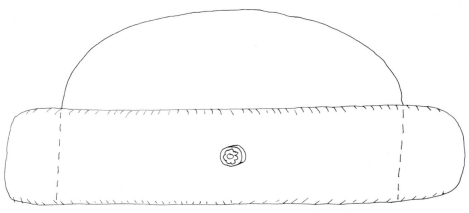

10   Pillow cap for travellers. Walter Jessop, Cheltenham, 1860

men. The lack of female waterproof clothing was understandable in view of the restricted lives led by most women. The first such garment for a woman was registered by Donald Nicoll & Co. of St Paul's Church Yard, the new firm founded by the younger of the Regent Street Nicoll Brothers. Nicoll's 'Registered Dryad' of 1871 heralded a new era of freedom and mobility for women, who were beginning to enjoy foreign travel, country rambles and even (in some cases) mountaineering. Manufacturers were quick to exploit this growing market, and by the 1880s, a substantial number of women's waterproof garments were being registered each year. The designs show how, in order to attract this fashion conscious clientèle, waterproof garments became increasingly stylish. New attractive fabrics were registered, such as the frosted pink, blue or green rubberised cloth made by Philip Frankenstein & Son of

11   Annie Matilda Wood's 'storm cap' must have been a fearsome sight on a dark night. 13 Delahay Street, Westminster, 1888

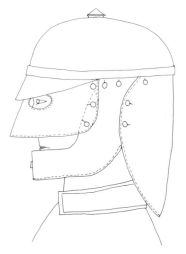

190

Manchester in 1885. The fashionable silhouette was carefully followed. Some of these mantles had a waterproof frill at the neck, while others had small triple collars. A great deal of top stitching was used, but on parts which did not need to be waterproof. The dolman sleeve of the 1880s, formed from an extension of the back so that the arm was held down, was much used by macintosh manufacturers: the loose sleeve pieces would be particularly waterproof and few seams were needed.

12 'Trouser protector', John White, 51 High Street, Manchester, 1867. Throughout most of the Victorian period, trousers were worn nearly touching the ground. This invention avoided the indignity of turning up one's trouser bottoms in wet weather

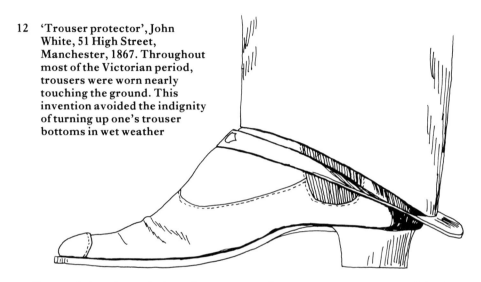

Some of the nicest designs for waterproof garments were registered by Joseph Mandleburg & Co., one of the many firms making them to start up in Manchester from the 1850s. Macintosh & Co.'s long experience there had created a pool of expertise which later entrepreneurs, many of whom like Mandleburg and Frankenstein, were East European Jews, were able to build on. Soon, Manchester and macintoshes were inextricably linked. In the 1880s, Mandleburg was one of Manchester's largest producers, with branches in London, Glasgow and Dublin. From when he started business in 1856, Mandleburg's aim was to make waterproof garments for men and women which were more stylish than ever before, and his attempts to make rubberised clothing acceptable led to experiments to control its smell, which was still a problem. His first trademark, registered in 1889, was F.F.O., which stood for free from odour. Unfortunately, the truth of this claim can never be ascertained.

While railway travel must have been far more comfortable than travelling by stage coach, by modern standards, it was still arduous. Judging by the number of 'railway wrappers' registered throughout the century, it must have been a cold and wet business, particularly in third class carriages. The 'Traveller's Wrapper' was registered in 1868 by the North British Rubber Company, which was financed by

American industrialists. It featured an oval waterproof base raised up on ribs.

Many special travelling hats were registered: Walter Jessop of 4 Royal Crescent, Cheltenham, registered his 'pillow cap for travellers' in 1860; the object being:

> To form a soft pillow or cushion round the head so that the same may rest easily against the back or side of the carriage or other place and thus afford additional ease to the wearer when sleeping or otherwise. The rim is composed of an annular airtight bag provided with a nozzle or valve.

Fellow travellers would have been given even more of a fright if one donned Annie Mathilda Wood's 'storm cap' of 1888. She was styled 'gentlewoman' of 13 Delahay Street, Westminster. More frequently used, but no less sinister looking, were 'respirators' – face masks worn to keep out fog. These were registered by several firms. In 1886, Jacob Ballin, an Aldersgate Street furrier, registered a magnificent chinchilla respirator by a sample. It was held on by elastic loops round the ears. Another sample, registered by Louisa Nice of 74 Gresham Road, Brixton, in 1888 was a knitted black egg-cup shaped bag with elastic loops, which can only be interpreted as a nose cosy. Chest protectors were another commonly worn garment, inside or outside the shirt. Moses & Son's 'Sternophylon' of 1851 was typical: a double layer of heart-shaped fabric fastening with elastic. Finally, no sensible traveller should be without his trouser protectors, as registered by John White of 51 High Street, Manchester, in 1867. Leather loops prevented the trouser bottom from dragging in the mud, while avoiding the usual indignity of having to turn them up.

18
A Nation at Play

CHANGES IN fashion such as the adoption of less formal, tweed clothes and waterproof garments seen by the end of the century were largely brought about by the upsurge of interest in outdoor pursuits evident among all classes. The English gentlemen who had always gone into the country to hunt, fish and shoot were joined by plebian sportsmen. Everywhere, by the 1890s, groups of cyclists and walkers could be seen. These were as likely to be working class members of the Clarion cycling club and mill workers enjoying a day out on the moors as enthusiasts from the middle classes. Then as now, a lot of pleasure was derived from 'doing it right', by purchasing the proper equipment. For the rambler, this included breeches, woolly stockings and enormous boots. Kilvert was appalled by the sort of things worn by invaders into his beloved countryside. On 4 April 1870 he recorded: 'To our horror saw two tourists with staves and shoulderbelts all complete, postured among the ruins in an attitude of admiration.'

Specially designed garments and appliances were eagerly sought after for all sports. The 'official sanction' of a patent or registration made them particularly attractive.

Maintaining horses had always been a luxury, especially when they were kept not as a means of conveyance from place to place, but just for the pleasure of riding round town and country parks and fox hunting. It was one of the few sports in which women traditionally participated, and many did so to the full and were famed for their courage. This was despite the fact that their side-saddle position and habit, which in the 1830s and 40s touched the ground when mounted, made riding for them arguably one of the most dangerous sports ever invented.

Since riding habits were closely tailored from woollen cloth along masculine lines, they were generally made by men's tailors. While the top-notch horsewomen would obviously patronise exclusive private houses in the West End, it was the wholesale clothier's ambition to boast a 'ladies' habit room', showing that his customers were rich enough to have horses. Moses & Son were advertising riding habits from 2s to £4 10s.

H. J. & D. Nicoll kept abreast of the latest equestrian fashions, which were, however, sometimes considered in dubious taste by the best circles. Their registered riding waistcoat of April 1852 heralded the summer's craze for elaborately decorated habits in pale colours. The fashion correspondent of *The Ladies' Cabinet of Fashion* commented unfavourably on this vogue in August of that year:

1 'The Alpine shooting boot' by
H. Salomon & Co., 44 Princess
Street, Edinburgh, 1870

I maintain that the proper riding costume, while modified to a certain degree by the reigning style, ought to preserve a strict simplicity and exquisite neatness to be in good taste, and that light colours, showy cuts, laces and embroidery, are quite out of place, embarrassing to the rider, and contrary to the rules of true elegance.

Most designs registered for riding habits were not so much decorative as concerned with various safety features and improvements which were introduced from the 1850s. Stout riding breeches of matching fabric began to be worn under the skirt: the one piece habit was often replaced by a long jacket and skirt, but most importantly, the

2   H. J. & D. Nicoll's riding vest in questionable taste, 1852

3 Riding habit advert from 'The Ladies' Newspaper', 1851

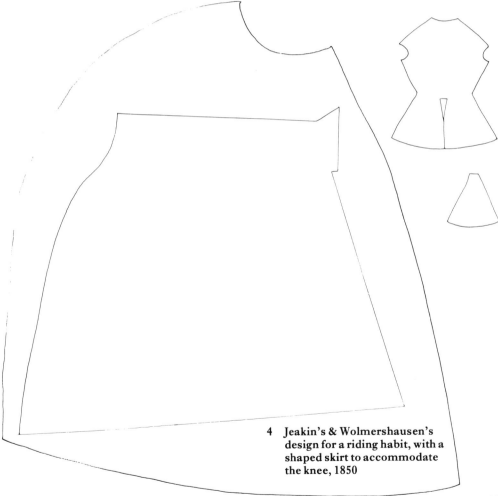

4 Jeakin's & Wolmershausen's
design for a riding habit, with a
shaped skirt to accommodate
the knee, 1850

195

5 'The Princess' riding habit.
Swears & Wells, Regent Street,
London, 1877

Coat. *Rider Mounted*   Coat. *Rider Dismounted*

Complete Pattern of Skirt in flat

Pocket for foot   *Pocket for foot*

6   Riding macintosh, John Phelps Mashoba, Dulwich, 1888

7   Ladylike tennis jacket. S. Whincup & Co., 25 Cheapside, City, 1886

skirt began to be cut so that it fitted the figure when mounted. At this time, the rider started to sit with her right leg higher on the saddle, looped over a curved pommel. This affected the 'sit' of the skirt, and a pouch was cut into it to accommodate the knee.

One of the new habits was registered by Jeakins & Wolmershausen, high class Mayfair tailors, who advertised it in *The Ladies Newspaper* for 1851:

> To Ladies, the new riding habit, registered by Jeakins, late foreman and successor to Mr Hutton, and Wolmershausen, late foreman to Mr Ford. Tailors and habit makers, 11 Curzon St., Mayfair. J. and W. respectfully solicit the attention of ladies to their new Registered Riding Habit, which has no seam in the waist, and displays in its form the most striking grace and elegance. The skirt also has a fall different from that of other habits; does not twist, and forms a straight horizontal line at the hem, being thus graceful in appearance and less liable to tear.

The registered design shows that the waist referred to was of the jacket, and that the skirt had a curved seam forming a knee pouch. This marked the beginning of a long career for Wolmershausen. He registered another habit in 1885, and so did his daughter Emily, for the shape of a riding skirt:

Whereby it is effectively prevented from 'riding up' without the use of footstraps, by dispensing with which the rider can more readily disengage herself from the habit in the event of being thrown.

The skirt was commonly fastened to the saddle, with the result that many riders were killed by being dragged after the horse. Important developments had been made since 1875, when the first 'safety skirt', which was slit up the back, was worn. From then on, many designs like Emily Wolmershausen's were patented and registered.

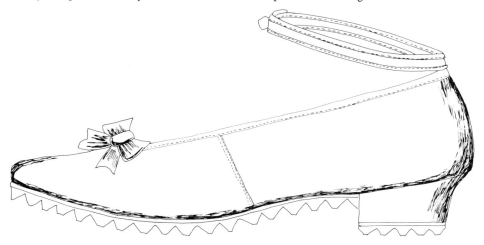

8 'The Watteau lawn tennis shoe', Samuel Winter, 22 Sussex Place, South Kensington, 1878. By naming the design after the famous painter, Winter latched on to the current vogue for all things eighteenth century

Lawn tennis was also regarded as an aristocratic pastime when first introduced in the 1870s. As in riding, women, or rather young girls, participated from the start. Speculative mamas soon discovered the usefulness of tennis parties, at which their daughters could disport themselves among eligible young men with the utmost propriety. While men wore their standard outfit for summer sports, of blazer and open-necked shirt with an attached collar, female players were handicapped, having to wear normal dress. In the late 1870s and early 80s, this was a tight sheath from shoulder to knee, to be succeeded by a cumbersome bustle. Kate Gielgud wrote of her girlhood in the 1880s in *An Autobiography*:

Our tennis dress consisted of ankle length flannel or serge skirts closely pleated, and plain long sleeved blouses with starched linen collars, and we wore wide leather belts and stiff brimmed boaters. Later the Huxley girls introduced us to stockinette jerseys, woollen and light, which left our necks free though we were not allowed to roll up our sleeves. The change definitely improved our play.

A collection of bodices specially designed for tennis were registered by S. Whincup &

PROFESSIONAL JEALO

Miss Matilda (referring to her new Lawn-Tennis Shoes, black, with india-rubber soles). "THE WORST OF IT IS, THEY DRAW THE F... *Our Artist (an ingenuous and captivating youth).* "AH, THEY MAY DRAW THE FEET; BUT THEY'LL NEVER DO JUSTICE TO YO... MATILDA!"

9 *Punch* 1878

10 Novelty tennis shoe with cut out balls and raquets, Joseph Dawson & Sons, Northampton, 1891

Co. of 25 Cheapside in 1886. Even these appear quite constricting. While normal clothing was worn in other respects, it was found that serrated rubber soled shoes were safest for running around on grass. The name 'Plimsoll' for a canvas shoe with a rubber sole was first suggested in 1876. From 1878, different types of rubber soled shoes were registered, starting with the 'University Lawn Tennis Shoe' submitted by Jefferies & Co. of Woolwich in January of that year. A female version, incongruously named the 'Watteau Lawn Tennis Shoe', was registered in March 1878 by Samuel

11 Bicycle motif on belt. D. B. Harris & Son, Birmingham, 1897

An Ornamental Design

for

A Jersey Bicycle Suit to be called
The "Fred Wood Champion Suit"

N. Corah Sons & Cooper
St. Margaret's Works
Leicester

12   'The Fred Wood Champion Suit', Corahs of Leicester, 1883

13   Tricycling dress. William James Harvey, Nottinghill, London, 1884

Winter, court and millitary bootmaker of South Kensington. This select establishment made them in patent leather or kid, and advertised them at 14s 6d post free by mail order. (Sylvia Druitt, *Antique Personal Possessions*). As tennis shoes went, this was expensive. In *How to Dress Neatly and Prettily on £10 a Year* of 1881, E. W. Allen wrote: 'For lawn tennis, of course, I wear lawn tennis shoes. 3s will procure a pair, for all ordinary purposes, quite as good as one at 15s.

Serrated rubber soles continued to be popular. The many versions registered exhibited more and more wonderful complexities in the serrations.

The sporting mania which gripped late Victorian society not only gave rise to a new generation of clothes for sporting needs, but also supplied a completely new and rich source of decorative motifs, which were used to embellish garments, jewellery, and every conceivable novelty. The crossed rackets which were cut out of the upper of a man's tennis shoe, registered in 1891 by Joseph Dawson & Sons of Northampton, were popular motifs, as were cricket bats and stumps, nautical emblems and, of course, all things equine. If one could not own a horse, then at least one could have a horseshoe brooch, or one like a hunting whip, even if it was only cheap tin from Birmingham. The 1880s saw the first of countless generations of horsy jewellery, and in the 1890s fancy belts made to look like saddlery, with buckles like bits and curb chains worn to set off nipped in waists.

14 Tricycling skirts tastefully depicted. Fébes Wahli, 144 Westbourne Grove, Kensington, 1894

When in the 1840s a blacksmith added pedals and brake to the 'hobby horse', the age of the bicycle came into sight. But it was another thirty years before the penny-farthing, combining comparative lightness and speed with a thrilling sense of danger, started the cycling craze. Flora Thompson remembered seeing them in her country lanes in the early 1880s:

> The first high penny-farthing bicycles were already on the roads, darting and swerving like swallows heralding the summer of buses and cars and motor cycles which were soon to transform country life. But how fast these new bicycles travelled and how dangerous they looked! Pedestrians backed almost into the hedges when they met one of them . . . yet it was thrilling to see a man hurtling through space on one high wheel, with another tiny wheel wobbling helplessly behind . . .
>   Cycling was looked upon as a passing craze and the cyclists in their tight navy knickerbocker suits and pillbox caps with the badge of their club in front were regarded as figures of fun. None of those in the hamlet who rushed out to their gates to see one pass, half hoping for and half fearing a spill, would have believed if they had been told, that in a few years there would be at least one bicycle in every one of their houses . . .
> (*Lark Rise to Candleford.*)

The early cyclists wore their special outfits with pride. Streamlined close fitting garments which allowed free movement were considered essential when pitching body and bicycle against the elements. Cycling as a competitive sport evolved hand in hand with the vehicle itself, and when Corah's of Leicester marketed their jersey bicycling suit in 1883, it was named the 'Fred Wood Champion Suit' after the Leicester cyclist who had become world champion in June of that year.

The first women to master the art did so on tricycles, which appeared in the late 1870s. Riding a penny-farthing in a skirt could have been impossible, and to avoid accidents, special clothing was worn on the tricycle, to the delight or disgust of onlookers. Two registered designs for cycling skirts, one plain with a pleated front, the other divided with a draped front, were in line with the list of garments recommended by the cyclists' touring club, given in Professor Hoffmann's *Tips for Tricyclists* of 1887. The fullness facilitated pedalling. Flat shoes and gaiters were the standard footwear, and breeches were worn under the skirt. By the next decade, the intrepid wore wide bloomers alone. But special clothes for ordinary cyclists were short lived. The invention of the safety bicycle in 1885 with equal wheels, the back one driven by a chain, and the pneumatic tyre patented by John Boyd Dunlop in 1888, encouraged more and more people to use bicycles as a convenient means of getting about rather than for sport. In 1895, over 800,000 bicycles were made in England. Peculiar get-ups that could not be worn for work, shopping or visiting were clearly inappropriate. Instead, everyday informal dress with slight modifications, was preferred. Men tended to wear tweed Norfolk jackets and knickerbockers with flat caps and women simply shortened their skirts and relied on a skirt guard over the back wheel.

Until the last twenty years or so, except at schools, football was almost a game of the past, and was rarely seen or heard of. In these days, special trains are run for grand matches, and 15,000 people are assembled to see a match.

... anyhow, football deserves the thanks of thousands of young English men, and of those to whom they belong, for promoting health and amusements in the dead of winter, and sending out into the pure air those who have the hardihood to face wet and cold with no protection but a jersey and a pair of flannel knickerbockers, and who are not afraid of a roll in the mud with the best good humour in the world. (Fred Gale, *English Sports: Their Use and Abuse.*)

The sudden rise to popularity of soccer in the late nineteenth century was entirely due to the general rise in living standards by which working men could afford the price of travelling to and seeing matches, and more importantly, which gave them enough free time to watch or play in them. Mass communications also played their part — without newspaper reports there could have been no sense of belonging to a league, and individual clubs would not have acquired such charisma.

The public schools developed football from traditional street games, but by the 1860s, town clubs were emerging. Nottingham County, Nottingham Forest, Sheffield Wednesday, Chesterfield and Queen's Park, Glasgow, all date back to that decade. Football as a national game grew out of the heartlands of the nation's industries. It had nothing to do with gentlemanly amateurism, big business being involved from the start. Huge matches were arranged between far flung teams; the first international between England and Scotland was held in 1873. Footballers were built up into heroes, and the allegiances of fans were exploited by the growing souvenir market, itself dependent on the working classes having spare cash. A printed cotton handkerchief registered in 1886 depicted the English team in action in their long breeches and elastic sided boots.

Corah's of Leicester had mass produced football jerseys since the 1870s; their rotary frames turned out miles of striped jersey which clothed all the greatest teams until the 1930s, in both football and rugby. The All Blacks wore 'St Margaret' jerseys for their 1906 British tour. Registered designs for football jerseys show how closely they were based on ordinary woollen undershirts. In fact, this type of long sleeved striped jersey was worn for many other sporting activities in the last century as well as football.

Football was always a rough game. Shinpads were introduced by Sam Widdowson of Nottingham Forest in 1874. Although Fred Gale, 'The Old Buffer', maintained that they 'were never dreamt of in days gone by, as a good player rarely, if ever, kicked anything but the ball in the game' this was clearly unlikely. Knee protectors were less common. Whose injured knee did Nurse Angelina Coles of Battersea have in mind when she registered hers in 1891? The hairy leg so tenderly depicted must undoubtedly have been that of a footballer!

Adequate footwear was especially important when playing football. Allegiances were built up to favoured makes, many of which were registered. Unlike today's footballer with his low cut boots, participants preferred to sacrifice dexterity in the

15   Sporting heros of 1886, from a cotton printed handkerchief showing the English
football team. Samuel Higginbotham, Glasgow

16 Nurse Angelina Coles' 'Knee
protector'. Battersea, 1891

interests of avoiding sprains. Boots came well up to the ankle, and in the 1890s tended
to be laced, rather than elasticated, for a firmer fit. The registrations seem to have
been mainly for reinforcements, such as extra bands across the upper, and pads at the
anklebone.

17 Towards the perfect football
boot: Owen Tilley, Shepshed,
Leicestershire, 1896

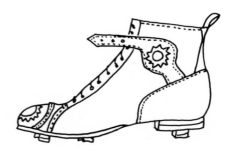

18 Football boot. Benjamin Ladds,
Rushden, Northants, 1892

19   'The Cert', a football boot without a sole. Broom & Foster, Manchester, 1894

Cricket is a popular game of much greater antiquity than football. Even in W. G. Grace's day, cricketers looked back with nostalgia to the great names of the 1830s and 40s. However, like football, by the end of the century, the game was attracting vast crowds and was being played on an international level. Most of the designs registered for cricket dress concerned ways of protecting the body. Cricket pads appeared in the 1830s. This was during a transitional period when modern rules were being drawn up. Underarm bowling was giving way to overarm, and the ball was being bounced higher. The pad was developed in response to this. By the 1850s, when cricketing dress was

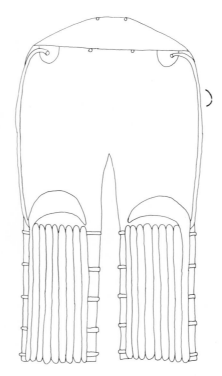

20 'The Registered Cricket guard', inflatable pads by William Redgrave, Grafton Street, London, 1852

beginning to be registered, pads were quite frequently worn. The usual type were made from horsehair but the 'Registered Cricket Guard' made by William Redgrave of Grafton Street and registered in 1852 was inflatable. The description stated:

The small elastic pipe leads up a side seam of trousers to a pocket made on purpose to hold it. When the wearer wishes the guard inflated, the pipe being elastic, it is easily stretched to the mouth, when by blowing down the mouthpiece, it becomes inflated in

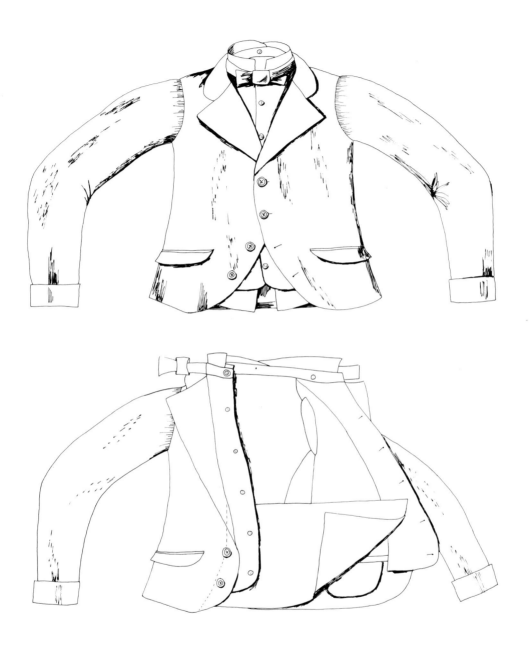

21 Rowing and cricketing jacket with many layers in one. Ben Nicoll, Regent Circus, 1849

the course of a second or so, with very little trouble, when the mouthpiece is again returned to the pocket. Even when inflated it is so very light that it does not occasion the slightest inconvenience to the wearer.

It is interesting to note that a similar inflatable pad was patented by Henry Emanuel in 1865. This is a reminder that the system for investigating both patents and registered designs was imperfect and superficial for most of the century.

Rubber was also used to greater effect for the backs of batting gloves like those registered in 1866 by Edward Brett and Henry Whale. It is an excellent shock absorber, and was widely used for this purpose. As the game grew more vigorous, more protection was needed. Fred Gale complained in 1888:

> Pads and gloves were invented rather more than forty years ago, and capital things they are, but pads now are like mats, and double the size of the leg, and many of the modern school, if the ground is not like a billiard table, make such a fuss about it, that you would think they were storming the Redan. (*Sports and Recreations in Town and Country.*)

Special cricket costume developed slowly. In the 1840s, top hats were seldom

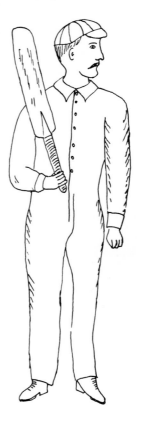

22 Cricket dress as envisaged by
Robert Shaw, gentleman, 22
Baker Street, London, 1890

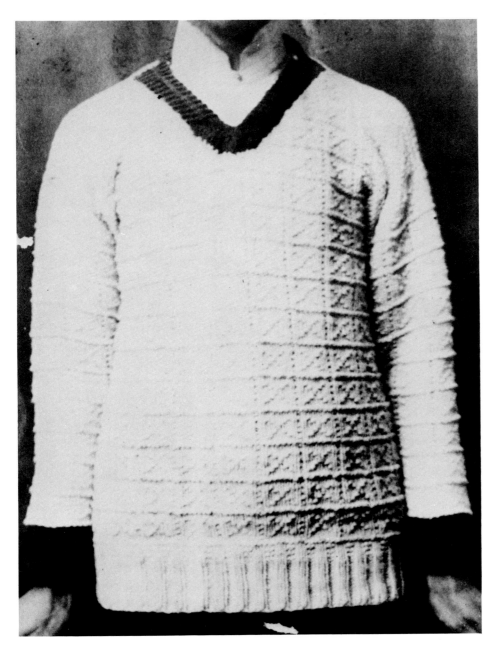

23 The essential cricket jumper, William Thomas Pitchers, Church Street, Surrey, 1893

discarded, and players had to take care not to offend against propriety, for instance, by taking their jackets off. The celebrated shirtmaker Ben Nicoll of Regent Street registered a clever solution to this problem in 1849. His cricket jacket looked like a jacket, waistcoat, shirt, collar and tie, but was, in fact, one garment. Special sports jackets in light colours, cut short at the waist, were worn for some occasions. In 1857 Leonora Louisa Toll of Holloway Road, Islington, registered a knitted cricket or rowing jacket, and attached a sample of tightly knitted white cotton thread to her drawing. In the same year, Welch Margetson & Co. registered their 'University Jacket' which was clearly intended for sports.

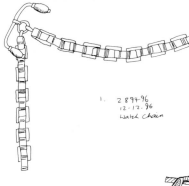

24 Sporting motifs from the 1890s:
(a) Bicycle watch chain, Saunders and Shepherd, Holborn Circus, City, 1896

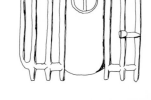

(c) Golf club brooch, James Fenton, 74 Great Hampton Street, Birmingham, 1892

(b) Horseshoe button, Speyer Schwert & Co., Monkwell Street, City, 1894

(d) Cricket buckle, Fergusson & Key, Stamford Street, City, 1894

(e) Tennis buckle, Alf Stanley, Wednesbury Road, Walsall, Staffs, 1892

By the 1860s, light, comfortable clothes were worn, but the colour was not white — national teams were covered in huge spots and patterns from top to toe. An experimental cricket costume, inspired by the fashion for combination under-garments perhaps, was registered in 1890, by Robert Shaw, Gentleman, of 32 Baker Street, Pentonville. Needless to say, it never caught on. By that time, the cricket dress which was to survive until the 1970s had evolved, of white flannels, white shirt, dark cap and V-necked cable stitched pullover.

19
Postscript

THIS BOOK has told a story largely of growth and optimism. Nineteenth-century industrialists were rightly proud of their many achievements. Against a background of grinding poverty, the lives of many ordinary men and women slowly improved. As their working and living conditions got better, their spending power and general standard of clothing rose.

But this is a story tinged with sadness. Very little is now left of that industrial heart of the City of London. Even by 1900, the area's heyday was coming to an end. The very prosperity which the warehouses helped to create drove them out as property values rose. Bulky goods could no longer be stored economically there, and the clothing trade began to be supplanted by the banking and insurance companies which characterise the area today. The Blitz extensively damaged those warehouses which remained, and after the Second World War many moved out of London altogether. Today, hardly any are left, since the redevelopment of the 1960s and 70s. Little Britain, one of the last islands of Victorian warehousing and courtyards in a sea of concrete, is being demolished at the time of writing.

Throughout the country, similar streets and warehouses are now empty, where once goods were dispatched across the world.

In all industries, firms are founded, rise to prosperity and come to an end. But in recent years the British clothing trade as a whole has declined dramatically. Just as the old warehouses have gone, so too have many of the once mighty enterprises they housed. To some extent this was inevitable. The industry grew up in the last century to supply the British Empire, and those countries which were once customers are now our suppliers.

But while researching the firms which registered designs in the nineteenth century, I became increasingly aware of the devastating effects of the current recession. Time after time, I found that firms survived two world wars and the lean years between, only to disappear without trace in the 1970s – in some cases, they took with them records which may have gone back well over a century. I would like this book to be seen as a tribute to the old days, and the firms that are no more, but also to the small number still surviving and flourishing.

The subsequent histories of several of the firms mentioned in this book are well known: Clarks shoes, Hepworths the tailors and Blakey's Malleable Castings are household names today. Other companies were taken over by firms climbing the ladder to success: G. H. Lee & Co.'s Liverpool dress shop is now a John Lewis Partnership store, and the corset makers Footman Pretty & Co. of Ipswich are part of

Debenhams. The great house of Welch Margetson & Co. still retains its individual identity, but the survival of this historic firm is entrusted to the hands of Carrington Viyella, now themselves part of the Vantona group. With its 'Buy British' policy, Marks & Spencer PLC has benefited several, including Welch Margetson and Corah's of Leicester. In the glove making industry, Dents and Fownes are rivals no more, but have amalgamated and operate from Warminster.

Appendix: a complete list of registrations referred to in the text and illustrated callmarks at the Public Record Office, Kew

NOTE: B.T. = Board of Trade. BT42 = designs 1839–1841. BT43 = ornamental designs 1841–1883. 112 and 113 refer to registration classes. BT45 = useful designs 1842–1883. BT50 = all designs after 1883. Where town is not given, this is a London address.

Registrations in Part I

W. J. Adams Lichfield Road Aston	General Gordon Heel plate	BT50	18998	1884
Charles James Appleton Hamilton, Ontario	'New style Stocking'	BT43/12	274301	1873
Alesbury, Major & Barret, Jewin Crescent, Fore St.	The Acme Lappel Collar	BT45	6023	1878
William Bacon & Henry Higginbotham 7 King St., Coventry	The Albert Edward Scarf	BT45	4550	1863
W. Blenkiron & Son 123 Wood St.	The Livingstone Brace Buckle	BT45	4920	1867
Henry Darcy & Co. Noble St.	The Beaconsfield Bow Tie	BT43/13	395197	1879
John Derring 85 Strand, London	adjusting galvanic band	BT45	404	1845
Noel Jeffery Dixon Billacomb Hymstock, Devon	Galvanic hat	BT45	394	1845
Farcy & Oppenheim Paris	Embroidered Corsets	BT50 BT50	87698 87784	1887 1887
George John Flamank 39 Wolverhampton Rd., Stafford	Stars & Stripes braces	BT50	73130	1887
Foster Porter & Co. Wood St., City	The Lady Peel Jacket	BT43/13	87222	1852
George Edmund Geach 4 Champion Terrace, Camberwell, London	Leg shaped necktie	BT50	56976	1886

Roger Gresty 77 Packington St., Islington	Tie & Waistcoat	BT43/13	234793	1869
Graham & Hummel 3 Trump St., Cheapside, London	Embroidered Jubilee corset panels	BT50	55579–80	1886
Joseph Sparkes Hall Regent St.	The Victoria & Albert Elastic Gaiter	BT45	1990	1849
John Heather 3 Bedford Court, Covent Garden	Madame Blangy's Parisian Hindoo Cloth Petticoat	BT45	1964	1849
Thomas Holland 40 South Audley St., Grosvenor Square, London	Jubilee Slippers	BT50	63465	1886
Ellen Lefroy The Priory, Limerick	Inflatable rubber boot	BT45	5523	1874
Frederick Lack 90 Strand	The Anuphaton Cloak	BT45	2991	1851
John Lyon Field 28 Winchester Crescent, Chelsea	The Dane Shirt Cuff	BT45	4650	1864
John McPherson Chicago, USA	toboggan caps	BT50	78403–7	1887
Alfred Webb Miles 73 Brook St., Hanover Sq.	The Dicanum trousers	BT45	4427	1861
Welch Margetson Cheapside, City	Trouser fastener	BT42	786	1841
Richard Mullins Moody 21 Aldermanbury, London	Combined collar and tie	BT50	25003	1885
E. Moses & Son Minories & Aldgate	The Sternophyon Chest protector	BT45	1729	1849
Mulloney & Johnson Priory Row, Coventry	False Hair	BT43/13	209079– 082	1867
Louisa Nice 74 Gresham Rd, Brixton	Nosewarmer	BT50	113596	1888
Newland & Potter 57 New Western St., Bermondsey	Cardboard shirt front	BT43/13	240411	1870
Orr & Co. Glasgow	Women's collars; machine stitched	BT43/13	118635–7	1859
William Blackmore Pine Strand, London	The Mimosa or flower cornet	BT45	1897	1849
Henry E. Randall Lady's Lane, Northampton	Stars & Stripes bootlace	BT50	115665	1888
Roberts & Metham Sheffield	Mr Punch Umbrella Handle	BT43/13	30658	1845

	Cobden Umbrella handle	BT43/13	32545	1845
	Shakespeare Umbrella Handle	BT43/13	37987	1846
Russell Bowlett & Russell Welford Place, Leicester	Fingerless Mitten	BT43/12	307670	1877
Sharp Perrin & Co. 40 Old Change	The Registered Royal Ladies' Drawers	BT45	4324	1861
George Shore 488 New Oxford St., London	Great Exhibition Glove	BT43/13	75741	1851
Smallpage & Son 41–3 Maddox St., Bond St.	The Kaiser Cape	BT45	5600	1874
John Smith 3 Lawrence Lane, Cheapside London	Combination Shirt Waistcoat	BT45	1808	1849
George Statham Coventry	Disraeli Braces	BT50	39322	1885
R. & W. Symington Market Harborough, Leicestershire	The Registered Radiating Side Steel Corset	BT45	6521	1882
Walter Thornhill 144 New Bond St.	Anti-Garrotting Cravat	BT45	4530	1862
Thomas Harris Toms Staining Lane, City	The Elcho Necktie	BT45	4357	1861
John Tucker Birch House, Old Lenton, Nottingham	Belt for keeping the mouth closed while sleeping	BT50	39994	1885
Wareham & Hollingworth Hyde	Paris International Exhibition hat tip	BT43/13	329784–5	1878
Wellington Williams 34 Gutter Lane, City	Box lining paper	BT43/13	86655	1852

Registrations in Part II – Chapter 5

Rebecca & Emma Alcock Doctor's Commons, City	Bust Improvers	BT45	1754	1849
Charles Bayer London Wall, City	Lady's belt	BT50	108967	1888
	Chemise/bodice	BT51	93919	1888
J. F. I. Caplin 58 Berners St., London	Dummy for Stays	BT42	669	1841
	The Hygean or Corporiform Corset	BT45	1995	1849
Madame Cavé (Ann Maria Cavé) 35 Union Grove, Clapham	Corset	BT45	6267	1880

Charles Cross Hallatrow near Bristol	Improved Chest Expander	BT45	5284	1871
Footman, Pretty & Co. Ipswich	Corset	BT45	5934	1877
Galbraith, Stewart & Co. 43 Mitchell Street, Glasgow	Chemise	BT43/13	220963	1868
Walter Helby Portsea	Corset	BT50	46392	1886
Hurst & Reay Little Britain, City	Corded white cotton petticoats	BT43/13	296324–7	1874
Caleb Hill Cheddar, Somerset	Stay clasp	BT45	3409	1853
Mrs Hornblow 12 St Ann's Square, Manchester	Chemise	BT45	4867	1867
W. Hull King & Son 35 Percy St., Rathbone Place, Oxford St., London	Maternity Corset	BT50	286830	1896
George Lander Cheltenham	The Dress Extending Zephyr	BT45	1470	1848
George Langridge & Co. Bristol	Ladies' combination garment	BT43/13	313247	1877
	Corset fastener	BT43/13	262665	1872
Theresa Lawrence Ludgate Hill, City	Lady's belt	BT45	1978	1849
F. Parsons 30 Gracechurch St., London and 'Sunnybank', Chipping Norton	Corset with expansible busts	BT45	6400	1881
Sarah Pearce 6 New Bond St., Bath	Sevigné Stay	BT45	2703	1851
Thomas Foot Piper 94 Cheapside, City	Ladies' Bussel; material air-proof	BT43/13 BT43/13	9851 10226	1843 1843
William Rushton 101 Malins Rd., Landport, Hants.	Corset with suspenders	BT43/13	407594	1883
Salomons & Sons 42 Old Change, City	Crinoline- horsehair	BT43/13	96767	1854
Léonce Bernard Schmolle 55 Aldermanbury, City	Crinolettes and bustles	BT43/12 BT43/12	253280–1 279441–3	1872 1874
Messrs Simister & Holland 66 Cheapside, City	The Ladies' petticoat or dress dilator	BT45	1161	1847
Southcombe Bros. North St., Stoke under Ham, Somerset	Drawers	BT50	349046	1899

Registrations in Part II – Chapter 6

George Barnett 39 Jewin St., London	Waistcoat fastener	BT42	758	1841
Alf Breese 34 Brewer St., London	Sock suspender	BT50	9766	1884
	Suspenders	BT50	8189	1884
John Checkley 20 Green Walk, Blackfriars Rd.	Garter	BT43/12	88900	1853
George Harborrow 340 Holborn Bar, London	Braces	BT45	1523	1848
Richard Kew Snowhill, Shude Hill, Manchester	Combined brace and chest expander	BT50	17858	1884
Christopher Nickells York St., York Rd., Lambeth	Elastic	BT43/12	49763	1848
William Rushton 101 Malins Rd, Landport, Hants.	Corset with suspenders	BT43/13	407594	1883
Alfred Robert Shirley 53 All Saints Rd, Westbourne Park	'The Shirley Brace' Combined braces and chest expander	BT50	5469	1873
John Smerton 9 Edmond Place, London	Waistcoat back-fastener – elastic	BT42	646	1841
Samuel Taylor 56 Lever St., Manchester	Braces	BT50	32830	1885
Archibald Turner Bow Bridge Works, Leicester	Elastics	BT50	81150–2	1887
Luke Turner Deacon St. Works, Leicester	Elastics	BT50	81012–26	1887

Registrations in Part II – Chapter 7

Adams Fryer & Co. Downend, Bristol	Grey Flannel Shirt	BT43/12	275472	1873
Thomas Richard Barlow 143 Tooley St., Southwark, London	The New Uniform Shirt front	BT45	4122	1858
Behrens & Co. Glasgow	Sewed Muslin Collar	BT43/12 BT43/13	91304–6 91248	1853 1853
Brown, Davis & Co. Love Lane, Aldermanbury City	Front Fastening Shirt 'The Figurate Shirt'	BT45	5242	1871

Edward Robinson Buck Egerton St., Irwell St., Salford	Sports shirt	BT50	175362	1891
James Carter Belfast	Blouse	BT50	147000	1890
A. K. Cook & Co. Taunton, Somerset	Shirt front	BT50	180855	1891
Cooks St Paul's Church Yard, City	The Aginoria Shirt	BT45	5174	1870
Richard Copley 252 West Derby Rd., Liverpool	Leg fitting Shirt	BT45	5951	1877
John Crawley & Son 82 Wood St., City	Collars	BT43/12 BT43/12 BT43/12	55721 111876–7 116034	1848 1857 1858
Dawson & MacNicol Buchanan St., Glasgow	Raglan sleeved shirt	BT45	4155	1859
Dent Allcroft & Co. 97 Wood St., City	Collars The Devonshire The United Service Dent's Perfected	BT45 BT45 BT45	3653 3937 3840	1854 1857 1856
Donaldson, Hirsch & Spark 33 Spencer St., Goswell Rd., London	Undershirt	BT45	3758	1855
Richard Adams Ford 38 Poultry, City	Collars	BT43/12 BT43/13	111876–7 113223–4	1857 1858
John Edward Ford Addle St., City	Embroidered shirt	BT43/13	104176	1856
Foster Porter & Co. 47 Wood St., City	The Lorne shirt	BT45	5216	1871
Alexander Grant Bros. St Clement's Court, City	'The Volkommen Shirt'	BT45	3797	1855
Hancock & Leighton Houndsgate, Nottingham	Blouses	BT50 BT50	205236–7 320542	1892 1898
David Hesse Back Piccadilly, Manchester	Imperial Patent Shirt Collars	BT45	413	1845
C. G. Hill & Co. Plantagenet St., Nottingham	Neckfrills	BT50	205720–1	1893
John King & Co. 57 Buchanan Street Glasgow	Machine stitched collars	BT43/13	118054–60	1859
George Longland Furniture Salesman 26 Beech Rd, Sale, Cheshire	Collar	BT50	290934	1896
May & Edlich 116 Newgate St., City	Paper Turndown Collar	BT45	6176	1879

McIntyre Hogg & Co. 26 Addle St., London and 120 Brunswick St., Glasgow and Foyle St., Londonderry	The Epaulette Shirt	BT45	4094	1858
Edmund Potter & Co. Ltd 10 Charlotte St., Manchester	Striped shirt	BT50	352976	1900
I. & R. Pritchard & Co. 9 Madeira Court, Argyle St., Glasgow	Child's dress	BT50	142744	1890
Adolphe Rosenthal & Co. Ltd 30 London Wall, City	Blouse	BT50	295518	1897
John Smith 3 Lawrence Lane, Cheapside	Combination shirt waistcoat	BT45	1808	1849
Dorothy Taylor (Manufacturer) 5 John St., Manchester	Blouse	BT50	285416	1896
Thacker & Radford Hodson's Square, Manchester	Demi-shirt	BT45	952	1847
E. & H. Tideswell 2 Wood St., City	Blouses	BT50 BT50	202537 344990	1892 1899
Tillie & Henderson 39 Miller St., Glasgow	The Abercorn Regd shirt	BT43/12	203362	1866
Albert Wacker 44 Landgrabben Strasse, Nuremberg	Tie holder for celluloid collar	BT50	354057	1900
William Westlow 73 Wood St., City	The Aptandum shirt	BT45	1349	1848
Welch Margetson & Co. 132 Cheapside, City	Side-fastening shirt	BT45	3873	1856
	Necktie and Scarf retainer	BT45	6711	1883
	Collar	BT45	133	1844
	Collars			
	The West End	BT45	3943	1857
	The Oriental	BT45	3990	1857
	The Corded Leopold	BT45	4010	1857
	Shirt front	BT45	1439	1848

Registrations in Part II – Chapter 8

Felix d'Alsace & Co. 24 Rue St Marc, Paris	Jacket Dress	BT50 BT50	316676–9 316676–9	1898 1898
Andrews & Williams 3 Old Fish St., City	Complete dress to be sold as one	BT43/13	143282	1861

224

Brickley & Lodge 16 City Rd., Finsbury, London	decorated fabric	BT43/13	89911	1853
James Collett 1 Vere St., Oxford St., London	decorated fabric	BT43/13	106432–5	1856
George Hitchcock & Co. St Paul's Church Yard, City	Dress fronts	BT43/12	84174	1852
James Houldsworth & Co. Portland St. Mill, Manchester	Dress fronts	BT43/13	79986–9	1851
John Hunt 349 Edgeware Road, London	Skirts for ball gowns	BT43/13	249999– 250002	1871
Jay's Mourning Warehouse (Jay & Smith) 246 Regent St., London	decorated fabric	BT43/13	108684	1857
Jay's Mourning Warehouse 247 Regent St., London	Mantle	BT43/13	109792	1857
	Eutheima Bodice	BT45	4760	1865
George Henry Lee & Co. Liverpool	dresses	BT43/13	397083 397226	1883
Lyons & Co. West Square, Lambeth London	Mourning bodice front	BT43/12	25888–90	1845
Thomas Toms 5 Kings Square, Goswell Rd., City	black crape collar	BT43/12	41204	1847
William Saunders 5 Gloucester St., Hoxton, London	widow's cap	BT43/12	43460	1847
George Macbeth & Son 19 King St., Manchester	Woman's Nautical Outfit	BT50	178460	1891
Barnet Marcus 37 Conduit St., City	Braided Costume	BT50	8227	1884
E. Moses & Son Aldgate, City	Dress Front	BT43/12	86483	1852
H. J. Nicoll Regent St., London	Combination mantle and skirt	BT45	5031	1869
Roberts & Heaven Back Piccadilly, Manchester	dress fronts	BT43/13	88876–9	1853
Henry Robinson 12 Watling St., City	costume	BT43/13	227521	1869
Henry Robinson 12 Watling St., City	The Princess Costume	BT43/12	288198	1875
Rosa Salter 2 Crombie Row, Commercial Rd., London	dresses	BT43/13	274653–4	1873

Scott & Son 8 Cannon Street, City	Mantle	BT43/13	302858	1876
Spencer, Wicks & Co. 4, 5, 6 Watling St., City	Mantles	BT50	144495– 503	1890
Thomas Vyse & Sons 76 Wood St., City	Mantles	BT43/13 BT43/13	151288–9 166179	1862 1863
Walley & Hardwick 55–7 Oxford St., London	Mantle	BT45	1428	1848
Wellington Williams 34 Gutter Lane, Cheapside City	Mourning box lining papers	BT43/13	56482	1848
George Bayless Yates St Mary's Gate, Nottingham	Mourning bonnet veils	BT43/13	55070 57439 70924	1848 1849 1850

Registrations in Part II – Chapter 9

Charles Clark 10 Austin St., Hackney, London	Bonnet	BT43/12	117397	1858
Thomas Ebbs 21 Pierpoint Row, Islington	tulle caps	BT43/13	21869–71	1844
John Farmer St Mary Gate, Nottingham	Bonnet Shapes	BT43/13	8976	1853
Fisher & Watson 20 Milk St.	Tulle cap	BT43/13	62178 62412	1849 1849
Henry Heath Oxford St.	Women's Hats	BT43/13	395380–7	1883
Robert Heath 18 St George's Place, Hyde Park Corner	Hats	BT43/13	118664–5 138430	1859 1860
Jay's Mourning Warehouse Regent St.	Hats	BT43/13	276800–5	1873
G. Long Loudwater, High Wycombe, Bucks	Bonnets	BT43/13	59293 59816 and unnumbered 5.4.49–10.4.49.	1849 1849
John Macintosh 3 Foster Lane, Cheapside, City	Knitted Tam O'Shanter	BT50	6022	1884
Simeon Miles 89 Bunhill Row, City	Paper hat	BT43/13	239531	1870
Henry Alexander Mullard 1, 2 & 3 Penn St., Hoxton, London	Paper hat	BT43/13	235832–6	1882
Caroline Martin 19½ Haberdasher St., Hoxton, London	Bonnet trimming	BT43/12	48122	1847

Munt Brown & Co. 85 Wood Street, City	Hats	BT43/13	131825–6	1860
Sadok Schneiders & Son Buck's Row, Whitechapel, London	cloth hat	BT50	102675	1888
G. Smith Union Hall, Union Street, Borough, London	Bonnet	BT43/13	91703	1853
Welch & Son 40 Gutter Lane	Straw Plait	BT50	62798–9	1886
White & Auborn 57 Upper Princess St., Luton	Sailor hat	BT50	289671	1896

Registrations in Part II – Chapter 10

John Barran & Sons Leeds	Boys' Suits	BT43/13	268775–80	1872
		BT43/13	268946–75	1873
		BT43/13	333150–61	1879
		BT50	134–5	1884
		BT50	150239	1890
		BT50	353029	1900
		BT50	9168	1884
Benjamin Benjamin 74 Regent St., London	Oude Wrapper: Cape or Coat	BT45	3878	1856
W. Cutler 25 St James St., London	Duplexa Coat	BT45	2453	1850
George Doudney 17 Old Bond St., London	Tailor's Measure	BT45	115	1844
Joseph Hepworth & Sons Wellington St., Leeds	Boy's Suit	BT50	1470	1884
Lewis's & Co. Ranelagh St., Liverpool	The Traveller's Friend	BT43/13 BT45	214598 4913	1867 1867
E. Moses & Son Minories & Aldgate, London	Duplex Waistcoat	BT45	1718	1849
Macbeth & Co. King St., Manchester	Boy's Suit	BT43/13	339153	1879
Donald Nicoll & Co. St Paul's Church Yard, City	Boy's Suit Ground Sheet	BT43/13 BT45	238638 5278	1870 1871
H. J. & D. Nicoll Regent St., London	Paletôts	BT45	393	1844
		BT45	1389	1848
		BT45	2691	1851
		BT45	3530	1853
	Cape	BT45	4582	1863

	Riding Coat	BT45	5105	1870
	Cape	BT50	38577	1885
	Cloak & Skirt	BT45	5031	1869
	Coat	BT45	1739	1849
Samuel Shirley 28a Market St., Manchester	Convertible Overcoat	BT50	19357	1884
Stewart & MacDonald Park Lane, Leeds	Boy's Sailor Suit	BT50	177248	1891
Stone & Forster 5 York St., Saint James' Sq., London	Overcoat	BT43/12	287517	1874
John H. Wilson & Co. 24 Love St., Liverpool	Overcoat	BT43/12	303583	1876

Registrations in Part II – Chapter 11

Andrew & Watson 403 Gallowgate, Glasgow	flat cap	BT50	348161	1899
James Bickerton Junior 36 Stamford St., Blackfriars, London	Opera Hat	BT45	107	1844
J. W. & A. Blair 125 Trongate, Glasgow	Compass set in hat	BT45	1554	1848
T. W. Bracher & Co. Stockport	Hat band	BT50	200766	1892
T. W. Bracher & Co. 3 Waterloo Rd., Stockport	Hat leathers	BT50 BT50	116485–6 258593 260188	1888 1895 1895
James Butt Stroud, Gloucs.	Hat suspender	BT45	5124	1870
S. & J. Carrington Stockport	Corrugated ventilating hat anti-macassar pad	BT45	4593	1863
J. & E. Christy & Co. 35 Gracechurch St., City	Gutta Percha hat top hats	BT45 BT43/12	1321 89065–7	1848 1853
Marks Doninger 18 Miller St., Shude Hill, Manchester	Smoking cap to be carried inside hat	BT50	28055	1885
Flanagan & Co. York Chambers, Liverpool	Aeolian hat	BT45	3527	1853
Edward Newman Fourdrinier 9 College Place, Camden Town, London	Hat suspender	BT45	1782	1849

John Fuller 95–6 Long Lane, Southwark	Bonafide Ventilating hat	BT45	1823	1849
John Fuller Southwark, London	Neoteric Ventilating hat	BT45	2907	1851
James Hague Hooley Hill, Near Manchester	Hat	BT50	53409	1886
Thomas Higgins 5 Warrington Gardens, Maida Hill, London	Improved hat brush to be carried inside hat	BT45	5061	1869
J. Langlen 9 Howard St., Glasgow	Hat guard showcard	BT50	15324	1884
Daniel Lever Denton, Cheshire	Hat ventilator	BT50	105809	1888
James Marlor & Sons Denton, Cheshire	Hat ventilator	BT50	23407	1885
David Nyman St James' Barton, Bristol	cap	BT43/13	78453	1851
Charles Rider 61 Red Cross St., Borough, London	Hat pocket	BT45	1241	1847
Wm. Ruttenau 50 Princess St., Manchester (1884) Springbank Works, Audenshaw (1886)	Hat leathers	BT50 BT50 BT50	7980 48751 75005	1884 1886 1887
Wm. Ruttenau Audenshaw & Ashton under Lyme, Cheshire	Hat band	BT50	345786	1899
Sadok Schneiders & Son 7 St Mary St., Whitechapel, London	'The Perfection Roll Curl for Soft Hats'	BT45	5094	1870
Wm. Twigg Birmingham	Hat clip for ticket, stethoscope or pencil	BT45	5816	1876
Wareham & Hollingworth Hyde, Cheshire	Hat tips	BT43/13 BT43/13 BT43/13 BT43/13	305666–9 C18 couples 319398– 400 Hardy Napier & Worsley 320570 Paris Exhibition 329784–5 Courting Couples	1876 1878 1878 1878
Samuel Wareham & Co.	Hat tips 18th century scenes. Soldiers in Africa	50 50	12995 18813	1884 1884

Registrations in Part II – Chapter 12

Biggs Brothers	Undershirts	BT45	49	1843
Leicester		BT45	3024	1854
Billson & Haines	Child's striped	BT43/12	99152	1855
Leicester	stocking			
Alfonso Boccardo	Jerseys	BT50	68165–70	1887
16 Rue des Petit Champs,		BT50	142894	1890
Paris		BT50	107317	1888
Nathaniel Corah & Sons	Jersey Bodices:			
Leicester	The Fedora	BT43/12	401081	1883
	The Princess	BT43/12	401082	1883
	The Louise	BT43/12	401083	1883
	The Iolanthe	BT43/12	401084	1883
	The Scarborough	BT43/12	401657	1883
Nathaniel Corah & Sons	The Saint	BT43/12	397640	1883
Leicester	Margaret's Gem			
Nathaniel Corah & Sons	Knitted trousers	BT43/12	400171	1883
Davies Moore & Co.	Stockings	BT50	81998	1887
Leicester		BT50	114821	1888
Geary & Sultzer	Nightcap	BT43/12	30664	1845
Norwich				
William Goddard	Singlet	BT45	628	1846
Nottingham				
Richard Harris & Sons	Polka Jacket	BT43/12	68377	1850
Leicester				
Hurst & Cane	Man's Pullover	BT50	285423	1896
49 Friday St., City				
Sarah Nathan	Crocheted	BT43/13	80590–1	1851
20 London Rd., Southwark	Undersleeves (with			
	net trimming			
	registration in			
	between)			
Robertson, Higginson, Lowe	Coat shaped	BT50	27035	1885
& Co.	wrapper			
Manchester &				
Loughborough				

Registrations in Part II – Chapter 13

John Biggs & Sons	Knitted glove	BT43/12	95297	1854
Leicester				
Robert Black	Press stud type	BT45	6361	1880
Park St., Worcester	fastener			
Dent Allcroft & Co.	Kid Gloves with	BT43/13	344836	1880
Worcester and	Machine Embroidery			
97 Wood St., City				

Fownes Bros & Co. Talbot St., Worcester	Glove	BT50	316238	1898
George Lewis Silver St., Worcester	The Alice Gauntlet	BT43/13	102459	1853
John Glover Nicol Worcester	Press-stud type fastener	BT45	6154	1879
George Shore 488 New Oxford St., London	Great Exhibition Glove	BT43/13	75741	1851
Topham & Fawcett Derby	Gloves	BT45	146	1843
W. & R. Coltman Leicester	Ringwood Gloves	BT50	24201–2	1885
Ward, Sturt & Sharp 89 Wood St., City	The National Rifle Glove	BT43/13	130668	1860
Whitby Brothers Yeovil, Somerset	Embroidered leather glove backs	BT43/13	308141–3	1877

Registrations in Part II – Chapter 14

Ebenezer Baines 55 Newgate St., City	Scarf retainer	BT45	4552	1863
Henry Coppin 69 Wood St., City	Ace of clubs tie	BT43/13	334086	1879
John Edward Ford 15 Addle St., City	Stock	BT43/13	97650	1853
William Robert Evans 48 Brighton Road, Stoke Newington, London	necktie	BT50	354058	1900
Foster Porter and Co. 47 Wood St., City	'Gentleman's scarf'	BT43/13	235140	1869
Alexander Grant & Bros. 2 Clements Court, Wood St., City	Stock	BT43/12	52486	1848
Henry Tucker Greenlaw 135 London Wall, City	Ties	BT50 BT50 BT50 BT50 BT50	7866 103182 105294–5 105296 345478	1884 1888 1888 1888 1899
Hall and Dutson Birmingham	scarf retainer	BT45	4642	1864
Joseph Hill Birmingham	scarf retainer	BT45	4935	1868
Moses Levi Jacob and Lewis Woolf Birmingham	scarf retainer	BT45	4567	1863

Henry Jagg 70 Hatton Garden, City	scarf retainer	BT45	5027	1869
John Compton Weeks Jefferys 19 Hargrave Park Rd., Holloway, London	Bow tie fastener	BT50	86712	1887
Lloyd Attree & Smith 28–9 Wood St., City	Tie	BT43/13	150199	1862
Richard Mullins Moody 21 Aldermanbury, City	Collar & Tie	BT50	25003	1885
I. & R. Morley 18 Wood St., City	Waistcoat cum necktie	BT43/13	235396	1869
Rix & Bridge 126 Cheapside, City	Firework Scarf	BT43/12	234140	1869
Robert Sayle St Andrew St., Cambridge	'The Sailor' cravat	BT43/12	274059	1873
Slater Buckingham & Co. 35 Wood St., City	The Duke of Edinburgh Cravat	BT43/13	204507	1866
Slater Son & Slater 35 Wood St., City	Waistcoat cum necktie	BT43/12	235177	1869
Hannah Smith Halifax	Stock Stiffener	BT45	929	1846
Charles Tighe & Sons 42 Lombard St., City	Necktie	BT50	200914	1892
James Ward 2 Vere St., Oxford St., London	The Cobweb Scarf	BT43/12	213852	1867
Welch Margetson & Co. 132 Cheapside, City	The Aerial Stock	BT45 BT45	1786 1847	1847 1849
Bryant Ratray & Bryant 10 Fore St., London	White Mouse tie	BT43/13	361143	1880

Registrations in Part II – Chapter 15

William Ashby & Sons Elm St., Leicester	Woman's shoe	BT50	229767	1894
John Barker & Co. High St., Kensington, London	Woman's shoe	BT50	146037	1890
John Blakey & Co. Lady Lane, Leeds	Heel tips	BT45 BT50	6616 2170	1863 1884
Fred Bostock Victoria St., Northampton	Man's shoe	BT50	348997	1899
Brightman Bros. Bristol	Woman's boot	BT43/13	227445	1864
Joseph Box 187 Regent St., London	Beaded shoe decoration	BT50	73426	1887

Cyrus & James Clark Street, Somerset	Elastic Shoe	BT45	2530	1850
	Front	BT45	2992	1851
	Boot elastic	BT45	3190	1852
	The Osborne Boot	BT45	3818	1856
	The Lorne Lace Boot	BT45	5296	1871
Derham Brothers Bristol and Northampton	Woman's boot	BT50	176319	1891
Joseph Sparkes Hall 308 Regent St., London	Elastic sided boots	BT42	310	1840
James Hamilton & Son Dundee	Woman's shoe	BT50	230907	1894
Jesse Harrison 15 Broad St., Northampton	Elastic sided boot	BT50	17118	1884
Lutwyche & Co. 136 Borough High St., London	Crocodile Hide Shoe	BT50	40931	1886
John Maddock & Co. Great Western Nail Works, Oakengates, Shropshire	Heel Plate	BT50	152543	1890
H. Marshall The Green, Northampton	walking boot	BT45	3642	1854
Richard Hodgson Southall & William Hallam 19 Swan St., Manchester	'The Wellington Blucher Shoe'	BT45	4609	1864
W. H. Staynes & Smith 9a and 192 Belgrave Gate, Leicester	Heel plate	BT50	61216	1886

Registrations in Part II – Chapter 16

Barber & Henton Wellington St., Leicester	Guernsey	BT45	5370	1872
John Blandy 22 Sloane Terrace, Chelsea, London	Baker's outfit	BT50	119151	1889
George Bayley 37 Upper Thames St., London	Ventilated Waterproof Cap	BT45	3959	1857
W. Dixon & Co. 26 Holborn Viaduct, City	Bell Boy's Outfit	BT50	115330	1888
Duncan & Black Cellardyke, Fyfeshire	Oilskin trousers	BT50	72958	1887
Fraser, Fraser & Co. Kilmarnock, Ayrshire	Knitted long men's drawers	BT50	93707	1888
Charles Hindley Cleaton Moor, Cumberland	Miner's clog	BT50	69172	1887
Irwell India Rubber Co. 6 Billiter St., London	A Combination garment	BT50	21098	1885

Lee, Fred William 46 Southampton Buildings, Holborn, City	Lee's Marine Life Preserver	BT45	242	1844
Joseph Park 37 Oldfield Rd., Salford	Clog	BT50	109753	1888
Samuel Reston Aldersgate St., City	The Life Preserver braces	BT45	1865	1849
Ridgard & Thompson Nottingham	Parlourmaid's caps & aprons	BT50	289670	1896
	Apron	BT50	320330	1898
	Cap	BT50	232588–9	1894
W. E. Sparling 66 West Smithfield, City	Butcher's smock	BT50	2826	1884
Arthur Thomas Umfreville 19–23 Baches St., Hoxton, London	Maid's cap	BT50	262684	1895
R. Walker & Sons Rutland St., Leicester	Miner's suit	BT50	60403	1886
Captain John Ross Ward, RN Inspector of Lifeboats to RNLI 14 John St., Adelphi, London	Cork Life Jacket	BT45	4708	1865

Registrations in Part II – Chapter 17

Jacob Ballin Aldersgate St., City	Respirator	BT50	63730	1886
A. B. Cow Hill & Co. 46–7 Cheapside, City	Waterproof Ventilated Garment	BT45	5233	1871
Philip Frankenstein & Son Manchester	Frosted rubberised fabrics	BT50	21414	1885
Walter Jessop 4 Royal Crescent, Cheltenham	Pillow Cap for Travellers	BT45	4321	1860
Joseph Mandleberg & Co. 3 Macdonald's Lane	Waterproof	BT45	5444	1873
	Ventilating	BT50	1651	1884
	Overcoat	BT43/13	335164	1879
J. Mandleberg & Co. Ltd. Pendleton, Manchester	Mantle	BT50	351597	1900
Joseph Mandleberg & Co. 3 Macdonald's Lane, Manchester	'Lady's Waterproof Cloak'	BT50	2908	1884
James Martin Walworth, London	The Protector	BT45	1598	1848
L. Mistorski 94 Shudehill, Manchester	Lady's reversible waterproof princess cloak	BT50	1998	1884

Maurice & Edward Moses 87 Tower Hill, London	The Janus Coat	BT45	3047	1851
Louisa Nice 74 Gresham Rd., Brixton	Nosewarmer	BT50	113596	1888
Donald Nicoll & Co. St Paul's Church Yard	Registered Dryad	BT45	5265	1871
North British Rubber Co. Castle Mills, Edinburgh	The Traveller's Wrapper	BT45	4952	1868
Osmond Brice & Chidley 14 Cannon St., City	'Arm opening flap in circular macintoshes'	BT50	28558	1885
George Spill 65–7 St George's St., St George's East, London and Bristol	Thorough Metallic Ventilated Coat	BT45	2871	1851
John White 51 High St., Manchester	Trouser Protectors	BT45	4898	1867
Annie Matilda Wood 13 Delahay St., Westminster	Storm Cap	BT50	92854	1888

Registrations in Part II – Chapter 18

Edward Brett & Henry Whale 30 Edward Sq., Caledonian Rd., London	The Skeleton cricket gloves	BT45	4779	1866
Broom & Foster Manchester	Football boots	BT50	231307	1894
Nurse Angelina Coles 20 Simpson St., Battersea, London	Knee protector	BT50	179925	1891
N. Corah & Sons & Cooper St Margaret's Works, Leicester	The Fred Wood Champion Suit	BT43/12	405298	1883
Joseph Dawson & Sons Overstone Rd., Northampton	Tennis Shoe	BT50	181527	1891
Charles East Britannia Works, Kettering	Football boots	BT50	52834	1886
James Fenton 74 Great Hampton St., Birmingham	Brooch like golf clubs	BT50	202534	1892
Alexander Black Fergusson & Robert John Key 42 Stamford St., London	Buckle like cricket bat, ball and wickets	BT50	233186	1894
John Turpin Waller Goodman 47 Albemarle St., Piccadilly, London	Tricycle shirt	BT50	6674	1883

Grant & Watson 112 Buchanan St., Glasgow	Football Jersey	BT50	179702	1891
D. B. Harris & Son 73–5 Newhall, Birmingham	Bicycle motif on belt	BT50	292015	1897
William James Harvey 14 Victoria Gdns., Nottinghill, London	Tricycle Skirt	BT50	1195	1884
Higginbotham Sons & Gray Glasgow	Cotton handkerchief with football team	BT50	56984	1886
Jefferies & Co. Wood St., Woolwich, London	The University Lawn Tennis Shoe	BT45	5992	1878
Benjamin Ladds Wellingborough Rd, Rushden, Northants	Football boot	BT50	201017	1892
John Phelps Mashoba Croxted Rd, Dulwich, London	Man's riding macintosh	BT50	114473	1888
Ben Nicoll 42 Regent Circus, London	Cricket Jacket	BT45	1833	1849
H. J. & D. Nicoll Regent St., London	Registered riding vest	BT43/13	84781	1852
William Thomas Pitchers Regent House, Church St., Surrey	Cricket Jumper	BT50	205687	1893
William Redgrave Grafton St., London	Registered Cricket guard	BT45	3390	1852
H. Salomon & Co. 44 Princess St., Edinburgh	The Alpine Shooting Boots	BT45	5148	1870
Robert Shaw 32 Baker St., Pentonville, London	Combination suit for cricket	BT50	142588	1890
Saunders & Shepherd Bartletts Buildings, Holborn Circus, City	Watchchain like bicycle chain	BT50	289496	1896
Speyer Schwert & Co. 35 Monkwell St., London	Button like horse shoe	BT50	231758	1894
Alf Stanley Wednesbury Road, Walsall, Staffordshire	Buckle like tennis racquet and balls	BT50	202938	1892
Swears & Wells 192 Regent Street, London	Riding habit	BT43/12	312260	1877
Owen Tilley Shepshed, nr Loughborough	Football boot	BT50	286706	1896

Leonora Louisa Toll Holloway Rd., Islington	Knitted cricket or rowing jacket	BT43/13	79323	1851
Fébes Wahli 144 Westbourne Grove	Bicycling skirt	BT50	231582	1894
Welch Margetson	University jacket	BT45	1826	1851
S. Whincup & Co. 25 Cheapside, London	Tennis Jackets	BT50	48761–4	1886
Samuel Winter 27 Sussex Place, South Kensington	The Watteau Lawn Tennis Shoe	BT45	6008	1878
Emily Wolmershausen 49 Curzon St., Mayfair	Riding habit	BT50	40127	1885
G. S. Wolmershausen 49 Curzon St., Mayfair	Riding habit	BT50	22668	1885
Jeakins & Wolmershausen 11 Curzon St., Mayfair	Riding habit	BT45	2538	1850

Books referred to in Part I

British Parliamentary Papers, Committee to Inquire into the Best Means of Extending a Knowledge of the Arts and Principles of Design among the Peoples of This Country. BPP 1835 Vol. V p.375 and BPP 1836 Vol. IX p.1.

Copyright of Designs Act 1839, c. 17.

Copyright of Designs Act 1842, c. 100.

Patents, Designs and Trademarks Act 1883, c. 57.

Jane Welsh Carlyle, *Letters and Memories 1834–66*, (ed. J. A. Froude), 1883 (October 1864).

Lady Dorothy Nevill, *Under Five Reigns*, (ed. Ralph Nevill), Methuen, 1910, p.173.

Anon, *How to Dress Well*, C. T. G. Routledge & Sons, 1868, p.23–6, p.52.

G. and W. Grossmith, *Diary of a Nobody*, 1st edn, 1892.

H. G. Wells, *Kipps: The Story of a Simple Soul*, Macmillan & Co., 1905, p.65.

E. W. Allen, *How to Dress Neatly and Prettily on £10 a Year*, 1881.

'Sylvia', *How to Dress Well on a Shilling a Day*, Ward Lock, c. 1875.

Robert Roberts, *The Classic Slum: Salford Life in the First Quarter of the Century*, Manchester University Press and Pelican, 1971, p.76.

Cooperative Working Women, *Life as We Have Known It*, (ed. Margaret Llewellyn Davies), Virago and Chatto & Windus, 1977, p.6.

E. Moses and Son, *The Growth of an Important Branch of British Industry*, Moses, 1860, p.4.

E. Moses and Son, *The Exhibition of 1851 for all Nations*, Moses, 1851, p.38.

Henry Mayhew, *The Unknown Mayhew*, (ed. E. P. Thompson and Eileen Yeo), Merlin, 1971 (Pelican Books, 1973, p.42).

Robert Finch, *The Flying Wheel*, I. & R. Morley, 1924, p.73.

Rev. Thomas Lomas, *A Memoir of the Late R. Harris MP*, B. L. Green, 1855, p.83, p.60.

British Parliamentary Papers, 1887, Vol. LXXXIX (331), Report to the Board of Trade on the Sweating System at the East End of London, p.1.

British Parliamentary Papers, Reports of the Royal Commission on Children's Employment in Trades and Manufactures, 1843 (430), Vol. XII, 1843 (432), Vol. XV and 1843 (431), Vol. XIV.

British Parliamentary Papers, 1845, Reports of the Royal Commission on the Condition of the Framework Knitters, BPP, 1845, 609, 618, Vol. XV.

British Parliamentary Papers, Reports of the Royal Commission on Children's Employment. 1863 (3170), Vol. XVIII, 1864 (3414), Vol. XXII, 1865 (3548), Vol. XX, 1866 (3678), Vol. XXIV, 1867 (3796), Vol. XVI.

British Parliamentary Papers, Reports from the Labour Correspondent of the Board of Trade on the Sweating System (London and Leeds), 1887 (331), Vol. LXXXIX and 1888 (c. 5513), Vol. LXXXVI.

British Parliamentary Papers, Reports of the House of Lords Select Committee on the Sweating System, 1888 (361), Vol. XX, 1888 (448), Vol. XXI, 1889 (165), Vol. XIII, 1889 (331), Vol. XIV, 1890 (169), Vol. XVII.

Andrew Wynter, *Our Social Bees*, R. Hardwicke, 1861, p.333.

Books referred to in Part II

Chapter 5

E. E. Perkins, *The Lady's Shopping Manual and Mercery Album*, T. Hurst, 1834, p.80.

Christopher Page, *Foundations of Fashion: The Symington Collection – Corsetry from 1856 to the Present Day*, Leicestershire Museums, 1981, p.7.

E. E. Perkins, *Treatise on Haberdashery and Hosiery*, William Tegg, 1874, 9th edn, p.92.

Edward J. Tilt, *Elements of Health and Principles of Female Hygiene*, Henry G. Bohn, 1852, p.196, p.272.

Roxy Anne Caplin, *Health and Beauty or Corsets and Clothing Constructed in Accordance with the Physiological Laws of the Human Body*, Darton & Co., 1856, p.51.

Roxy Caplin, *Woman and Her Work: The Needle, Its History and Utility*, William Freeman, 1860, p.60.

James Torrington Spencer Lidstone, *The Londoniad: A Grand National Poem on the Arts*, published by Universal Patronage, 1856, p.59.

Alison Adburgham, *Shops and Shopping*, George Allen & Unwin, 1964, new edn 1981, pp.91–2.

Lady Dorothy Nevill, *The Reminiscences of Lady Dorothy Nevill*, (ed. Ralph Nevill), Thomas Nelson & Sons, 1906, p.96.

Punch, vol. 32, p.60, 1857, poem on inflatable crinolines.

Chapter 6

Thomas Hancock, *A Personal Narrative of the Origin and Progress of the Caoutchouc and India Rubber Manufacture in England*, Longman etc., 1857, p.25, p.67.

The Great Exhibition, Catalogue, 1851, p.593.

J. W. Hayes, *The Draper and Haberdasher*, Houlston's Industrial Library, 4th edn 1878, p.70–71.

Perkins, 1834, ed. p.101.

Tilt, p.197.

Baroness Stoffa, *The Lady's Dressing Room*, Cassell, 1892, p.246.

Anon, *Progress and Commerce*, The London Printing and Engraving Co., 1893, p.210.

Charles Goodyear, *Gum Elastic and its Varieties*, published for the author, New Haven, 1855, p.294.

Chapter 7

Thomas Hood, 'The Song of the Shirt', *Punch*, vol. V, 1843.

James Grant, *Lights and Shadows of London Life*, Saunders & Otley, 1842, p.201.

British Parliamentary Papers, Report of the Royal Commission on Children's Employment, 1864, vol. XXII, p.66ff.

R. S. Surtees, *Ask Mama*, 1858.

Charles Dickens, *Pickwick Papers*, 1837, Chapter XXXII. p.440.

A Major of Today, *Clothes and the Man*, Grant Richards, 1900, p.131, p.64.

Charles Dickens, *The Old Curiosity Shop*, 1840, Chapter XLIX, p.380.

Arnold Bennett, *The Old Wives' Tale*, 1908, p.305, p.20.

Arnold Bennett, *Anna of the Five Towns*, 1902, p.48.

Anon, *How to Dress, or Etiquette of the Toilette*, Ward Lock & Tyler, 1876, p.11.

Rylands and Sons, Catalogue, c. 1870, Rylands, p.103ff.

H. G. Wells, *Kipps*, pp.110–11, p.58.

H. G. Wells, *Love and Mr Lewisham*, Harper & Row, 1900, Chapter 8.

Robert Roberts, *The Classic Slum*, Pelican, 1971, p.40.

Chapter 8

E. E. Perkins, 1834, ed. p.101 and 1874, p.73.

Anon, *How to Dress Well*, 1868, p.79.

Daniel Puseley, *Commercial Companion*, Warren Hall & Co., 1858, p.218.

Anon, *The Guide to the Trade: The Dressmaker and Milliner*, Charles Knight & Co., 1842, p.92.

British Parliamentary Papers, 1843 (431), Vol. XIV, p.283.

Henry Mayhew, *Shops and Companies of London*, The Strand Printing and Publishing Co., 1865, p.218.

British Parliamentary Papers, 1864 (3414), Vol. XXII, p.189ff.

Illustrated London News, 1866.

E. Moses and Son, *Spring and Summer Manual*, Moses, 1857, pp.20–1.

J. W. Hayes, *The Draper and Haberdasher*, 4th edn 1878, p.40.

'Sylvia', *How to Dress Well on a Shilling a Day*, c. 1875, p.25.

Anon (M.M.), *How to Dress and What to Wear*, Methuen, 1903, p.158.

Chapter 9

F. Talbot, *Etiquette: The Philosophy of Manners, the Principles and Practice of True Politeness and the Courtesies of Life*, W. R. M'phun, Glasgow, 1857, p.50.

Arnold Bennett, *An Old Wives' Tale*, 1908, p.104.

Chapter 10

Henry Mayhew, *The Unknown Mayhew*, (ed. E. P. Thompson and Eileen Yeo), Merlin, 1971 (Pelican, 1973, p.227, p.43).

George Augustus Sala, *Gaslight and Daylight*, Chapman and Hall, 1859, p.59.

E. Moses and Son, *The Past, the Present and the Future*, 1846, pp.16–17, p.8.

E. Moses and Son, *Spring and Summer Manual*, 1857, p.1.

D. Puseley, *Commercial Companion*, 1860, ed. p.221.

Charles Dickens, *Dombey and Son*, 1846–8.

H. G. Wells, *Kipps*, p.52.

Compton Mackenzie, *My Life and Times*, Octave One, 1883–97, Chatto & Windus, 1963–71, p.178.

Chapter 11

Frederick Engels, *The Condition of the Working Class in England*, 1845, new edn Granada, 1982, p.99.

Robert Roberts, *The Classic Slum*, p.40.

Healthy and Artistic Dress Union, *The Dress Review*, 1900–1910.

Charles Dickens, *Little Dorrit*, 1855–6, Chapter XXVI.

Charles Dickens, *The Old Curiosity Shop*, Chapter LIX.

Rev Francis Kilvert, *Kilvert's Diary: Selections from the Diary of the Rev Francis Kilvert 1870–79*, (ed. William Plomer), Jonathan Cape, 1944, 16 December 1872.

Charles Goodyear, *Gum Elastic and its Varieties*, 1855, p.298.

The Hatters' Gazette, 1886, vol. XI, 1.12.86, p.697.

A Cavalry Officer, *The Whole Art of Dress*, Effingham Wilson, 1830, p.51.

H. G. Wells, *Bealby*, Methuen & Co., 1915, pp.815–16.

Cooperative Working Women, *Life as We Have Known It*, (ed. Margaret Llewellyn Davies, p.88.

Anon, *Modern London*, Historical Publishing Co., c. 1890, p.100.

G. and W. Grossmith, *Diary of a Nobody*, 1892, p.158.

Chapter 12

British Parliamentary Papers, 1845 (609) (618), Vol. XV, Reports of the Royal Commission on the Condition of the Framework Knitters. Appendix II, p.247 and p.93.

British Parliamentary Papers, 1863 (3170), Vol. XVIII, Report of the Royal Commission on Children's Employment, p.265.

Rev C. Coe, *The Friend of the Poor in his Prosperity and Affliction: John Biggs*, published privately, 1871, p.26.

Great Exhibition 1851, Reports of the Juries, p.478.

British Parliamentary Papers, Report of the Royal Commission on Children's Employment, 1843 (430), Vol. XIV, p.267.

Rylands & Sons, Catalogue, c. 1870s, p.189.

Anon, *Leicester in 1891*, Robinson & Pike, 1891, p.34ff.

D. H. Lawrence, *Sons and Lovers*, 1913 (Penguin edn pp.40–1).

Chapter 13

Anon, *How to Dress, or the Etiquette of the Toilette*, 1876, pp.57–8.

Anon, *Etiquette for Gentlemen*, Warner's Bijou Books, 1866, p.17.

E. W. Allen, *How to Dress Neatly and Prettily on £10 a Year*, p.38.

E. E. Perkins , *The Lady's Shopping Manual and Mercery Album*, 1834, p.53.

W. M. Thackeray, *The Book of Snobs*, (ed. John Sutherland), University of Queensland Press, 1978 (1st edn 1847), pp.60–1.

J. W. Hayes, *The Draper and Haberdasher*, 4th edn, 1878, p.92.

Anon, *Modern London*, Historical Publishing Co., c. 1891, pp.178–9.

Chapter 14

Charles Dickens, *Bleak House*, 1853, Chapter XIV.

James Grant, *Lights and Shadows of London Life*, 1842, p.199.
British Parliamentary Papers, 1843 (431), Vol. XIV, p.761.
Punch, 1854, p.10.
Anthony Trollope, *Barchester Towers*, 1857, Chapter 10.
Lloyd, Attree, Smith and Co., *100 years*, Lloyd, Attree Smith & Co., 1957.
A Major of Today, *Clothes and the Man*, 1900, p.145.
G. and W. Grossmith, *Diary of a Nobody*, 1892, p.198.

Chapter 15

Joseph Sparkes Hall, *The Book of the Feet*, Simpkin Marshall & Co., 1846, pp.129–32 and
    p.87.
Punch, 1848, p.128.
Arnold Granger, 'History of the Boot and Shoe Industry in Leicester 1750–1950', *British Boot
    and Shoe Institute Journal*, March 1965, p.9.

Chapter 16

Anon, *The Lady's Maid*, Houlston's Industrial Library, c. 1878.
S. P. Dobbs, *The Clothing Workers of Great Britain*, Routledge, 1928, p.XI.
Charles Dickens, *The Old Curiosity Shop*, Chapter LIV.
Factory Act information provided by John Smart of the Science Museum.
D. H. Lawrence, *Sons and Lovers*, p.82.
Charles Goodyear, *Gum Elastic and its Varieties*, pp.265–6, p.267.
A Lady, *Common Sense for Housemaids*, J. Hatchard & Son, 1850, p.61.
M. M. *How to Dress and What to Wear*, p.6 and p.31.

Chapter 17

Thomas Hancock, *A Personal Narrative of the Origin and Progress of the Caoutchouc and India
    Rubber Manufacture in England*, 1857, p.53, p.55, p.87.
The Gentleman's Magazine, 1836, quoted in C. W. and P. Cunnington, *Handbook of English
    Costume in the 19th Century*, Faber & Faber, 1959, p.142.
Great Exhibition, 1851, Reports of the Juries, p.593, p.594.
R. S. Surtees, *Plain or Ringlets*, 1860, p.62.
H. G. Wells, *Kipps*, Book III, Chapter 2.
Rev Francis Kilvert, *Kilvert's Diary: Selections from the Diary of the Rev Francis Kilvert 1870–79*,
    (ed. William Plomer), Jonathan Cape, 1944.

Chapter 18

Kilvert's Diary, 4 August 1870.
E. Moses & Son, *Spring and Summer Manual*, 1857, p.11.
Kate Terry Gielgud, *An Autobiography*, The Bodley Head, 1953.
Sylvia Druitt, *Antique Personal Possessions*, Blandford Press, 1980, p.105.
E. W. Allen, *How to Dress Neatly and Prettily on £10 a Year*, p.34.
Flora Thompson, *Lark Rise to Candleford*, Oxford University Press, 1945 (Pelican edn p.476).

Professor Hoffmann, *Tips for Tricyclists*, 1887, (Quoted in Jeanne Mackenzie, *Cycling*, Oxford University Press, 1981).

Fred Gale (The Old Buffer), *Modern English Sports: their Use and Abuse*, Sampson, Low, Marston, Searle & Rivington, 1885, p.49, p.54, p.53.

Fred Gale, *Sports and Recreations in Town and Country*, Swann, Sonnenschein & Co., 1888, p.28.

General Bibliography

Alison Adburgham, *Shops and Shopping*, George Allen & Unwin, 1964, 2nd edn 1981.

David Alexander, *Retail Trading in England during the Industrial Revolution*, Athlone Press, 1970.

Anon, *Etiquette for Gentlemen*, Ward Lock, c. 1880.

Anon, *The Lady's Maid*, Houlston's Industrial Library, c. 1878.

Anon, *Milestones in the History of Mandleburg and Co., 1856–1946*, Mandleburg, 1954.

Anon, *A Visit to Regent Street*, H. J. & D. Nicoll, c. 1860.

William Barber, *The Chronicles of Canal Street*, Christy & Co., 1868.

Klaus Boehm, *The British Patent System*, Cambridge University Press, 1967.

James D. Burn, *Commercial Enterprise and Social Progress*, Piper, Stephenson & Spence, 1858.

Duncan Bythell, *The Sweated Trades: Outwork in Nineteenth Century Britain*, Batsford, 1978.

British Parliamentary Papers, Copyright of Designs Act, 1839, c. 17.

British Parliamentary Papers, Report of the Select Committee Appointed to Inquire into the Expediency of Extending Copyright of Designs, BPP 1840, Vol. VI, 1.

British Parliamentary Papers, Copyright of Designs Act, 1842, c. 100.

British Parliamentary Papers, Patents, Designs and Trademarks Act, 1883, c. 57.

British Parliamentary Papers, Board of Trade: Report of the Departmental Committee on Industrial Designs (gives summary of legislation), Command 1808, 1961–2, Vol. XX, p.29, HMSO, 1962.

Alison Beazley, 'The Heavy and Light Clothing Industries 1850–1920', *Costume*, VII, 1973.

Penelope Byrde, *The Male Image: Men's Fashion in England 1300–1970*, Batsford, 1979.

Cooks of St Paul's, *150 Years 1807–1957*, Cooks, 1957.

Grace Rogers Cooper, *The Sewing Machine: Its Invention and Development*, Smithsonian Institute Press, 1976.

C. W. Cunnington, *English Women's Clothing in the Nineteenth Century*, Faber & Faber, 1957.

C. W. and P. Cunnington, *A Handbook of English Costume in the Nineteenth Century*, Faber & Faber, 1959.

Phillis Cunnington and Alan Mansfield, *English Costume for Sports and Outdoor Recreations*, Faber & Faber, 1969.

Phillis Cunnington and Catherine Lucas, *Occupational Costume in England*, Faber & Faber, 1967.

Fiona Clark, *Hats*, Batsford, 1982.

Valerie Cumming, *Gloves*, Batsford, 1981.

Dorothy Davis, *A History of Shopping*, Routledge & Keegan Paul, 1966.

Charles Dickens, *Nicholas Nickleby*, 1838–9.

Charles Dickens, *Pickwick Papers*, 1836–8; *The Old Curiosity Shop*, 1840; *Dombey & Son*, 1848.

Charles Dickens, *Bleak House*, 1852–3.

William Ewers and H. W. Baylor, *Sincere's History of the Sewing Machine*, Sincere Press, Phoenix, Arizona, 1970.

Michael Fysh, *Russell–Clarke on Copyright in Industrial Designs*, 5th edn, Sweet & Maxwell, 1974.

Elizabeth Gaskell, *Mary Barton*, 1848.

Madeline Ginsburg, *Clothing Manufacture 1860–90*, in High Victorian.

Kenneth Hudson, *Towards Precision Shoemaking: C. & J. Clark Ltd and the Development of the British Shoe Industry*, David & Charles, 1968.

Patricia Hudson, *The West Riding Wool Textile Industry*, Passold Foundation, Eddington, Wilts, 1975.

Hyam, *The Gentleman's Illustrated Album of Fashion*, 1851.

James B. Jefferey, *Retail Trading in Great Britain, 1850–1950*, Cambridge University Press, 1954.

W. G. Jones, *Leicester Stockingers 1680–1890*, Spencer's illustrated Almanac, Leicester, 1891.

Keith Jopp, *Corah of Leicester, 1815–1965*, Corah, 1965.

Claudia Kidwell, *Suiting Everyone: The Democratisation of Clothing in America*, Smithsonian Museum, 1974, USA.

Leicester Footwear Manufacturers' Federation, 100th Annual Report and Centenary Supplement, 1871–1971.

George Macintosh, *Biographical Memoir of the Late Charles Macintosh*, printed privately, Glasgow, 1847.

Peter Meinhardt, *Inventions, Patents and Trade Marks*, Gower Press, 1971.

David Ryott, *John Barran's of Leeds, 1851–1951*, Barrans, 1951.

June Swann, *Shoes*, Batsford, 1982.

Joan Thomas, *A History of the Leeds Clothing Industry, Yorkshire Bulletin of Economic and Social Research*, Occasional Paper 1, 1955.

Jane Tozer and Sarah Levitt, *Fabric of Society: A Century of People and Their Clothes, 1770–1870*, Laura Ashley Ltd, 1983.

Christina Walkley, *The Ghost in the Looking Glass: the Victorian Seamstress*, Peter Owen, 1981.

Norah Waugh, *The Cut of Men's Clothes 1600–1900*, Faber & Faber, 1964.

C. W. Webb, *An Historical Account of Corah's of Leicester*, Corah's, c. 1940s.

Prof. F. A. Wells, *The British Hosiery and Knitwear Industry; Its History and Organisation*, David & Charles, 1935, 2nd edn, 1972.

Bill Williams, *The Making of Manchester Jewry, 1740–1875*, Manchester University Press, 1976.

Ralph F. Wolf, *The India Rubber Man: The Story of Charles Goodyear*, Caxton Printers, Caldwell, Idaho, 1940.

W. G. Woolmer, *100 Years Round Your Neck*, privately published by H. T. Greenlaw, 1970.

Index

(Numbers in italic refer to illustrations)